MEDIA COMMENT

MW01107279

Bad Medicine *is an insider's look at the failure of the justice system in its dealings with Aboriginal lawbreakers. Alberta Provincial Court Judge John Reilly spares no one, including himself, in his belief that a different and non-racist approach would serve First Nations more effectively. He makes a compelling case for "good" medicine to replace the "bad." A must read for anyone connected with Canada's legal system.*

—Catherine Ford,
Author of *Against the Grain: An Irreverent View of Alberta*

Bad Judgment *is an angry book and Reilly pulls no punches in naming names.*

—Eric Volmers, *The Calgary Herald*

Reilly makes no pretence towards his book being a scholarly one, and this is possibly one of its greatest strengths. He has a message to deliver, not just for academics and policy makers, but for Canada and possibly the world at large. He disavows the often mysterious and arcane jargon that academia insists must be correct, in order to make his message accessible to anyone who may venture to read it, from the most educated to the least educated.

—David Milward, School of Law, University of Manitoba,
The Windsor Yearbook of Access to Justice

For anyone who is still learning about the very real issues Indigenous Canadians face, [Bad Medicine] will be an eye opener. If you are interested in the concept of restorative justice, this is a must-read.

—Edmonton Public Library,
Indigenous Stories and Reconciliation: 11 Must-Reads

... here's a judge willing to speak out and actively engineer alternatives and swim bravely against powerful societal currents.

—Bill Kaufmann, *Calgary Sun*

[John Reilly's] crusade has touched off a nationwide debate about government policies that are designed to foster native self-determination but may condemn another generation of Indians to lives of dependency and despair.

—Steven Pearlstein, *The Washington Post*

Judge John Reilly wanted to expose wrongdoing on the Stoney reserve. What he didn't realize was that powerful forces – in Ottawa, in Edmonton, and in the band itself – had a vested interest in ignoring the problem.

—Gordon Laird, *Saturday Night*

... government dollars flow in and many reserves get huge oil and gas revenues, but housing is pitiful, in some cases water is unclean, and social problems, unemployment and crime are all high. Why is this? Reilly had the courage to ask. He's not alone.

—Linda Slobodian, *Calgary Sun*

Judge Reilly's order was a brave and crazy political stunt. There is little chance that his order will hold up on appeal, but that's not the point. This man, this powerful white man who makes his living moving people from the scenic ghettos we quaintly call "reservations" to the even worse environment of prison, tried to do the right thing.

—Nick Devlin, *FFWD*

At first it appeared little would come of Provincial Court Judge John Reilly's order for an investigation into physical and political squalor on the Stoney Indian reserve, 30 miles west of Calgary.... But now it seems Judge Reilly's intervention has unleashed a maelstrom of activity: in the courts, in Ottawa – and especially in band offices, where frustrated Indians are taking matters into their own hands.

—*Alberta Report*

BAD JUDGMENT

*The Myths of First Nations Equality and
Judicial Independence in Canada*

Revised and Updated

by John Reilly

RMB

For information on purchasing bulk quantities of this book, or to obtain media excerpts or invite the author to speak at an event, please visit rmbooks.com and select the "Contact" tab.

RMB | Rocky Mountain Books Ltd.
rmbooks.com
@rmbooks
facebook.com/rmbooks

Cataloguing data available from Library and Archives Canada
ISBN 9781771601962 (paperback)
ISBN 9781771601979 (electronic)

Printed and bound in Canada

Front cover: adapted from a painting by Stoney artist Roland Rollinmud

We would like to also take this opportunity to acknowledge the traditional territories upon which we live and work. In Calgary, Alberta, we acknowledge the Niitsitapi (Blackfoot) and the people of the Treaty 7 region in Southern Alberta, which includes the Siksika, the Piikuni, the Kainai, the Tsuut'ina and the Stoney Nakoda First Nations, including Chiniki, Bearpaw, and Wesley First Nations. The City of Calgary is also home to Métis Nation of Alberta, Region III. In Victoria, British Columbia, we acknowledge the traditional territories of the Lkwungen (Esquimalt, and Songhees), Malahat, Pacheedaht, Scia'new, T'Sou-ke and W̱SÁNEĆ (Pauquachin, Tsartlip, Tsawout, Tseycum) peoples.

We acknowledge the financial support of the Government of Canada through the Canada Book Fund and the Canada Council for the Arts, and of the province of British Columbia through the British Columbia Arts Council and the Book Publishing Tax Credit.

Disclaimer
The views expressed in this book are those of the author and do not necessarily reflect those of the publishing company, its staff or its affiliates.

For Alan Hunter, QC
(1937–2010)
❖

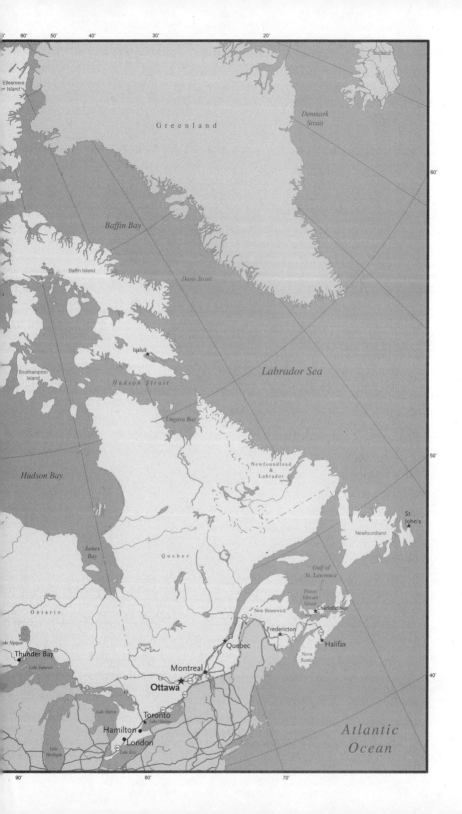

CONTENTS

ACKNOWLEDGEMENTS

I don't really consider myself an author, but I had a story to tell and it was only through the encouragement and support of many of my friends that I was able to tell part one of it in my first book, *Bad Medicine: A Judge's Struggle for Justice in a First Nations Community.* That work had its genesis at the Georgetown Research Institute when Bob Sandford facetiously told me that the institute was a literary club and in order to be a member I would have to publish.

The Georgetown Research Institute is the impressive sounding name used by a group of learned Canadians who gather weekly at the Georgetown Inn in Canmore and solve the world's problems over a few glasses of ale. Bob initiated the discussion, but I have also appreciated the support and encouragement of the other members of the institute: Joost Aalsberg, Paul Carrick, Sally Guerin, Rick Hester, Peter Nichol, Lawrence Nyman, Dave Palmer, Keith Paynter, Brent Pickard and Peter Rollason.

Bob Sandford is the author or editor of over 25 books on environmental policy and on the history and heritage of the Canadian West. He began his work with UN-linked initiatives as chair of the United Nations International Year of Mountains in 2002. He also chaired the United Nations International Year of Fresh Water and Wonder of Water Initiative in Canada in 2003–04. He is currently the Epcor Chair of the Canadian Partnership Initiative in support of United Nations "Water for Life" Decade.

It was Bob who introduced me to Don Gorman, the publisher of Rocky Mountain Books, now called RMB. Don suggested the title *Bad Medicine*, and in doing so, also gave me the inspiration for the title of the present book.

Also at RMB, editor Joe Wilderson has been a pleasure to work with. His improvements on my somewhat amateurish manuscripts have transformed them into very professional appearing books.

I would like to thank John Martland, QC, for reading and commenting on the manuscript. His remarks had me remove some unnecessarily inflammatory material, which may allow the book to be published without litigation.

Thanks also to retired Judge Doug McDonald, who took the author photo used on the back cover. He won second place with that image at the Sooke Annual Fair. I'm embarrassed by how much I like it.

It was difficult for me to focus on writing this account. I found it almost impossible to work at home, because there were so many distractions and easy excuses to do something else. For this reason I did much of the writing away from home: with my son, Sean, and his wife, Alice, in Taichung, Taiwan; at Alan and Jacquie Kay's condo in Kaslo, British Columbia; at Ron England's home on South Pender Island, BC; and at Nancy Spratt and Mark and Jack Robinson's weekend home in Canmore, Alberta. I thank you all for giving me the space I needed.

I wish to acknowledge as well the many people who encouraged me, both in the events described and in the writing about those events: Carmen Beck; John Chief Moon; Keith Chief Moon; Ron Davey; Mary Lou Davis; Mike and Lise Dove; Charlotte England; Chris Evans, QC; Harley and Lois Frank; Tina Fox; Anne Georgeson; Cheryl Goodwill; Sandra Hamilton; Warren and Mary Anna Harbeck; Paul and Sharon Hatfield; Susan Kurtz; Floyd Many Fingers; Martha Many Gray Horses; Lorraine Parker; Gail Patrick; Marjorie Powderface; Peter Poole; Donna Potter; Roland Rollinmud; Ron and Sally Starchuck; Judy Tilley; Greg Twoyoungmen; Helmer Twoyoungmen; Preston Twoyoungmen; Syd and Frances Wood and many others who pressed me to get the next book out.

INTRODUCTION

My 33 years as a judge, and especially the 20 years during which I had jurisdiction over the cases arising on the Stoney Indian Reserve at Morley, were a very painful learning experience. They made my life much more difficult but much better. More difficult because they brought me into conflict with my chief judge, the court administration, many of my fellow judges, the government of Alberta and the federal Department of Indian Affairs and Northern Development (as it was then called). Better because they gave me a focus and a purpose. The focus was real justice and the purpose was to improve the delivery of justice to the Indigenous People in my jurisdiction.

My friend Donna Kennedy-Glans advised me not to write this book. Her reason was that to relive the events of which I speak might be bad for me psychologically. I met Donna in her capacity is the founding director of Bridges, an NGO she had established while working in Yemen for Nexen Inc. She was a Conservative MLA at the time we had this discussion, and while the thought crossed my mind that she didn't want me to write about things that would reflect negatively on the Conservative government, I was confident that her motive was my happiness and mental health. She may have been right. Writing this book was tremendously difficult, it generated a lot of negative emotion for me, and I didn't like the result. But I had made a commitment to Don Gorman and Rocky Mountain books to have it written by the fall of 2014, so I submitted it for publication in spite of my negative feelings about it.

Bob Sandford once told me that as an author you never really finish a book; you just reach a point where you abandon it. I confess that I abandoned the first version of this book without feeling that it was really finished.

I'm doing this rewrite with much more positive emotion because I believe the circumstances of the Indigenous People of Canada are improving. The release of the interim report of the Truth and Reconciliation Commission, *Honouring the Truth, Reconciling for the Future*, and newly elected Prime Minister Justin Trudeau's promise to work towards a new relationship with Canada's Indigenous People, have given me new optimism.

I am much happier with the present revision.

When I wrote the first edition, I was thinking mostly about the lawyers and judges who would read it and who had been critical of my conduct throughout the time that I describe. So I wrote largely in the form of a legal argument. A number of non-lawyer readers of the first edition have commented that they found it difficult to read because of its legal and technical nature. I do this rewrite with a view to telling the story to readers who do not have a legal background, and are just interested in the story.

There are number of reasons why I want to tell this story. One is simply that it was part of the plan. When I talked to Bob Sandford about my ambition to write a book, I told him I wanted to write about the people and the cases that changed my understanding of Indigenous People, my struggle with my court administration, and my changed view of the law of Canada. I said that all of this seemed like it would be a tome that would rival *War and Peace* in length, and I was so overwhelmed by the whole project that I just couldn't get it started. Bob suggested I break it up and write three books. So *Bad Medicine* was book one, this is book two, and book three, which hopefully will appear in 2019, will be titled *Bad Law*.

The more serious reason is that I believe the story of my own struggle is important because it demonstrates the difficulties of the Indigenous People of this country in our so-called justice system.

The bad judgment I refer to is, of course, that of the chief judge in ordering me to leave this jurisdiction. There may be those who think the title more aptly fits my own conduct in the events described. I will leave that conclusion to the reader.

The subtitle, "The Myths of First Nations Equality and Judicial Independence in Canada," was chosen to underscore two facts: that there is still a real problem of inequality for Indigenous People in the Canadian justice system; and that judicial independence, which should be sacred as a bastion of protection for all citizens, is not as sacrosanct as one might expect. The story I will tell here will show how this inequality inherent in our criminal justice system results in unjust bias against Indigenous People. And since judicial independence is fundamental to the system that protects the rights and freedoms of every person in Canada, this story will also show that one of the most serious threats to that protection is posed by politicians who seek to control judges.

In a civilized and democratic society the legislative arm of government passes laws to maintain public order. The administrative arm of government creates police agencies for the purpose of enforcing those laws. The judicial arm of government ensures that the enforcement of law is fair. Without the judiciary there would be no protection from oppressive legislation or from the abuse of police power.

Because the judiciary has this unique function, any attempt to control it is a threat to the rights and freedoms not only of every person who appears in court but of every person in Canada.

I was appointed to the bench in 1977 and had my office in Calgary until I moved to Canmore in 1993. From 1981 to 1986 I was the circuit judge from Calgary for Cochrane. This gave me my first experiences with the Stoney people. In those five years, I dealt with many Stoney offenders but knew nothing about them.

No one would fault me for this, because it was part of being objective, which is what a judge should be.

After I was transferred to Canmore in 1993, Cochrane was added to the Canmore assignment and I again became the circuit judge with jurisdiction over cases arising on the Stoney Indian reserve at Morley.

This time I made a diligent effort to learn about Indigenous People in general and Aboriginal justice concepts in particular, and to apply the Criminal Code of Canada with cultural awareness of the circumstances of such offenders as required by a then new amendment to the Code.

In attempting to deal with Aboriginal offenders in a culturally sensitive way, I wrote lengthy judgments trying to explain the concepts I was learning to other judges, especially judges of the Court of Appeal, so that they might understand my reasoning. My judgments and the resulting media attention made me something of a hero to many Aboriginal people across Canada.

This media attention also caused me considerable anxiety. I knew it was not looked on favourably by many of my fellow judges. The chief judge told me I was an embarrassment to the court. My anxiety proved justified when on May 26, 1998, he ordered me to move from my home in Canmore to be assigned to courts in Calgary. His reason for the transfer was that I had lost my "objectivity with Aboriginal offenders."

The *Oxford English Dictionary* defines "objectivity" as "... the ability to consider or represent facts, information etc. without being influenced by personal feelings or opinions; impartiality; detachment." The opposite of objectivity is subjectivity, which is personal bias or opinion.

My adversaries accused me of loss of objectivity because of my efforts to deal with Aboriginal offenders in a culturally sensitive manner. Their position was that I was biased in favour of such accused and therefore unfit to hear their cases. But what

I had come to see was that the system itself is biased against these offenders. What's more, I saw a huge bias in the position of my adversaries, namely their assumption that the system treats everyone fairly and gives equal justice to all by treating everyone the same. One of the most important lessons I learned during my efforts to improve the delivery of justice to Aboriginal people is that "same" is not "equal." When you treat people who are unlike as if they are alike, you are practising systemic discrimination. You can only achieve true equality when you take account of the differences.

The most common symbol of Justice is a blindfolded woman holding a set of scales. The scales of course are the judicial system: everything in favour of the offender goes on one side; everything against him goes on the other. When everything is properly weighed, a decision will be made for or against the accused. But what do we do if the scales are weighted against the accused before we even start? We either take weight off the heavy side or we put some onto the light side, or perhaps a little of each, to bring them into balance. In the case of Aboriginal offenders we can unweight the heavy side by acknowledging the inherent bias in the system, or we can weight the light side by acknowledging the right of these offenders to be treated differently. This is not to give the Aboriginal accused an unfair advantage but rather to give them equality by taking away disadvantage.

In my work as a judge of the Provincial Court of Alberta I was faced with a hugely disproportionate number of Aboriginal accused, and in trying to comprehend why this was, I believe I gained a bit of an understanding about the reasons for it.

The coming of the Europeans destroyed a way of life that had sustained Indigenous Peoples – without gunpowder, metallurgy or the written word – for thousands of years. When Anthony Henday met the Stoney in the mid-1700s, he commented on how peaceful their society was and how well cared for their children were.

He must have been very impressed. In the England of his time, children as young as 10 and 12 were being made to work in factories and mines. His society could be extremely cruel, while the people here in North America were living in a peaceful society that must have appeared utopian compared to his own.

Today, however, the majority of Aboriginal people in Canada are living in poverty (see, for example, the 2016 report "Shameful Neglect," by David Macdonald and Daniel Wilson, listed under Further Reading), and their communities experience a disproportionate incidence of addictions, crime, suicides and children in foster care.

Whether the European newcomers were well intentioned, or just outright malicious in what they did, is not the issue. Whether they legitimately wanted to help the Indigenous People advance from what Europeans saw as primitive living conditions, or just wanted to control them so they could take their land, is not nearly as important a question as what can be done today to repair the harm that was done to their social structure.

I have heard too many people from the settler society say that the problems of Aboriginal peoples today simply come from the fact that they have been required to move through 5,000 years of human advancement in 500 years and that all that is required is more time. If you mention residential schools to people who express this attitude, you will almost always be met with the argument that those schools were all closed 50 years ago and they should just be forgotten. To me, this is like saying that when a forest fire has stopped burning, the harm is gone. The harm done to Aboriginal families and Aboriginal society by residential schools is not gone, and it is incalculable. Generations of children were taken from their families and institutionalized, often in abusive circumstances.

The Canadian government and the Christian churches justified these schools as an effort to educate the children so they could move from their "primitive" conditions into the "advanced" conditions of white society. But the stated intention was to "take the Indian out of the Indian child," and in practice many of the children going into those schools became little more than free farm labour, made to work long hours on the pretext of being taught the arts of agriculture and animal husbandry.

The Indigenous people were ordered to give up their children, and those that did not were prosecuted as criminals. Many of the children taken into those schools died there. The people in the villages, left without the children, were also lost, and it is little wonder that many of them succumbed to addictions and violence. When the children who survived were released and allowed to return, many of their villages were in turmoil, and the children, who still didn't belong in white society, didn't belong there either.

The results of this disruption of their way of life did not disappear with the closing of the schools. Today Indigenous communities have a hugely disproportionate number of children being taken into foster care because many parents are unable to properly look after them. This is the legacy of the residential schools: generations of institutionalized Indigenous People, unable to learn the traditional customs of parenting, and children still suffering from their parents' lack of Traditional Knowledge.

I believe one reason for the continuing suffering and dysfunction in Aboriginal communities is that it is so easy for the non-Aboriginal to ignore it. Yet awareness of it is the first step in finding a solution. This why I have written this book and why I wrote *Bad Medicine*.

Cori Brewster, a well-known local songwriter and singer, told me that my book inspired her to write a song she titled "Bad Medicine." I was impressed by its haunting beauty and appreciative of her doing this. It supports the growing awareness of the plight of First Nations that I hope will eventually lead to change. I asked Cori if I could include the lyrics in this introduction and she kindly agreed:

Bad Medicine

My grandfather was a good friend
To the Stoney Nakoda
They were neighbours, traded horses, Watched the same sun
rise upon Yamnuska

My grandfather would be troubled
By all these white wooden crosses on the hilltop
Prairie grasses around those fresh mounds, Pain and sorrow
leaning in the wind

All those young men, all those young lives
Alcohol and suicides
And that hopelessness within
Bad medicine

Plastic flowers, little teddy bears
Dreamcatchers tied upon the cross
Silver necklace from her sisters
As the sun goes down on Devil's Thumb

All those young girls, all those young lives
Alcohol and suicides
And that hopelessness within
Bad medicine, bad medicine

We need the elders for their wisdom
We need the youth to feel hope
We need to walk in their footsteps
We need to hear the beating of their drums

All those young ones, all those young lives
Alcohol and suicides
And that hopelessness within
Brittany Bearspaw, Oliver Rollinmud, Conrich Holloway,
Dallas Stevens, Sherman Labelle, Killian Poucette, Barney
Twoyoungmen, Cree Rollinmud

The treaties failed them, governments failed them
Their Chiefs failed them, we have failed them, we have failed
them
All those young ones, all those young lives
Alcohol and suicides
And that hopelessness within

Bad medicine, bad medicine, bad medicine
My grandfather would be troubled

❖ I ❖

HOW THIS ALL STARTED

From the time I became a lawyer, I had wanted the position of resident judge for Banff. The dockets were usually light and the judge lived in Banff amid the majestic Canadian Rockies, in Banff National Park. In 1993, when I obtained the posting in Canmore, with Banff as part of my circuit, it was like I had won a lottery.

My initial interest in obtaining a judicial appointment had been sparked by Judge Gary Cioni. I think it is ironic that Gary at that time had the distinction of being the youngest judge appointed to the court. His suggestion to me that I seek an appointment ultimately resulted in his losing that distinction. He had been appointed a few months after his 31st birthday, and I was appointed a few days before my 31st. At 30 years of age I was the youngest appointment ever made to the Provincial Court of Alberta.

This was after just seven years of practice. I had articled with Daniel M. McDonald, who had been a student of my father's in junior high school. When he heard I was going to graduate in law he invited me to his office. Unfortunately he left private practice shortly after and our association was brief. He did, however, give me great training in courtroom procedure and turned over all of his criminal work to me.

This resulted in my getting my most famous, or infamous, client, Paul Joseph Cini. On November 12, 1971, Cini had hijacked an Air Canada flight out of Calgary. At some time before this, McDonald had acted for Cini on some other, minor matter, and

Cini asked McDonald to again represent him. The file was turned over to me.

I had less than two years of experience as a lawyer when I took this trial, and I was unsuccessful in my effort to have Cini declared not guilty by reason of insanity. However, the trial was national news, and it gave me a certain profile which didn't do me any harm. The notoriety it gave me was likely a part of the reason I was appointed to the bench at 30 years of age.

Judge Cioni may have been more interested in unloading the Drumheller work than he was in my being appointed a judge. In the mid-'70s, the Provincial Court, Criminal Division, in Calgary consisted of five judges: Verne Reade, Fred Thurgood, John Harvie, Gary Cioni and Leo Collins. Collins was the circuit judge and only sat occasionally in the city. The judge at Drumheller had retired and not been replaced. The Calgary judges were covering Drumheller and the circuit courts in that jurisdiction, and it was a burden for them.

I liked the idea of being appointed a judge, and I followed up by speaking to the assistant deputy minister of justice, Bill McLean. I asked him about Drumheller. Then, in conversation, I asked him if the Banff position would be available on Judge Graves's retirement. I speculated that Judge Lou Justason might take it. He had a home in Harvie Heights, just west of Canmore, and commuted to Calgary. McLean's comment was that he didn't think the department would "inflict Lou Justason on the citizens of Banff."

We had this conversation in about 1976, and my appointment to Canmore 19 years later was the fulfillment of my ambition.

Bill Graves, the Banff judge, was a retired RCMP officer who had been appointed a magistrate prior to the passage of the Provincial Court Act. There were still a number of lay magistrates in the '70s who were subsequently "grandfathered' into the position of provincial judge

The evolution of the Provincial Court of Alberta was taking place during the years in which I practised law and sat as a judge. When I began going to court as a student at law in 1969, I went to what was called the Magistrates Court, often referred to as "the police court." In Calgary these courtrooms were located on the second floor of the downtown police station.

The Provincial Court of Alberta was created by the Provincial Court Act of 1971, which came into force in 1973. In the mid-'70s, Justice Cam Kirby conducted a review of the administration of justice in the Provincial Court. His report, released in August of 1975, made a number of recommendations, one being that non-lawyers no longer be appointed to the court.

Another recommendation of the Kirby review was that courtrooms be located in places separate from police facilities, to avoid the appearance that the court was simply an adjunct of the police. This was a huge change from the original "police magistrates." Historically, the commanding officer of each police detachment was ex officio a police magistrate. It probably didn't give an accused much confidence in the "independence of the judiciary" when the constable who arrested him took him in front of the constable's own commanding officer for trial and sentence.

In every case where an accused faces a maximum penalty of more than two years imprisonment, he can choose, or "elect," to be tried in the lower court without a jury and without a prelim-inary inquiry, or to be tried in a higher court, either by a judge alone or by a court composed of a judge and jury. This step in the procedure is referred to as the "election." When I started going to court the election used the word "magistrate" to designate the lower court. This wording was later changed to substitute "prov-incial court judge" for "magistrate."

When Judge Graves retired he was replaced by Albert Aunger, who had practised law in Grande Prairie and been appointed a "magistrate" in 1971.

This was during Allan Cawsey's tenure as chief judge, and it was his policy that when a vacancy occurred, sitting judges were given the opportunity to fill that vacancy and new appointments would take the positions that thus became available. Pursuant to this policy Aunger was offered and took the opening in Banff. That seemed to foreclose any possibility that I would ever be the resident judge for Banff. Aunger was only 40 years old and judges could sit until age 70.

Then, in 1991, at age 57, Aunger retired. He left Banff and moved to Nanoose Bay on Vancouver Island. I again inquired about the possibility of taking the position, but the assistant chief judge for Calgary and area, Hubert (Bert) Oliver, told me Aunger was not going to be replaced by a resident judge. Banff would be covered as a circuit from Calgary. So again it seemed the position was unavailable. Then it was announced that Robert Henry Davey had been appointed a judge and assigned to the Banff circuit. His official residence was to be Canmore.

I was a little upset by this development. I had been a judge for 14 years. I had made many inquiries about being assigned to this position and it was going to a newly appointed judge. Allan Cawsey had been appointed to the Court of Queen's Bench in 1979, and the new Provincial Court chief judge, Edward R. Wachowich, was evidently not continuing Cawsey's practice of making new openings available to sitting judges.

Then I learned that Davey didn't even want the position. He wanted to be in Calgary. So I contacted him and proposed that we make a joint application to have our residences redesignated so that we could trade places. He agreed and we made the request to the chief judge in the summer of 1992.

What seemed straightforward became somewhat complicated, however. We needed the agreement of Chief Judge Wachowich and an order from the minister of justice. Wachowich didn't want to make the order without the agreement of the assistant chief judge, but Assistant Chief Judge Oliver was going to retire that year, and we had to wait for the appointment of his replacement.

We also had to wait for the appointment of a new justice minister. On September 9, 1992, Don Getty resigned as premier and that seemed to put the government on hold. On December 5, Ralph Klein was elected the new party leader, and he was sworn in as premier on December 14.

In December Brian Stevenson was confirmed as the new assistant chief judge, and he agreed to the proposed move.

On December 8, 1992, Chief Judge Wachowich requested the redesignation of our residences from the attorney general, Ken Rostad. That request was not answered until January 6, 1993, when a new attorney general, Dick Fowler, finally made the order, to be effective May 1, 1993. (In the provincial election held barely six weeks later, Fowler lost his seat and a newly re-elected Ralph Klein reinstated Rostad as attorney general.)

This was like a dream come true. It was also a tremendous relief, because my wife Laura and I had purchased a house in Canmore in the expectation of getting the transfer, and we were somewhat concerned about what we would do with it if we did not get the transfer.

The transfer did come through, though, and it was like a new lease on life. I moved from a small office in the Calgary Provincial Court building, with windows looking onto the roof of the police station on the other side of an alley, to an office in Canmore, where the windows looked out on trees and mountains.

The house we had purchased in Canmore backed onto a public reserve where Policeman's Creek separated us from a golf course. It was within "canoe-carrying" distance of the Bow River. I would keep a kayak strapped to the roof of my van, and on days when court finished early I would have one of the clerks drive me down to the river below Bow Falls and I would paddle home. Gail Kazimer lived in the next cul-de-sac over from us, and she would willingly drive my van back to our house and walk the short distance home. It was an idyllic lifestyle.

Things were not so idyllic for the court generally in those years, however. It was a time of cutbacks, and the court was being reorganized and required to do the same work, or increasing work, with fewer judges.

In the spring of 1994 the Calgary region had its complement of judges reduced from 21 to 19. The 19 included myself in Banff and Judge Gordon Clozza in Drumheller.

Again the proposal was made to close Banff and have all the cases arising there be heard in Canmore instead. I was now a resident of the Bow Valley and becoming attuned to the views of the locals, which included concerns that favoured keeping the court in Banff. Dennis Shuler, the mayor, pointed out that when police officers were required to appear as witnesses, they could be attending to their regular duties until they were called to court, if court were in Banff. If court were in Canmore, they would have to go there and perhaps spend the day waiting to be called. Mayor Shuler saw it as the provincial government downloading tax burden onto the town of Banff.

Also, the court facility in Banff, on the third floor of the Cascade Plaza, was only in the second year of a 10-year lease. If the government were going to have to honour that commitment, the change might not amount to much of a saving.

I also told Judge Stevenson that it was my understanding there might be some federal–provincial considerations to closing the court in Banff. Judge Oliver had told me that there was a federal–provincial agreement requiring the province to maintain a court in the national park. I had never seen any documentation to this effect, and when the court was subsequently closed, there was no mention of it. Whether that suggestion contributed to keeping the court open for another few years or not, I don't know. In any event, I liked the trips to Banff and didn't want to give them up, and I was pleased to see that it didn't happen at that time.

Judge Stevenson also suggested that Airdrie be added to the Canmore circuit. I argued against this. Taking over Cochrane had already doubled my caseload. I felt that adding Airdrie was requiring me to accept an unfair portion of the increased workload for judges generally. I won that argument, but this may have been the beginning of difficulties I subsequently had with Judge Stevenson.

I met with the Attorney General, who at the time was Brian Evans, the MLA for Banff–Cochrane, and on my initiative Cochrane was added to the Canmore circuit. This added all the clerical work for Cochrane to the Canmore office. The staff was increased by about 25 per cent, but the workload was almost doubled.

The court administrator, Cheryl Dubuc, suggested doing "court users meetings" to find ways to streamline the work. These would be conferences of all the players in the system, aimed at finding out what worked and what didn't.

It was a new experience for me to be doing this. In the years I had spent in Calgary, I didn't really know anything about what all those people in the clerks office did. Now I was faced with helping them with a situation I had been instrumental in creating, when none of the staff had had any say in the changes that so significantly affected them.

It was in preparing for these administrative meetings that I became aware of the magnitude of the problem with Aboriginal accused. Before this I had not seen the forest for the trees. I knew there were a lot of Aboriginal people appearing in Cochrane, but in preparing for the meetings I actually counted them and calculated the percentages.

The RCMP detachment in Cochrane is responsible for the town itself and the rural area stretching some 70 kilometres from Bragg

Creek north to Cremona and about 30 kilometres west, to and including the Stoney Indian Reserve at Morley. We estimated that the total population thus serviced by the court was about 30,000. The population of the reserve was about 3,000, so proportionately the Stoneys should have constituted about 10 per cent of the caseload. They were closer to 80 per cent.

We had our first meeting in Cochrane on June 21, 1996. I was in the chair and Cheryl Dubuc attended in her role as court administrator. We had invited all three Stoney Chiefs, but Chief Ken Soldier of the Chiniki band was the only one to attend. Peter Wesley and Harley Crowchild represented the Tsuu T'ina Nation/ Stoney Corrections Society. Roy Barclay, the chief probation officer, and Ken Haggle, the Cochrane probation officer, were also present. Others in attendance were Harold Hagglund, the senior Crown prosecutor; Staff Sergeant Bob Wheadon, the commanding officer of the Cochrane RCMP; Roy Pennoyer, the chief of the Stoney Tribal Police; Marjorie Powderface, the Indigenous court worker; Ron Davey, house counsel for Legal Aid; Martin Siller, pretrial coordinator for Calgary; Dave Paul, Provincial Court manager for Calgary; Jim McLaughlin, the Provincial Court's regional director; Jodi Guertin, the RCMP court liaison; non-sitting justices of the peace Sherry Titheridge and Greg Buchanan; and defence lawyers Shelley Mabbot, Donna Morris, Mary Jo Rothecker, Guy Cochrane, Robb Beeman, Sheldon Kaupp and Karen Gainer.

These meetings enabled us to begin to do a little streamlining to make the operation of the court a little more efficient. One of the most obvious problems to be dealt with was adjournments by Aboriginal accused. Marjorie Powderface explained that it was in her job description to get adjournments for her clients, and so that is what she did. Many of the adjournments were to allow her clients to get legal aid, which was difficult because they had to go into Calgary to the Legal Aid office and transportation was often a problem.

As a result of the discussions, the RCMP agreed to begin giving arrested persons contact information for Legal Aid at the time of arrest. In turn the Legal Aid Office arranged to have application forms at the court so they could be completed without the need to go to Calgary, and to appoint a permanent duty counsel. This allowed accused persons to deal with the same lawyer on every appearance, which resulted in fewer court appearances.

For the first time in my judicial career I was doing something that went beyond hearing individual cases. It gave me a sense of accomplishment and challenged me to do more.

❖ 2 ❖

ABORIGINAL AWARENESS IN THE 1990S

The 1990s were a time of growing awareness of the plight of Aboriginal people in Canada.

In June 1990 Elijah Harper prevented the Manitoba legislature from approving the Meech Lake Accord. He was the province's only Aboriginal MLA and spoke against the accord because it was created without input from Aboriginal people and did not make any provision for them.

From July 11 until September 26 Mohawk warriors were in an armed standoff with the Sûreté du Québec and later the Canadian army. The dispute had arisen when the town of Oka was going to expand a golf course and residential development onto land claimed as Traditional Territory of the Mohawk at Kanesatake. The land contained ancestral graves and had been contested by the band since 1717.

In August and September a group of Piikani in Alberta known as the Lonefighters, led by Milton Born With a Tooth, Devalon Small Legs and Glen North Peigan, attempted to prevent completion of a dam on the Oldman River, resulting in armed intervention by the province of Alberta. It was a dispute rooted in Treaty 7 (1877), the surrender of Piikani reserve land for irrigation headworks in 1922, a blockade in 1978, and continuing frustration at dam construction continuing in the 1980s despite a court order to halt it.

These events resulted in a number of studies by governments across Canada. In Alberta there was the Task Force on the

Criminal Justice System and Its Impact on the Indian and Métis People of Alberta. The report of the task force, written by Justice Allan Cawsey and referred to as the Cawsey Report, was published in 1991.

Nationally there was the Royal Commission on Aboriginal Peoples, known as RCAP. The commission's report, in five volumes, was published in 1996.

I described the impact the information in these reports had on me in the chapter "My Aboriginal Education" in *Bad Medicine*. Here, it is sufficient to say I was overwhelmed by what I learned from these reports, and by the dysfunction and suffering I saw in the Stoney community. There was no doubt in my mind that the many violent offences I dealt with in my courtroom were the result of social conditions which were the result of a history of colonialism.

The Family Group Conferencing program I attended in Edmonton in January 1997 also had a huge influence on my thinking about justice. This program gave me my first glimpse of the concept of restorative justice and its potential for making a real change in human behaviour without the need for imprisonment. I was impressed by the statistics on reduced crime rates in places where it was used, and I wanted to put it into practice in my jurisdiction. The concepts it embraces are what the Aboriginal peoples used in their society before Europeans came here.

The Eurocentric justice system is punitive. In England it goes back to the 11th century, after the Norman invasion. Henry I, son of William the Conqueror, set out conduct that was seen as a "breach of the king's peace." Victims became secondary to the state in the prosecution of crime. It was only in 1996 that the Criminal Code of Canada moved away from that with its victim impact statement provisions.

While the English have a history of using brutal punishments for offending behaviour, Aboriginal people used restorative methods. These methods, where they are being used today, are seen to be much more effective. I wanted to use these methods at Morley. My request that the chief judge support me in this was the beginning of my conflict with him.

❖ 3 ❖

THE *HUNTER* MATTER

The case of *R. v. Hunter* is dealt with at length in *Bad Medicine*. Both the June 1997 judgment (ordering the investigation) and the November 28 judgment (the reasons for sentence) are included as appendices there. The present story is about the aftermath of that case, so I will summarize it briefly.

On January 1, 1997, Ernest Hunter and his common-law partner went to a party, got drunk and got into an argument and he beat her severely. On May 27, 1997, he pleaded guilty to a charge of assault causing bodily harm, and the Crown and defence made submissions on sentence.

The Criminal Code had recently been amended to allow victims of crime to make a victim impact statement. Hunter's victim had not made a statement but I asked her if she wanted to say anything. She said the accused was a good man when he wasn't drinking and he should get treatment.

Hunter's lawyer, Jim Ogle, told me his client had been taking an anger management program but was unable to complete it because his funding had been cut by the tribal government.

I adjourned to June 26, 1997, to allow for the preparation of the presentence report.

The reason I was able to maintain my sanity in more than 30 years on the bench is that I made my decisions in court and didn't take them home with me. There are some who would argue that I did not in fact maintain my sanity. That is another discussion.

Hunter was an exception. The case was typical of much of the violence I heard described over the years in that courtroom. Yet his victim said he was a good man, and his lawyer said he had been taking an anger management program but couldn't finish it because the tribal government had cut off his funding.

The standard sentence for this man's offence was 18 months imprisonment, and earlier in my career I would have imposed that without giving it a second thought. If I didn't, the Court of Appeal would.

But my thinking was changing, and another new section in the Criminal Code was causing me to look beyond the isolated incident before me. That section was s. 718.2(e):

> All available sanctions other than imprisonment that are reasonable in the circumstances should be considered for all offenders, with particular attention to the circumstances of Aboriginal offenders.

Circumstances of this Aboriginal offender that were relevant to his sentencing included his community situation. He was a dysfunctional individual because he had grown up and was living in a dysfunctional community. In his community, alcoholism, family violence, suicide and other social problems existed at many times the rate of the general population, and nothing was being done about it.

I believed it would be simply a further injustice to send this man to prison for being the natural result of the dysfunctional social system he came from, especially when nothing was being done to remedy the conditions to which he had succumbed.

His lawyer's statement that he had been taking an anger management program but had not been able to finish it because funding had been cut was something I thought was very important in this matter.

The connection between tribal funding and domestic violence may have seemed very tenuous to my chief judge, but in my view it was a crucial factor. I had wanted to see programs established to help the disproportionate number of Aboriginal accused that were appearing in my court. The Rev. Dr. Chief John Snow had told me that this would not be possible because of lack of funding. Other people who had inside knowledge, and whose information I trusted, told me there were millions of dollars being misappropriated.

Although I was confident of my information, I couldn't just say these things for the record. In our legal system evidence doesn't come from the judge; it is supposed to come from the Crown. But another recent amendment to the Criminal Code now allowed a judge, after hearing submissions of the Crown and the defence, to order further evidence. So on June 26, 1997, when the matter came back to court, I again adjourned it and ordered the Crown to provide me with a report on social conditions on the reserve, including political corruption and financial mismanagement.

It was my expectation that the order would force the Crown prosecutor's office to take a look at the abysmal social conditions on the reserve and the causes thereof. In my total naïveté, I even hoped they might see fit to lay charges against those who were misappropriating tribal funds for personal use. This, of course, did not happen. Even when the *Calgary Herald* later exposed specific abuses, such as Chief Philomene Stevens taking her salary as Chief but using welfare money to pay her babysitter, no action was taken and poorer Stoneys continued to live in poverty.

What did happen was tremendous media frenzy, and the provincial government appealed the order. *Bad Medicine* devotes a whole chapter to the media coverage, but it is useful to recap some of it here.

On June 28, 1997, the *Calgary Sun* ran an article headlined "Judge's order appealed." It quoted Justice Minister Jon Havelock as saying it was the government's position that I had exceeded my jurisdiction in ordering the investigation.

On July 8 the *Herald* ran an article headlined "Klein queries judge's power." Premier Klein was quoted as saying I had overstepped my authority and that the tribal governments would be dealt with on a government to government basis.

On the same day, there was an article in *The Globe and Mail* headlined "Klein slams judge's call for review," in which the premier said I should have consulted the government first, and that the matter was being discussed in cabinet and caucus.

The July 11 *Herald* headlined "Lawyers say Klein wrong to rap judge's comments." The article quoted lawyers Sue Hendricks, Alain Hepner and André Ouellette saying that the premier had threatened judicial independence by publicly criticizing me.

That same month, Roland Emery Ear was murdered, the fifth violent death of a young Stoney since my order. A *Herald* article headlined "No probe despite murder charge" reported that Minister Havelock, asked if this would alter the government's position on the investigation, had answered, "Our position hasn't changed."

On August 18 and 21 Havelock was quoted in the *Herald* saying the Stoney reserve was federal jurisdiction and they should conduct an inquiry. My order was apparently putting a fair amount of political pressure on the Alberta government to do something about the problem, and they seemed to be doing their best to avoid doing anything about it.

One of the curious aspects of the appeal process was that I was named as a respondent along with the accused. I simply indicated to the Crown that I would not respond and would let the matter be determined on the submissions of the Crown and the defence.

The appeal was heard on September 26, 1997. It was successful in part. Justice LoVecchio of the Court of Queen's Bench ruled that I was entitled to some of the information I asked for, but not all of it. By the time the appeal was determined and the report produced, it was November before Ernest Hunter was back in court for sentencing.

❖ 4 ❖

THE *HUNTER* JUDGMENT

I spent a lot of time during the summer and fall of 1997 drafting reasons for judgment that I would give in passing sentence on Ernest Hunter.

I was confident that the information I had about social conditions on the reserve was accurate, and I had decided that I would, in accordance with the new provision in the Criminal Code mandating "particular attention to the circumstances of Aboriginal accused," impose a treatment-oriented sentence and not send him to jail.

I was also hopeful that if my judgment were appealed by the Crown and upheld by a higher court, my interpretation of the new provision would become a precedent. I reread the Cawsey Report and the whole Report of the Royal Commission on Aboriginal Peoples and quoted both in a lengthy judgment. I also quoted stories from the *Calgary Herald*. In my view the *Herald* had done the investigation the federal and provincial governments should had done, and the information they published confirmed my allegations of financial mismanagement.

While I was working on this, I was getting pressure not to say the things I was intending to say.

In the fall of 1997 the Alberta Provincial Court judges held their annual conference in Canmore. The investigation I had ordered was the subject of considerable conversation. Brian Stevenson was at first very supportive of what I had done. He said several times that my order had "made friends for the court."

Harry Gaede, a classmate of mine in law school, now the president-elect of the Alberta Provincial Court Judges Association, told me that in writing further judgments I should be careful not to criticize the Alberta government, because it might have an effect on salary negotiations.

Until then I had always thought that arguments about salary and judicial independence were just academic. But here was an example of pressure being brought to bear on my judicial function. The fact that Harry Gaede was in fact using the fear of possible effect on our salaries to influence what I would say in a judgment probably did not strike him as an egregious violation of judicial independence. The very essence of judicial independence is that judges should be able to write judgments without fear of repercussions from government, yet here I was being told by the president-elect of the judges association to be careful about what I wrote because it might result in all of us being paid less.

I was disheartened by how zealous my fellow judges could be about the principle of judicial independence when it came to their salaries and pensions, when many of them didn't seem to care about the pressure that was being put on me to refrain from saying things in my judgments that I felt I had a duty to say.

Judge John Maher, the outgoing president of the judges association, later told me about a meeting he had attended with Justice Minister and Attorney General Havelock and Chief Judge Wachowich. Judge Maher said the meeting had begun with Havelock virtually raging at the chief judge about trouble I was causing with my statements on Aboriginal justice. Gaede and the other members of the judges association executive probably knew about this, but I didn't. Apparently the threat was much more real than I realized.

Stevenson asked me if I would give him some warning of anything that would generate more media attention. He said he wanted to be prepared for it. Consequently I gave him a draft of my proposed judgment. He wrote a lengthy comment on it. I rewrote it with his comments in mind, and I think he actually helped me in making the judgment more credible.

Some time later, I had what I thought was just an accidental meeting with judges Cioni and Stevenson in the Provincial Court building in Calgary. They walked into the judges lounge while I was there. Stevenson told me he had given Cioni a copy of my draft and we talked about it.

Stevenson told me he and Cioni were in agreement that the judgment should not be delivered. They said my comments on the political situation went far beyond the scope of the case before me and were not relevant to the sentencing of an accused in a domestic assault. I argued that in my view they were very relevant, and that if any of us had grown up and lived in that dysfunctional environment, we could well be in the same situation. Cioni told me that in his opinion, if I delivered the judgment, I would probably end up in front of the Judicial Council. I said if I did, I would tell them the same thing.

I also sent a copy of the draft to Allan Cawsey and asked his opinion of it. I was particularly interested in knowing whether he had any comment on my references to his report. He too told me I shouldn't deliver it. If there was anyone I would have listened to, it was Allan Cawsey, but he went on to say: "There is no question that one of the worst aspects of reserves is corrupt tribal government, but we aren't allowed to say anything about it." I took this as his tacit approval.

On November 28, 1997, I sentenced Ernest Hunter to probation and gave my reasons for judgment. The Crown appealed.

On November 29 the *Herald* ran an article headlined "Judge's removal predicted." The story quoted University of Calgary law professor Chris Levy as saying: "Judge Reilly won't back down and there probably is enough public support that his job will be safe ... but the provincial government is not happy with what has gone on … And I have heard that Judge Reilly may be brought back into Calgary as a cost-saving measure."

Laura was concerned about the article and on December 2 she called Stevenson to ask him about it. Stevenson wrote to me the next day and assured me that any discussions related to the closure of the Canmore circuit would be based solely on cost effectiveness, and I would be consulted "prior to any final recommendations concerning the future of Canmore as a base point."

He also said he was disappointed that Chris Levy and the media would translate regular and ongoing examination of the cost-effectiveness of servicing circuit points into a "'punishment' scenario directed at you as a result of your work."

Chris Levy was a regular visitor in the judges lounge at the Calgary provincial courthouse and he often spoke with Stevenson. I suspected that the source of the professor's speculation might well have been things Stevenson had said to him directly. I would later learn that Stevenson's letter to me was disingenuous at best.

❖ 5 ❖

JUDICIAL INDEPENDENCE

My definition of judicial independence is this: judicial independence is not a perk for judges; it is the right of every person who ever appears before a court to have their case decided by the presiding judge and not by someone in some back room telling the judge what to do.

I had the privilege of discussing this with Justice John Bracco. He had been appointed to the Alberta District Court in 1975, to the Supreme Court of Yukon as a deputy judge in 1977 and later to the Alberta Court of Appeal and the Nunavut Court of Appeal. He worked on judicial ethics and judicial conduct topics with judges in Ukraine and was a member of the advisory committee re the Canada–Ukraine Judicial Reform Project in 1996–97.

Justice Bracco agreed with my comment. He told me that the opposite of judicial independence is something they had in the former USSR called "telephone justice." A judge would hear a case, and before giving judgment he would telephone the party boss, who would tell him whether to find the prisoner guilty or not and what sentence to impose.

I am afraid most of my fellow judges saw my attempt to exercise my judicial independence as judicial anarchy. The media referred to me as the "controversial judge," the "outlaw judge," the "renegade judge." (The latter term was the one my friends on "the rez" liked the best.)

Judicial independence does not mean judges are free to do as they please. Their job is to make findings of fact based on the evidence presented to them and decide cases according to their knowledge of the law, and the precedents.

Precedents are based on the principle that all people should be treated equally. Accordingly, if accused A was treated this way by court A, then accused B in similar circumstances should be treated the same way by court B. Part of the job of lawyers is to find precedent cases which support the arguments they are making in favour of their clients.

The control over a judge's judicial function, the safeguard against abuse of his power, comes from the appeal process in which all decisions are made according to the due process of law.

Section 11(*d*) of the Charter of Rights and Freedoms guarantees that anyone charged with an offence has the right to be "presumed innocent until proven guilty according to law in a fair and public hearing by *an independent and impartial tribunal.*" It is this right of "any person charged" that is the constitutional basis of judicial independence. The "independent tribunal" is the judge deciding according to the legal process and without outside influence.

In *Hunter* I made a decision that did not follow precedents. I distinguished the case on the basis of the amendment to the Criminal Code that required me to consider the available sanctions "with particular attention to the circumstances of Aboriginal offenders." It was those last nine words that changed the law in relation to Aboriginal offenders and changed my life. My promise was to improve the delivery of justice to the Stoney Nakoda people at Morley, Alberta. I saw this new provision as a mandate to do exactly that.

Judicial independence allowed me to make the decision I made. If I was wrong, the only correction I should have faced was a decision by the Court of Appeal saying I was wrong and replacing my ruling with theirs. The Court of Appeal did that, but I believe the Supreme Court of Canada ultimately upheld my position.

What went wrong in my case was the attempt of the chief judge, in his role as an administrator, not as a judge, to influence my judicial decision-making function. That attempt to control my decision-making was a real threat to judicial independence.

❖ 6 ❖

JUDICIAL REMUNERATION

There had been an ongoing dispute between the Alberta Provincial Court Judges Association (APCJA) and the Alberta government in relation to salaries. And it was a rather ironic twist in the litigation over this that gave Chief Judge Wachowich and Assistant Chief Judge Stevenson the mistaken impression that the chief judge had the power to order me to relocate.

The background to the dispute is this.

Alberta Provincial Court judges are appointed and paid by the provincial government, while Queen's Bench and Court of Appeal justices are appointed and paid by the federal government.

From 1980 to 1988 the salaries of Provincial Court judges were simply set at 80 per cent of the amount paid to Queen's Bench justices. But in 1988 Alberta unilaterally discontinued the practice of increasing the salaries of Provincial Court judges in tandem with the periodic raises granted to the federally appointed justices. The salaries of Provincial Court judges accordingly fell behind, eventually becoming significantly less than 80 per cent of their federally appointed counterparts.

By 1994 the APCJA was preparing to sue the Alberta government for the shortfall in salaries. Their claim would be based on breach of contract. The argument would be that it became a term of employment of all the Provincial Court judges appointed between 1982 and 1988 that their salaries would be 80 per cent of the Queen's Bench figure. The shortfall constituted damages arising from the breach of the employment contract.

In March of 1994 the government and the APCJA agreed to negotiate in good faith. The association would refrain from commencing proceedings pending negotiations, and the government agreed to waive any limitation periods.

At the end of March the government of Ralph Klein announced that all provincial employees, including the provincial judges, would have their salaries rolled back by 5 per cent as part of a program to balance the budget. The judges saw this as a violation of the agreement and commenced litigation against the Alberta government. They took the position that the reduction in salaries was a violation of the financial security aspect of judicial independence.

This argument was then raised in a number of criminal matters. One such was the case of Shawn Carl Campbell, charged with unlawful possession of nunchaku sticks and failing to attend court, both minor offences. He objected to the jurisdiction of the court on the basis that the judge did not have financial independence and therefore the accused was deprived of his right to an independent and impartial tribunal under s. 11(d) of the Charter of Rights. A supplementary argument was that s. 13 of the Provincial Court Judges Act violated judicial independence.

Section 13 was the provision that gave the Attorney General the power to designate the residence of a Provincial Court judge. It was this provision that had required me to get the Attorney General to approve my original transfer from Calgary to Canmore in 1993. The argument was that s. 13 gave the Attorney General the power to change a judge's residence without his consent and was therefore a power which could be used to punish a judge whose rulings were adverse to the government.

The Provincial Court ruled in favour of Campbell's argument and the Crown appealed to the Court of Queen's Bench.

In a lengthy judgment issued November 15, 1994, Queen's Bench Justice David McDonald ruled against the applications by

Campbell and the other two accused. He found that the power to fix salaries contained in s. 17 of the Provincial Court Judges Act was valid, but any application of that section to decrease salaries would be unconstitutional because of the violation of the financial security condition of judicial independence. However, the APCJA had successfully challenged the reduction in salary in their litigation, and Justice McDonald therefore found it was no longer an issue.

He ruled that s. 13 of the Provincial Court Judges Act was an unconstitutional violation of judicial independence. He ruled that the provision was of no force and effect and therefore no longer presented a violation of judicial independence.

Campbell's challenge to the court's jurisdiction therefore failed.

Another of the ironies in the case was that, even though the Crown had won the battle, it had lost the war. It was successful in having Campbell's challenge to jurisdiction set aside, but the provincial legislation had been struck down.

The Crown appealed to the Alberta Court of Appeal but the court refused to hear the appeal because the Crown had won the case.

The matter then came before the Supreme Court of Canada as an issue in a Prince Edward Island case dealing with the remuneration and judicial independence of Provincial Court judges there.

The Alberta Attorney General, the Canadian Association of Provincial Court Judges and the Alberta Provincial Court Judges Association, among others, appeared as interveners in this case, and the SCC considered the Alberta issue in relation to s. 13.

First, the SCC ruled that the Alberta Court of Appeal was wrong in not hearing the Crown appeal in *R. v. Campbell*. Even though the Crown had been successful in its effort to continue the trials, it had lost on the underlying findings of constitutionality, and the court should have heard the appeal.

Having made this finding, the SCC could either send *Campbell* back to the Alberta Court of Appeal with a direction that they decide it, or the SCC could rule on it themselves. They decided to rule on it themselves.

Their finding was that the salary reduction imposed by the payment regulation for Provincial Court judges was unconstitutional because there was no independent, effective and objective commission in Alberta to recommend changes to judges' salaries.

In striking s. 13, Justice McDonald had said that decisions to designate the place at which a judge shall have their residence and the days on which court will hold sittings are "administrative decisions that bear directly and immediately on the exercise of the judicial function," and that "the Chief Judge's and Assistant Chief Judges' ability to combine flexibility with cost-efficiency and other relevant considerations (such as avoiding travel fatigue, providing the community with a diversity of judges, enhancing collegiality and consistency within the court) must not be fettered."

Wachowich and Stevenson relied on what McDonald said as establishing the chief judge's authority to order a judge's change of residence.

Chief Justice Lamer in the scc judgment said he agreed with McDonald's ruling that s. 13 was unconstitutional, because it conferred powers on the Attorney General and Minister of Justice (or a person authorized by him or her) to make decisions which infringe upon the administrative independence of the Alberta Provincial Court. He said his concern was that "as it is presently worded, s. 13(1)(*a*) creates the reasonable apprehension that it could be used to punish judges whose decisions do not favour the government, or alternatively, to favour judges whose decisions benefit the government...."

The mistake Wachowich and Stevenson made, when they used McDonald's judgment as establishing the chief judge's power to move me, was to assume that because the result had been upheld his words had become law.

In relation to judicial remuneration, the result of the "Judges Reference" case was that judicial compensation commissions were established. The government and the judges association now make submissions to the commission, the commission makes recommendations to the government, and the government either accepts the recommendations or gives reasons for not doing so.

There was more litigation between the Alberta judges and the provincial government when the latter didn't accept recommendations, but the process seems to be working reasonably well now.

❖ 7 ❖

CPL. YOUNG

As if the events at Morley, and the media speculation about my possible removal from my circuit, were not causing me enough anxiety, RCMP Corporal Bill Young of the Banff detachment filed a complaint against me alleging that I was biased against him and asking the assistant chief judge to order me not to hear any cases in which he was a witness.

This complaint arose out of comments I made to Crown prosecutor Sarah Bhola in the presence of Cst. Buerkens after I had heard a couple of cases that caused me to be concerned about Young's use of force in making arrests.

In a trial I heard on December 15, 1997, the evidence was that Cpl. Young and Cst. Tracey Kennet arrested two young men at Lake Louise and transported them to Banff. En route one of the men was kicking at the interior of the police car. The police were not in any danger, as the "silent patrolman" (a metal screen between the front and back seats of the patrol car) protected them. However, when they were only a few minutes from Banff, Young and Kennet stopped the car and pepper sprayed the young man.

Then, the next February, a young Swiss man, Reto S., pleaded guilty to a charge of assaulting a peace officer, namely Cpl. Young. Young had arrested the man's friend, Andreas I., for some very minor thefts and was going to take him to the Banff detachment. Reto attempted to intervene. He said in court that he just wanted to help because Andreas did not speak English very well. Young ordered him to stay away. When Reto persisted, there was some shoving and Young charged him with assaulting a police officer.

Andreas pleaded guilty to theft of a souvenir licence plate and a Rose & Crown restaurant menu, Reto to assaulting a police officer.

This was the kind of case I hated dealing with. Any criminal proceeding can have onerous consequences for the accused. In my view, those consequences, in terms of future employment and international travel, when a criminal record is created, often go far beyond what is warranted by a minor offence such as a $10 or $20 theft. Many of these minor matters are in fact now being dealt with using alternative measures.

If Andreas had pleaded not guilty it is unlikely there would ever have been convictions. To prove the charge, the Crown would have had to call the owners to prove the items were stolen. It is unlikely they would have found the owner of the souvenir licence plate, and I suspected it would be unlikely that anyone from the Rose & Crown would have been able to say those menus are never given away and never sold. Unless they could say that, there would have been no proof the menu had been stolen.

So this young man, who was perhaps putting any further visits to Canada in jeopardy by incurring a criminal record, was being convicted because he had been co-operative.

As for Reto, he's trying to help a friend who does not speak English well, and this might even have assisted a police officer. The way I saw it, the whole matter could have been dealt with much differently if Young had been less aggressive.

In each case, I imposed a conditional discharge requiring a $200 charitable donation. Each accused paid his $200 that same day. The Crown appealed both sentences on grounds that they were inappropriately lenient, but the appeal was later withdrawn.

After court that day, I told prosecutor Bhola, who was with Cst. Buerkens, that I was concerned about Young's aggressive attitude and asked her to tell him so. My expectation was that Young might modify his behaviour accordingly. I was apparently quite wrong in my expectation. Young filed the complaint in a letter dated February 11, 1998.

My theory is that because I tended to take a somewhat "soft approach" to justice generally, this did not appeal to an authoritarian police officer like Young. He apparently saw my ill-advised comments as an opportunity to have a public dispute with me. He could thereby establish a bias on my part and he would never have to appear before me again. I have some grudging admiration for his bravado in doing so.

He must also have gone to local media with his complaint. The May 6, 1998, issue of the Banff *Crag & Canyon* published an item headlined "RCMP back Mountie." It said Alberta's Chief Judge Edward Wachowich was investigating a complaint filed by Young claiming I was unfairly biased against him in court. The officer in charge, Staff Sergeant Al McLeod, publicly supported Young and never even bothered to ask me about my concerns.

I think it is a sad comment on the ethics of the RCMP that when a judge is concerned about the conduct of one of its members, the officer in charge defends the member without any further inquiry. This, after all, was not something that came from gossip on the street. It arose from material that was before me in court.

Chris Levy again got back into action. In the May 12 issue of the Banff paper, an article headlined "Judge's comments raise legal question" quoted Levy: "The judge's acknowledgement of bias against Young should spark a re-evaluation by Justice Minister Jon Havelock and Chief Provincial Court Judge Edward Wachowich of the system of resident judges."

The article also contained further quotes from Levy saying that because I had acknowledged I had a problem with Young I would have to disqualify myself from hearing any case in which Cpl. Young gave evidence, because I would not give the Crown a fair hearing. He also said the incident raised a question as to whether it is appropriate to have a single judge.

I believe that if Young's letter had come to Bert Oliver, he would have called me into his office and told me to keep my opinions to myself. Then he would have written to Young and told him the file was closed.

However, from what I learned later, I know that Stevenson was working towards getting the chief judge to order my transfer and this played into his plan. He conducted a full investigation. He required statements from me, Bhola and Buerkens and sent a full report to Chief Judge Wachowich.

Chief Judge Wachowich then wrote to me and Young separately. He told me my remarks were inappropriate and that he would be hard pressed to hire counsel for me if action were taken against me for slanderous comments made off the bench. He said he hoped I would refrain from making such comments in the future and provided me with the letter he had written to Young.

He told Young my comments were inappropriate and that he had told me so. He went on to say:

> ... any opinions formed for or against a party from evidence or conduct occurring before a judge in a judicial proceeding do not constitute the prejudice required to disqualify the judge. Indeed the job of a judge is to judge – to weigh the credibility of witnesses and decide what is acceptable and what is not.
>
> As for your concern that Judge Reilly has lost impartiality vis-à-vis you, the assertion is too broad to be justified. Allegations of bias or lack of impartiality are serious matters and need to be raised in each individual case before the presiding judge to ask him to disqualify himself. The judge's decision to disqualify himself or not is a judicial decision.
>
> I note from a press report (*Calgary Herald*, April 29, 1998) that on March 23 in a trial in Banff the Crown requested Judge

Reilly to disqualify himself from a drug case on grounds of apprehension of bias and he did.

Blanket disqualification cannot be imposed administratively. To allow a litigant or a party to file a letter critical of a trial judge and assert that it is a basis for disqualification would encourage impermissible judge shopping.

I thank you for bringing your concerns to my attention. I trust I have addressed them and now I consider this matter closed.

I thought Judge Wachowich's letter was an excellent statement of the law. What he said to me was exactly what I had expected. What he said to Young went further than I would have expected, and I was somewhat gratified to see it. I was still inclined to think the matter would have received far less attention if the complaint had been made against a judge who enjoyed the favour of the court administration.

❖ 8 ❖

THE *HUNTER* SENTENCE APPEAL

The Court of Appeal delivered its judgment on the sentence appeal in *R. v. Hunter* on May 8, 1998, and true to form they maintained the status quo by adding an 18-month prison term to the probation I had imposed.

Aside from the fact that they allowed the appeal, they did not seem to make any criticism of my conduct in the matter. The court referred to cases decided after I had delivered my judgment, so I could hardly be criticized for not following them.

One of several references to one of those cases, *R. v. Brady*, is paragraph 13:

> As Hetherington J.A. in *Brady* supra at page 548 pointed out:
>
> > Sections 718, 718.1 and 718.2 codify but do not change the law in relation to sentencing. The purpose and principles set out [in those sections] have guided our courts for many years. The only provisions which could be said to bring about a change are [paras] (*d*) and (*e*) of s. 718.2. It is arguable that they place increased emphasis on the principle that incarceration should be the last resort.

The court referred to my order for the investigation, the fact that its scope had been reduced on appeal, that I had entered as an exhibit approximately 70 pages of newspaper and magazine articles regarding the Morley reserve, and that I delivered a written sentencing decision of 44 pages and imposed a two-year suspended sentence.

The court made no further comment on the investigation or my efforts to inform them about the social conditions at Morley by providing them with the newspaper reports. The comment they did make was, in my view, very neutral:

> [20] The sentencing judge in this case placed a great deal of emphasis on the circumstances of the Aboriginal offender and... interpreted this to mean a judge should consider the social, political, historical and cultural factors which play a role in the commission of offences by Aboriginals and contribute to the special difficulties that they experience before the courts.
>
> [21] Section 718.2(e), however, is only one of a number of principles and purposes to be considered in fixing a fit sentence. As pointed out in *Wells*, there is no suggestion that s. 718.2(e) is in any way paramount to the other parts of s. 718.2 or that s. 718.2 is paramount to ss. 718 and 718.1. An appropriate sentence must reflect all of the provisions in those sections.

I had hopes that this judgment might be appealed to the Supreme Court of Canada. I spoke to Hunter's counsel, Jim Ogle, about this possibility. He said he would like to take it to the Supreme Court, but he couldn't find Hunter to get instructions. The Court of Appeal delivered its judgment when Hunter was not present, and he remained at large until after the time for appeal had expired.

I had hoped this would be my equivalent of Stevenson's *Big M* case, but it was not to be. The interpretation of s. 718.2(e) subsequently came before the Supreme Court of Canada in *R. v. Gladue*. The high court confirmed that the purpose of this section was to change the law and to deal with the over-incarceration of Aboriginal people.

❖ 9 ❖

R. V. GLADUE

Some people say you always remember where you were when you heard really earth-shaking news. On Friday, April 23, 1999, I was driving back to Canmore on the Trans-Canada Highway, coming around the bend at Lac des Arcs, when I heard the news that the Supreme Court of Canada had released its judgment in *R. v. Gladue.*

Jamie Gladue had been charged with second degree murder in the stabbing death of her common-law partner, Reuben Beaver. She was born in McLennan, Alberta, in 1976, one of nine children. Her mother was Cree, her father Métis. Her mother left the family home when Jamie was 11 and died in a car accident when she was 14. Jamie and her siblings were raised by her father. She moved in with Reuben when she was 17 and they had their first child when she was 18.

On September 16, 1995, Jamie was celebrating her 19th birthday in the townhouse unit of a friend in Nanaimo, BC. Jamie was five months pregnant and she was drinking. Her blood alcohol content was subsequently determined to be between 155 and 165. She also had a thyroid condition that was said to cause exaggerated reactions to emotional stress.

During the course of the evening, Reuben and Jamie's sister Tara left and went to Tara's unit in the same townhouse complex. Jamie suspected they were having intercourse. She accused Reuben of having sex with her sister. He admitted that he had, and then told her she was "fat and ugly and not as good as the others."

She cut him with a small paring knife. Reuben ran to Tara's unit and was banging on her door when Jamie caught up to him and stabbed him in the chest with a larger knife. He collapsed on the floor in front of Tara's apartment and died in a large pool of his own blood.

A witness said Jamie was jumping up and down as if she had tagged someone and said, "I got you, you fucking bastard," but that she didn't seem to realize what she had done.

On the day scheduled for trial, the Crown consented to a plea of guilty to the lesser charge of manslaughter. This was justified by the provocation of the deceased's comments to her. There was evidence that Reuben had been abusive of her and in fact had served a sentence of imprisonment for an assault on her.

Sentencing took place on February 13, 1997, some 17 months after the event. In the interim, Jamie had been free on bail. She had taken counselling for alcohol and drug abuse and upgraded her education. Her lawyer argued for a suspended sentence or for a conditional sentence that could be served in the community. It was agreed she did not present a danger to the community.

The trial judge considered s. 718.2(*e*). In relation to the "particular attention to the circumstances of Aboriginal offenders" provision he said that although both the accused and the victim were Aboriginals, they were not living on a reserve and the offence occurred in an urban setting. He found that there were no special circumstances because of their Aboriginal status and gave no special consideration to their background in passing this sentence. He sentenced Gladue to three years in prison.

On appeal to the BC Court of Appeal, two of the panel upheld the trial judge, while the third, Justice Anne Rowles, wrote a dissenting judgment. She spoke at length on the unique circumstances of Aboriginal offenders and their cultural views on justice, and in the result said she would reduce the sentence imposed by the trial judge.

I read her judgment with interest. Justice Rowles said many of the same things I had said in my sentencing judgment in *R. v. Hunter*, and I was confident the Supreme Court of Canada would agree with her.

The matter did go to the scc and Justices Peter Cory and Frank Iacobucci wrote the judgment. They held that the courts below erred in taking an overly narrow approach to s. 718.2(*e*). The purpose of that provision is to address the historical over-representation of Aboriginals in the criminal justice system, and it applies to all Aboriginals regardless of place of residence or lifestyle.

The case demonstrated another irony of legal proceedings. In this case Jamie Gladue lost the battle but won the war. The court ultimately dismissed the appeal, but their reasoning set a huge precedent for Aboriginal accused.

The scc found that the sentence was fit given the seriousness of the offence, and in any event Gladue had been released on day parole after serving six months, had done well on an electronic monitoring program and been granted full parole. For these reasons it was not in the interests of justice to resentence her.

I took some satisfaction in comparing the comments I had made in *R. v. Hunter* with those of the scc in *R. v. Gladue*.

In *Hunter* I had ordered an investigation to put information on the record which in my view was relevant to the circumstances of the Aboriginal accused.

In *Gladue* the scc said that "even where counsel do not adduce this evidence... it is incumbent upon the sentencing judge to acquire information regarding the circumstances of the offender as an aboriginal person. ..."

In *Hunter* I said I was concerned about the conditions on the reserve at Morley, the futility of imprisonment and the cultural conflict between the law of Canada and Aboriginal people.

In *Gladue* the scc said "the background factors which figure prominently in the causation of crime by aboriginal offenders" are "years of dislocation ... low incomes, high unemployment, lack of opportunities and options, lack or irrelevance of education, substance abuse, loneliness, and community fragmentation."

The court continued:

> ... the judge who is called upon to sentence an aboriginal offender must give attention to the unique background and systemic factors which may have played a part in bringing the particular offender before the courts. In cases where such factors have played a significant role, it is incumbent upon the sentencing judge to consider these factors in evaluating whether imprisonment would actually serve to deter, or to denounce a crime in a sense that would be meaningful to the community of which the offender is a member. In many instances, more restorative sentencing principles will gain primary relevance precisely because the prevention of crime as well as individual and social healing cannot occur through other means.

In *Hunter* I spoke of the futility of imprisonment and the need to use alternatives.

In *Gladue* the scc said that

> ... the government position when Bill C-41 was under consideration was that the new Part XXIII [of the Criminal Code] was to be remedial in nature. The proposed enactment was directed, in particular, at reducing the use of prison as a sanction, at expanding the use of restorative justice principles in sentencing, and at engaging in both of these objectives with a sensitivity to aboriginal community justice initiatives when sentencing aboriginal offenders. ...
>
> ... The 1996 sentencing reforms embodied in Part XXIII

and s. 718.2(e) in particular, must be understood as a reaction to the overuse of prison as a sanction, and must accordingly be given appropriate force as remedial provisions.

In *Hunter* I said I would not follow the Court of Appeal sentencing guidelines, because in my view s. 718.2(e) had created a new consideration in sentencing Aboriginals.

In *Gladue* the scc said:

Section 718.2(e) is not simply a codification of existing jurisprudence. It is remedial in nature. Its purpose is to ameliorate the serious problem of overrepresentation of aboriginal people in prisons, and to encourage sentencing judges to have recourse to a restorative approach to sentencing. There is a judicial duty to give the provision's remedial purpose real force.

In *Hunter* I spoke of cultural differences and quoted the Royal Commission on Aboriginal Peoples report *Bridging the Cultural Divide*, which said at p. 281: "All evidence before the commission makes it clear that the non-aboriginal justice system has failed the Aboriginal peoples."

In *Gladue*, the scc quoted RCAP to the same effect and also said:

Statements regarding the extent and severity of this problem are disturbingly common.... the Royal Commission on Aboriginal Peoples listed as its first "Major Findings and Conclusions" the following striking yet representative statement:

'The principal reason for this crushing failure is the fundamentally different world views of Aboriginal and non-Aboriginal people with respect to such elemental

issues as the substantive content of justice and the
process of achieving justice.'

In *Hunter* I said that the new provision of the Criminal Code
required an emphasis on treatment and that not only justice but
morality required this to be emphasized in relation to Aboriginal
peoples.

In *Gladue* the scc said s. 718.2(*e*) "directs sentencing judges to
undertake the sentencing of aboriginal offenders individually, but
also differently, because the circumstances of aboriginal people
are unique." and "Judges may take judicial notice of the broad systemic and background factors affecting aboriginal people, and of
the priority given in aboriginal cultures to a restorative approach
to sentencing."

Alberta's Chief Judge Wachowich, in his letter to me of April
3, 1998, had said: "You want to justify your actions under 718.2(*e*)
which is an interpretation of that section by yourself whereby you
have greatly exceeded your jurisdiction."

My reading of *R. v. Gladue* tells me that the scc agreed with
my interpretation and that I properly exercised my jurisdiction.

In his March 30 letter to Wachowich, Stevenson commented
that I was a judge who had an "obsession to subjugate the law
to his perception of unjust social conditions on the Stoney First
Nation Reserve at Morley," and concluded that "when matters
before him involve aboriginal persons, he does not intend to act
objectively, judicially or in accordance with Canadian law."

Again, my reading of *Gladue* tells me that I was right to consider the social conditions, and that I was acting objectively, judicially and in accordance with Canadian law.

❖ IO ❖

A MEETING WITH THE CHIEF JUDGE

Wachowich and Stevenson did not wait for the scc judgment in *Gladue*. They may not even have been aware of the case. The week after the Alberta Court of Appeal issued its judgment in *Hunter* on May 8, Laurie Herron called to tell me the chief judge wanted to meet with me. We set the date for May 26, 1998.

.I asked her what it was about. She said she didn't know. The Cpl. Young matter was still outstanding. I assumed it was about that, and that it would just be a formality in which I would be told my comments were ill-advised and the matter would be at an end.

On May 14 I saw Judge Stevenson at the University of Calgary on the occasion of Justice Milton Harradence being conferred an honorary doctorate. We just happened to be walking from the parking lot at the same time, and I asked him what the meeting with the chief was all about. He replied: "I don't know, and I can't find out, because the chief is out of town." Trying to make light of the situation I asked him if I should have a lawyer with me. He replied in his usual flippant manner: "That might not be a bad idea."

I was still assuming it had to do with Young when I received the letter from Wachowich disposing of the Young complaint.

Again mystified as to what the meeting was about, I called Judge Stevenson's office and asked him again. His answer was something to the effect of "oh, it has to do with the new Tsuu T'ina court and possible changes to your circuit."

On May 26 I attended the meeting, still not knowing what it was about. I went into Stevenson's office. Wachowich and Stevenson were sitting on either end of a couch and I sat in a chair across from them. After we had exchanged greetings I asked what the meeting was about. Wachowich told me they had reviewed matters on my circuit and I was to move back to Calgary effective September 1.

I told them I thought they were being unfair and that I would talk to a lawyer. I accused them of political motivation. They denied they had any and told me they were concerned that I had lost my objectivity with Aboriginal offenders.

They criticized me for calling Stoney Chief John Snow a "crook" and for attaching 70 pages of newspaper clippings to my judgment in *Hunter*. I argued that I had not called Snow a crook but that he was one, and that the *Calgary Herald* had done the investigation the government should have done.

Wachowich and Stevenson said I was lucky the Court of Appeal had not been more critical of me in their judgment on the *Hunter* sentence. When I said the appeal decision might not be sustained on further appeal, the two of them chided me for thinking I knew more than the Court of Appeal and said this was just further proof of my loss of objectivity.

I challenged them on the matter of judicial independence and the impression that the people at Morley and the general public would have about this being a punishment for my efforts to improve the delivery of justice. They were not prepared to listen to me. The meeting was simply a formality to inform me of a decision already made. This was confirmed at the end of the meeting when Wachowich gave me a letter dated (and presumably signed) on May 25. It said:

> As a result of continuing and mounting concerns about your obsession to subjugate the law to your perception of

unjust social conditions of the Aboriginal peoples as well as your prejudgment attitude which can more frequently become grounds for application to disqualify yourself from presiding over a case on the basis of bias, Assistant Chief Judge Stevenson and I have decided to reassign you to sit in Calgary from the 1st of September 1998.

This entails a change of residence for you from Canmore to Calgary. Assistant Chief Judge Stevenson will assist you with the administrative details in this matter.

I may add that this move is the only honourable way of keeping you and the provincial judiciary out of harm's way. For the purposes of the executive branch, however, I have justified this move on administrative grounds. (See copy of enclosed letter to the deputy minister.)

The letter to the deputy minister included the following:

As part of our ongoing commitment to improve the efficiency of the justice delivery system, Assistant Chief Judge Stevenson has thoroughly reviewed the operations of the court circuit west of Calgary (Banff, Canmore and Cochrane). I enclose his report for your perusal.

I agree with Assistant Chief Judge Stevenson that the above-noted circuit can be run more efficiently from Calgary. This can be done by adjusting our sitting schedule on that circuit and by moving Judge Reilly from Canmore to Calgary.

Pursuant to the authority that I have under the existing laws, I intend to designate the sitting days on that circuit as suggested by Assistant Chief Judge Stevenson and reassign Judge Reilly from Canmore to Calgary, both decisions to be effective 1st of September 1998.

Whether Canmore should remain a base point or not is in your jurisdiction; my concern is the provision of facilities there to hold sittings of our court on designated days from 1st of September 1998.

This is to request you to do whatever is necessary to facilitate the changes that I am making, namely the change of residence of Judge Reilly from Canmore to Calgary and appropriate staffing and facilities at Canmore on the new sitting days there.

It was now apparent that the timing of Laurie Herron's call to me was because Wachowich and Stevenson had waited for the Court of Appeal decision in *Hunter* before taking action against me.

Later, when I received the chief judge's record in the course of my litigation against him, I read a memo from Herron to Wachowich dated April 29, 1998. In it she told the chief judge that I had been inquiring about the Young complaint. Her memo went on to say: "I believe he is anticipating some action being taken against him. He is not aware, of course, of the impending closure of the Banff/Canmore Base Point."

I can only guess that Laurie Herron knew what the meeting was about but had been told to lie to me about it.

❖ II ❖

AFTER THE MEETING

After the meeting I was feeling numb and confused. I needed someone to talk to. I called retired Assistant Chief Judge Hubert (Bert) Oliver.

His wife, Pam, made us tea, and we chatted for a considerable time. Bert was supportive of my efforts with Aboriginal offenders and did not approve of the action being taken against me. At the end of our discussion he recommended that I retain counsel to challenge the order.

When I left, I called Alan Hunter while I was still parked in front of Judge Oliver's house. I told him of my situation and asked if he would help me. He told me to make a record of everything I could remember of the meeting and to come to his office the next morning.

At home that night, Laura and I talked about what we should do. I was fed up with the conflict. I have often said I wanted to be a judge because I didn't like being an advocate in our adversarial system. I thought I would make a much better referee than a player. I suggested to Laura that maybe we should just give in and go back to Calgary.

Laura and I have since separated, but in spite of the unhappy differences that arose between us, I will always be grateful to her for her reply at that moment: "You started this fight to help the Stoneys. Are you just going to back out on them?"

She was right. And besides that, the thought of going back to the courthouse in Calgary and being under the thumb of

Stevenson, after he had pretended to be my friend and betrayed me, was unbearable.

I stayed up most of the night, reliving the meeting and recording every comment that came to mind.

The next morning the City page of the *Herald* headlined an article by Bob Beaty: "Judge's transfer lamented." It said a Stoney councillor and former reserve executive charged that Reilly was being punished by the provincial government for forcing it and Ottawa to take action on long ignored allegations of political and economic corruption on the once-rich reserve 60 kilometres west of Calgary. The article said Chief Judge Wachowich had confirmed the transfer, and quoted him as saying: "I can emphatically deny that governments had anything to do with it."

The story went on to review the history of my order for the investigation and the band management by Coopers & Lybrand, the sentence of probation I had delivered in *Hunter* and the fact that the Court of Appeal had overruled me and raised the sentence to 18 months imprisonment.

The article quoted Hunter's lawyer, Jim Ogle: "I think it is very regrettable for the Stoney community that they will lose a judge who has gone to such great lengths to learn about their culture and apply his knowledge to his sentencing practices."

Tina Fox was quoted as saying: "This makes me sad. John Reilly is fair and objective." She said other judges didn't look at the whole picture in cases involving Aboriginals. "They just kept sending our people to jail, but Judge Reilly looked at the whole picture, including our social situation, and passed sentences designed to heal those charged and the community."

Finally it quoted Warren Harbeck, a linguist who had worked in the community for 33 years: "For those who had been beaten down for so long and struggled to find ways to get on top of things, John Reilly has had the heart to extend a hand." He also said the courtroom I ran was known for its "justice, mercy and truth" and that "if those virtues proved to be the ground for punishing him, then this is indeed a sad day for all Albertans."

I found these comments comforting of course, but the fact that the article was in the paper concerned me. I didn't know how Bob Beaty had managed to get the story, but I was sure Brian Stevenson would accuse me of immediately running to the press, which in fact he did. As it turned out, it was Judge John James who had given Beaty the story. Judge James told me about it some time later and said he didn't want to see them railroad me quietly.

In the past I had found it relaxing to flip through the paper in the morning before heading off to court. I was far from relaxed the morning of May 27. I drove to Calgary and met with Alan Hunter and a junior lawyer, Megan McMahon. Alan read my notes. When he had finished he said, "You've been slimed, slammed and punished and they didn't give you a hearing."

Alan Hunter's life was pleading cases for his clients. For him the most egregious aspect of what had happened to me ("egregious" was one of his favourite words) was that I had not been given a hearing. This was a breach of procedural fairness, and in his view the order could be set aside for this reason alone.

McMahon added that what she saw as the fatal flaw was that my initial designation as the resident judge for Banff/Canmore was by ministerial order. The chief judge, regardless of whatever authority he had over me, did not have the jurisdiction to overrule the order of a minister.

I suggested that the most important issue was judicial independence. Wachowich and Stevenson obviously disagreed with my judgments in relation to Aboriginal offenders. They were relocating me to prevent me from making any further comments on injustices to the Stoney people. This was a real violation of judicial independence, as opposed to the theoretical violation that related to the salary issue. The order was so obviously faulty that I expected a simple chambers application, which might take an hour or two, would be all that would be necessary to have it set aside. This was yet another example of my own naïveté.

The next day saw another headline on the *Herald*'s City page: "Reilly hires lawyer to battle transfer." The article said I had hired Alan Hunter, one of Alberta's most prominent lawyers. Again it recited a brief history of the *Hunter* case and my order for the investigation. It quoted Harry Gaede, the president of the Alberta Provincial Court Judges Association, as saying that moving a judge might be an issue of judicial independence. Gaede went on to point out that the Supreme Court of Canada had dealt with one case where a government had relocated a judge, and said it was an affront to judicial independence. Gaede was further quoted as saying, "Certainly, the chief judge under the previous legislation believes he has the power (to reassign judges)."

The article concluded with: "Stoney councillor Aaron Young said Reilly gave First Nations people a voice, and it isn't surprising that attempts would be made to silence him."

❖ 12 ❖

THE LITIGATION BEGINS

Alan Hunter wasted no time in getting down to business. By letter dated May 29, he informed the chief judge that he would represent me in the matter and asked him to withdraw the order of transfer. In that letter the only grounds he stated were that the order had been made without notice to me and without hearing from me. He also commented that this was a delicate matter for the Provincial Court of Alberta and I had no desire to harm the Provincial Court by the public nature of a proceeding in the Court of Queen's Bench, but that there was no alternative if the chief judge was not prepared to withdraw his decision and all directions as to its implementation.

Alan was highly principled and he was legitimately concerned about the reputation of the court. He wanted to maintain its public respect. I was angry and might not have been so principled, but one of Alan Hunter's oft-repeated admonitions was "take the high road."

He also advised me to keep a low profile: "You know, John, I'm guessing that most judges read the newspapers. If you are seen to be too defiant or too close to the Stoneys, it may have an influence on the outcome of this case."

We discussed the Women of Distinction Awards, at which Tina Fox was being honoured with a Lifetime Achievement Award. Alan pointed out that the press would cover the event and just my attendance would likely be subject to comment in the media. Tina was my friend and she had gone out on a limb for me by publicly supporting my order for the investigation. I told Alan I would like to be an ideal client, but there was a limit to what I was prepared to do. Not going to Tina's event was beyond that limit. I think Alan agreed with me, even though I was not taking his advice.

The awards night was a fine evening. Tina made a great acceptance speech. No one from the media paid any attention to me.

I did take Alan's advice to withdraw from an event sponsored by the Aboriginal opportunities committee of the Calgary Chamber of Commerce's Native Awareness Week. I had agreed to speak on a panel entitled "A Moccasin in Two Worlds," scheduled for June 15, 1998. Barb Bedard had invited me the previous November, after I had delivered my sentencing judgment in *Hunter*. I had hoped matters would have settled down enough by June that I could do this, but the impending litigation changed that.

It was a disappointment to me to have to pass on the opportunity to be on a panel with Peter Meekison and Mike Cardinal, who had been members of the Royal Commission on Aboriginal Peoples. I had written what I thought was a great talk on my own personal awakening to the plight of Aboriginal people in Canada (see Appendix B). I wrote about hearing Aboriginal women tell of the horrors of residential schools and my not knowing what they were talking about. I wrote of the difference between the version of Canadian history I had learned at school and what my father had taught me at home. One example was the school version of the Riel Rebellion and my father's version, the Riel Resistance. I sent a copy to Chief Judge Wachowich and asked if he had any objection to my attending the panel discussion. He sent the request to Stevenson, who said my comments went beyond permissible public comment by judges and contravened judicial ethics.

Stevenson was not in a good position to be too critical. Some years before, as president of the judges association, he had made a very public speech in favour of capital punishment, which was severely criticized by some judges who disagreed with his position and were afraid that his remarks would be taken as being representative of the court when they were not.

Wachowich wrote confirming Stevenson's opinion. He said he found my proposed speech provocative and inaccurate and the reference to Hitler offensive. He too said my remarks would go beyond permissible public comment by judges and contravened judicial ethics.

I didn't see anything inaccurate or unethical about anything I said, but Alan Hunter's advice was that it might make the possibility of settlement more difficult. He asked me to withdraw, in the interest of a possible resolution, and I did.

In spite of this effort to appease the chief judge, settlement proved impossible. On June 26, 1998 (my 52nd birthday), a year to the day after I had ordered the investigation at Morley, I met junior counsel Megan McMahon in the coffee shop at Cochrane and swore the affidavit in support of my application for judicial review.

The affidavit was nine short paragraphs setting out that my official residence was Canmore, that the chief judge had ordered me to change my residence, and that in conversations prior to the meeting at which I was given the order, I was not informed of the reason for the meeting. It also said that I believed the respondent was biased in making the decision and that the decision infringed my judicial independence, took into account irrelevant considerations and was actuated by improper motives.

In addition to Wachowich's letter of May 25 mentioned in chapter 10, I also attached as Exhibit C a letter of April 3 which was in response to a letter I had written to Wachowich suggesting that his Polish background might make him more sympathetic to the Aboriginal people. His reply stated:

I applaud you for your conversion on the road to Damascus and the help you are prepared to accord the Aboriginal people but I strongly object to how you are improperly abusing your judicial position to achieve this end. Your judgments in *Hunter* and others recently are the most atrocious judgments that I have seen as Chief Judge of the Provincial Court. An example is making findings of fact where there is no evidence before you and there are many others. You want to justify your actions under 718.2(e) which is an interpretation of that section by yourself whereby you have greatly exceeded your jurisdiction.

On June 29, 1998, we started the litigation by an originating notice of motion for judicial review. The application was returnable in chambers on July 10, 1998.

The procedure for judicial review requires the person receiving the originating notice requesting the review to forthwith file all the documents that relate to the decision being challenged. In the ordinary course, we should have received the chief judge's documentation and been able to go into court to argue the matter. Such was not to be the case.

Alan Hunter was initially optimistic about settlement, because we expected Cliff O'Brien, of the firm of Bennett Jones, to be the chief judge's lawyer. Hunter told me that O'Brien was able counsel who would assess the issues and simply tell the chief judge that his order was bad for having been made without jurisdiction and without a hearing, and for being a violation of judicial independence.

Unfortunately that didn't happen. Bennett Jones was acting for the Alberta Provincial Court Judges Association in their lawsuit against the government over salaries. Ironically, because I was a member of the APCJA, Bennett Jones were, in effect, my lawyers too. A law firm cannot act for you on one file and against you on another. This would be a classic example of a conflict of interest. So, Cliff O'Brien was not eligible to act for the chief judge. Wachowich went so far as to ask the APCJA to consent to O'Brien representing him, but the association refused.

Because of this, the chief judge was required to go with his second choice, E. David Tavender, QC, of the firm of Milner Fenerty. The government of Alberta would pay Tavender and he could run up as big a bill as he liked. One of the worst aspects of civil litigation is that wealthy parties to a lawsuit can run up legal costs to such an extent that an underfunded party has no recourse but to give in, even if they have an ironclad case at law. It is my view that this is exactly what I was faced with. To be fair to David Tavender, Alan Hunter didn't like him, and this contributed to the impossibility of resolution.

"Judicial independence" was the slogan of the judges' litigation team, and there was animated support for it by most of the judges. The expectation of financial return from the litigation over salaries was a huge motivator. On the other hand, my interest in judicial independence was to be able to write judgments which I believed were a proper application of the law. I believed the government, through the chief judge, wanted to prevent me from saying the things I was saying. Those in power did not want the abuses in tribal governments and reserve communities to be made public, and I saw the overt action to prevent me from doing so as an absolute and real violation of my judicial independence.

My fellow judges, with some notable exceptions, were disinterested. Judges generally tend to be very conservative, and many were critical of my controversial comments and agreed with the chief judge's action against me. In any event, the main event for most of the judges was the salary issue. My criticism of all levels of government was not helping their negotiations.

When I first spoke to Alan about taking my case, I had asked him how much he thought it might cost. His reply was: "How long is a piece of string?" He told me he couldn't afford a lawyer himself, but that he would see the matter through and would not pursue me for payment. This wasn't exactly a promise of pro bono work. The legal expenses, which ultimately exceeded a quarter of a million dollars, were a huge source of stress for me.

This was a huge breach of my judicial independence. I became seriously indebted to a lawyer, which could have created the real possibility that the lawyer could expect favours from me.

There was in fact an occasion on which a lawyer from Hunter's firm was representing a man accused of a minor traffic violation. The violation had implications in a pending civil suit. I had no interest in the case and had never met the lawyer who was acting. I asked the Crown if they had any objection to my hearing the case and they did not. However, the lawyer said he would prefer another judge, to avoid the possibility that if he obtained a favourable result from me, it might be seen as having been influenced by my dealings with his firm. His position was absolutely correct and I adjourned the matter so it could be heard by a different judge.

Meanwhile, back in my own litigation, Chief Judge Wachowich's counsel, Mr. Tavender, had the July 10 return date adjourned to August 7.

On July 15 he made an offer of settlement that I found offensive. It proposed that I would accept the reassignment to Calgary but could maintain my residence pending a determination by the Judicial Council, and my expenses would be paid for travel from Canmore to Calgary until that determination was made. I would then withdraw my notice of motion without costs. I suggested to Alan Hunter that perhaps he should explain our position to Tavender and the chief judge using small words and short sentences. The unfortunate fact is that there was virtually no communication. Our position was that the order was faulty and should be withdrawn. Their position was that I should accept the order and move.

On July 16, Tavender filed a notice of motion on behalf of the chief judge challenging the jurisdiction of the Court of Queen's Bench to review the chief judge's decision. What I had naïvely expected would be a simple chambers application was becoming a very drawn out bit of litigation.

The lawyers went together to the office of Kenneth Moore, the Chief Justice of the Court of Queen's Bench, to select the QB justice who would hear the matter. It was agreed that it would be Justice Blair Mason.

Alan and I were both pleased with the assignment of Justice Mason. We discussed the matter at length. Alan commented that since judges tend to be pretty conservative, there would be a fair amount of peer pressure on the judge hearing the case to decide against me. As Alan put it, "You upset a lot of people with that *Hunter* decision, and a lot of them will be in agreement with Wachowich's move to shut you up. Everybody knows the social conditions on the reserves are horrible, but no one wants to deal with them. This will get a lot of media attention and if you talk to the press, we have to assume that judges will be reading the paper, and that could go against you."

I didn't say anything to anybody except Bert Oliver. Stevenson told some of the judges that he and Wachowich were moving me back to Calgary. Judge John James heard it in the judges lounge, and he told Bob Beaty, the *Herald* reporter.

"The quieter you are, the better it will be for you. Take the high road," advised Alan.

I told him Blair Mason was a Scots Presbyterian and I was confident that he would decide according to his conscience no matter how much pressure he might feel. I did agree to limit my public comment.

I told Alan that my mother had spoken highly of Blair Mason, that when she was in the choir at St. Mary's they had a joint

Christmas festival with his church and she was very impressed with his singing.

"What does your mother think of all the publicity you are getting?" Alan asked.

"She died 10 years ago. Good thing, too. If she were still alive, all the media excitement would probably kill her."

The conversation ended with a comment Alan often made: "Keep your powder dry."

During the litigation, I was often asked what I thought about the possibility that the matter would be decided against me on political grounds. To this I repeated what I'd said to Alan Hunter: I was confident Blair Mason would decide the matter according to his conscience and would be absolutely uninfluenced by any political consideration.

❖ 13 ❖

THE HEARING ON JURISDICTION

I shake my head when I think of how naïve I was to believe this matter would be disposed of quickly. It was just so patently obvious that the chief judge's order was bad, but that didn't deter Tavender.

It was now August 7, 1998, and we were in court for the purpose of determining whether or not the Court of Queen's Bench could even hear my application. The *Herald* ran an article headlined "Reilly's transfer battle heads to court today."

It was agreed that argument on the challenge to jurisdiction would take some time. Argument on the merits of the order itself would be adjourned to a later date.

Tavender filed a 31-page brief, citing 26 references to support his arguments. He then filed a supplementary brief adding another 14 references. The two binders totalled 447 pages. Hunter filed a 22-page brief, citing 16 references to support his argument. His one binder was 426 pages. The hearing took all day and the transcript was 182 pages. Justice Mason would have to assimilate over 1,100 pages of material in order to decide whether he even had jurisdiction to hear the real issue.

From my own experience as a judge, I think there would be an overwhelming temptation to find in Tavender's favour. If Justice Mason found he did not have jurisdiction, his work would be done. If he found he did, he would have to listen to more hours of argument and assimilate another thousand pages or more of material. Fortunately for me, Blair Mason was a very conscientious judge, and that temptation may not even have occurred to him.

My respect and admiration for Alan Hunter was becoming augmented by affection. He had a problem with his voice. His doctor had told him he had inflamed vocal cords, but beyond that, the doctor could neither tell him the cause nor suggest a cure. So Hunter talked with the aid of an amplifying speaker that hung around his neck, and his delivery seemed painfully strained. In spite of this, he spoke eloquently in my behalf.

Tavender argued that opening up the internal workings of the court to public scrutiny through a judicial review risked undermining public confidence in the system's independence. His main argument was that institutional independence should exclude the judicial review process.

He spoke easily, if not a little glibly. His arguments were basically these:

1. Institutional judicial independence requires the court to be free of any external control, including control by the higher court through judicial review of a chief judge's decision in any administrative or disciplinary matter.
2. Judicial review is a legal action against the chief judge, and s. 16 of the Provincial Court Judges Act prohibits any action against a judge.
3. Judicial review is not available where there is an alternative remedy. In this case the alternative was a complaint to the Judicial Council.
4. Judges cannot be required to testify in relation to the exercise of their judicial function. Because judges have this immunity, I should not be allowed to testify and therefore my affidavit should be struck out.

If Tavender's arguments were accepted, it would mean that a

chief judge could take any action against any judge on the basis of his administrative and disciplinary authority. Unless the judge could prove the action was taken with malice and without probable cause, there would be no recourse.

Tavender claimed the chief judge had the power, under his administrative and supervisory powers, "to assign Judge Reilly to Calgary or to High Level or wherever the other worst location or best location may be in the sittings of Alberta … ."

He argued that because the statute expressed no limit as to what the chief judge may do, the legislature intended that "the chief judge, in carrying out his section 9 discipline duties, be free of restraint, jurisdictional restraint, natural justice restraint and that, rather, he'd be entitled to act more or less as the Lord Chancellors in England have acted, in an informal way, with the object of trying to resolve the problem, without restraint."

In answer to Tavender's arguments, Hunter asserted that Tavender had completely missed the constitutional aspect of the matter – that the real issue was the constitutional protection of judicial independence, and that Tavender had failed to address the constitutional issue.

He argued that even if there was a clearly expressed intention by a legislature not to be bound by the Constitution, it would not prevail. He pointed out that since 1982, we have a constitutional democracy, not a parliamentary democracy, and that the authorities on which Tavender relied related to a sovereign Parliament which we no longer have, and that any law that is inconsistent with the Constitution is of no force or effect. I, of course, thought Hunter's analysis was brilliant.

During his submission I noted that Vijay Bhardwaj, the chief judge's legal adviser, looked extremely upset. He had counselled the chief judge on the procedure for transferring me. I believe he could see that Hunter was right, and he was now realizing how bad his own advice had been. I found Bhardwaj's discomfort amusing at the time, but I liked Vijay and it was upsetting to me that he was with my adversary in this matter. He died of a heart attack not long after this and I worried that the stress of this lawsuit may have contributed to it.

Hunter made several references to the chief judge's failure to file the record. He pointed out that the purpose of the chief judge's application was so that we don't see the record, and said: "It makes you wonder what's in the record."

He summarized the question before the court as: "Does the Queen's Bench of Alberta have the power to review an apparently unconstitutional action by a statutory delegate, and should it exercise it on the basis of the material that the court presently has?"

He said he would show that the issue was judicial independence, that the impugned decision was "constitutionally impermissible, as it infringes upon all of the judges of the court, for it will be a power not limited to Judge Reilly. If [the chief judge] can apply it to Judge Reilly, he can apply it to any judge absolutely and without judicial review."

Finally Alan said the material demonstrated that the chief judge had "acted without jurisdiction and upon improper motives and considerations and failed to govern himself in accordance with settled principles of fairness, including notice, hearing and impartiality."

In the course of his argument, Tavender had said, "I know of no authority that says the chief judge may not comment adversely on a past decision." To this, Hunter replied: "It's not a comment. It's more. It's the whole thing. It's the charge, the prosecution, the trial, the conviction and the sentence. It's not just a comment."

Justice Mason listened patiently to the arguments and then adjourned the matter so he could prepare a written judgment. In the meantime, he ordered a stay of the transfer order. This meant that while the matter was being decided, I would continue in my position in Banff/Canmore/Cochrane.

The *Herald*, of course, covered the hearing. The resulting article was headlined "Judge's transfer blocked till court rules" and was accompanied by what I thought was a great photograph of me and my wife, Laura, taken outside the courthouse when we went for lunch during the noon break. The article on the next page was headlined "Judge: Quote from letter draws gasp." This was a reference to the courtroom reaction to Wachowich's letter telling me that I was improperly using my judicial position, making atrocious judgments and being an embarrassment to the court.

I suppose I should have been embarrassed by the chief judge's critique, but I was so confident I was right that I thought those comments could only be an embarrassment to him. It was my ambition at all times to draw attention to the abysmal conditions on the reserve, and this article, as with almost all of the others the *Herald* printed, included the background to the story: "In June 1997, in ordering the provincial Crown to investigate social and economic conditions on the Stoney reserve, 60 kilometres west of Calgary, Reilly said a powerful elite ran the reserve like a 'banana republic' while two-thirds of its 3,300 residents lived on welfare." My naïve theory was that if the problems were public knowledge, something would be done about them, so I took satisfaction from the fact that the litigation was continuing to keep that issue alive. It also gave me some satisfaction that Stevenson, who had already scheduled me for sittings in Calgary in September, was now required to put me back on the Banff/Canmore/Cochrane circuit.

❖ 14 ❖

PRESERVING THE PUBLIC RIGHT

Alan Hunter would often start a conversation in a way that indicated he had been giving a matter deep thought. After the August 7 appearance before Justice Mason, he started such a conversation with me:

"What do you think would happen if you decided a case against a party who appeared before you, and he appealed the decision on the basis that his section 11 right to be tried by an impartial and independent tribunal was violated because your independence was compromised by the pressure being put on you by this litigation?"

"Well, I suppose he might have a successful argument," I replied.

"So what are you going to do about it?" Alan asked.

"I don't know. Chris Levy was quoted as saying I should be given a paid leave of absence until this is settled, but I don't think Wachowich is inclined to ask the government to send me on a paid holiday for upsetting them the way I seem to have upset them. However, I do see your point. This could take years, and if one litigant were successful in making that argument, every case I heard could be set aside. What do you suggest?"

"I think that every time you open court you should advise everyone present of your situation and give them the option of proceeding or not," Alan answered. "I don't think you have any choice in this. Members of the public are entitled to know what's going on and to make an informed decision on whether or not they want to have you hear their cases."

"I agree. I'll draft something and we'll discuss it further before I do this."

The statement we agreed on, which I first read aloud in court on August 11, 1998, was the following:

> Prior to dealing with any of the cases that are on the docket today I wish to make a brief statement relating to litigation in which I am involved with my chief judge. I do so because the litigation has raised the issue of my handling of cases, particularly those involving Aboriginal offenders, but it concerns everyone who appears before me. I would like to carry on the business of this court as usual, but I find it necessary to make this statement because the rights of everyone appearing before me may be affected by what is happening to me.
>
> Every accused person before the court has the right under section 11(d) of the Charter of Rights to a fair and public hearing by an independent and impartial tribunal. If my independence is compromised, that right is denied to those who appear before me. If I am subject to external control, then the right of every person who appears before me is compromised. The only control over my decision-making capacity should be courts of appeal, which may overrule my decisions if I have made an error in law or procedure or exceed my jurisdiction.
>
> On May 26 of this year the chief judge of the Provincial Court of Alberta directed that I be reassigned from my sittings in Banff, Canmore and Cochrane and that I accept assignments in Calgary from September 1, 1998, and move my residence from Canmore to Calgary. In doing so, he informed me – and this is now a matter of record in the Court of Queen's Bench of Alberta – that his reason was continuing and mounting concerns about my obsession to subjugate the law to my perception of unjust social conditions of Aboriginal peoples. It is also a matter of court record that he has also told me that my

judgments in *Hunter* and others are most atrocious, and that my handling of native matters is an embarrassment to the court, that I have lost my objectivity in relation to Aboriginal offenders, that I have a prejudgment attitude, that I am biased, and that I have abused my judicial power in respect to my handling of cases involving Aboriginal offenders.

The message I get from these statements and my transfer is that if I do not decide cases in a manner which pleases the chief judge, I will be subject to punishment by him. I regard the decision of the chief judge as wrong and I am challenging it in the Court of Queen's Bench. I do not intend to be influenced by these events, but those appearing before me should know this is happening and should not be required to have their cases heard by me while my independence in deciding cases before me is subject to this external pressure.

I will continue to hear cases according to my view of the law and what is right, and I will resist every external pressure in performing my judicial function, but people who appear before me should be aware of the pressures I am facing, and if anybody is uncomfortable about my ability, in these circumstances, to properly decide cases before me, they can simply request adjournments, and I will grant all requests, without requiring reasons, until such time as the cloud over my independence has been lifted.

There were in fact no requests for adjournment pursuant to my offer.

However, David Tavender saw my statement as an opportunity to again try to lift the stay of my transfer. On August 19 he filed a notice of motion to vary the stay of my reassignment. In support of the motion he filed a transcript of the statement from the court reporter, giving as his grounds "the need to ensure that the Provincial Court sittings at Banff, Canmore, Cochrane and

Calgary be effectively and efficiently administered pending the determination of these matters."

During most of this litigation, I pretty much assumed that the decisions would go in my favour. The whole proceeding against me was just so patently wrong that I couldn't imagine losing. But, for some reason, I found this application upsetting. I was in a campground on Okanagan Lake with Laura and my children, Carlyn, 4, and Jamie, 3. This was 1998 and my cell phone service was limited to Alberta, so I had called Hunter's office on the pay phone in the campground. His secretary, Louise McKay, told me the notice of motion had been filed.

The thought occurred to me that even though I knew I would be successful in the long run, the public spectacle of my fight with the chief judge was not doing the appearance of justice any good. Justice Mason might be influenced by this enough for him to find that a less conspicuous place for me to be sitting would be in the best interest of justice. I thought of the smug look on Stevenson's face the day he and Wachowich gave me the order. The possibility of having to work in the same courthouse with him destroyed my enjoyment of watching my children build sand castles.

When Alan and I discussed the matter, I told him I was upset by it, and I said with some degree of emotion, "If I were dealing with men of good will, I wouldn't have these problems."

He replied in his usual forceful way, "Well, you're not, so get over it."

The new motion was heard on September 2, 1998. Justice Mason heard that argument and then delivered a 26-page judgment on the question of jurisdiction, which had been argued on August 7. He went over the arguments of the chief judge's counsel and my counsel and gave a detailed ruling on each.

He distinguished between the chief judge's adjudicative independence as a judge and his decisions as a statutory delegate, and said the arguments on the chief judge's judicial independence did not apply to the latter. Justice Mason confirmed that the matter raised constitutional issues of the adjudicative independence of Provincial Court trial judges and the institutional independence of that court; that issues could not be limited by provincial legislation; that a chief judge does not have unfettered powers; and that adjudicative judicial independence is the freedom of individual judges to hear and decide cases without interference by the government, any organized nation or group, any individual or even any other judge.

Justice Mason then ordered the chief judge to file his return to my originating motion and extended the stay of the chief judge's order.

Again I was able to stay in Canmore and continue doing my circuit.

❖ 15 ❖

ATTEMPTED MEDIATION

Throughout my difficulties with the chief judge's office, Judge Ray Bradley was always the soft-spoken supporter who seemed to try and help me behind the scenes. Around the same time that I was trying to establish justice programs at Morley, Judge Bradley had worked with Judge Peter Ayotte in establishing a successful program on the Alexis Reserve, near Edmonton, which coincidentally is also a Stoney community.

The difference between Morley and Alexis was of course the community participation. At Alexis there was a group of more than a dozen community leaders who would accept referrals from the Provincial Court judges and work with offenders towards rehabilitation.

Ironically, in 2006 there was an article in the *Edmonton Journal* praising the program and Chief Judge Ernie Walter, who was about to retire, for work in trying to expand the program. While Judge Walter was getting the good press on this program, he was still actively opposing my efforts at Morley.

Judge Bradley sincerely wanted to end my fight with the chief judge's office. He prevailed upon Chief Judge Wachowich to participate in a mediation session in Calgary. It took place on September 21, 1998. The mediators were Judge Frank Maloney and Judge John Maher.

Laura and I arrived at the courthouse about 2:30 in the afternoon and talked with Maloney and Maher for a couple of hours.

They had already met with Wachowich and Stevenson in the morning.

This was an unusual format for mediation. I am aware of the process of a mediator shuttling back and forth between parties, especially where there is so much animosity that there may be a potential for violence if everyone is in the same room, but I don't think that applied here. In spite of our differences, I think we would have all been able to speak civilly. However, this was the format. Wachowich and Stevenson presented their case to the mediators; we presented ours; and then the mediators made a proposal for settlement. We told the mediators we were sure the order for transfer was politically motivated and said we were not going to accept it.

It was in this context that Judge Maher told us about the meeting with Justice Minister Jon Havelock in the summer of 1997. His reason for recounting the incident was to demonstrate that Wachowich was doing his duty as chief judge. He also said Wachowich was determined to protect his jurisdiction from review by the higher court, and that he would take that issue to the Supreme Court of Canada if necessary. What Maher wanted me to know was that Wachowich had resisted the pressure to take action against me. What I concluded was that there had in fact been political pressure to take the action.

Judge John James suggested to me that Wachowich wanted to remain on good terms with the minister because he wanted post-retirement employment as the coordinator of the justices of the peace program.

I mentioned this to Judge Phil Ketchum one day when he and I were paddling down the Bow River from Banff to Canmore. He told me that Judge Sam Friedman had been appointed coordinator by Chief Judge Wachowich on the condition that he would retire when Wachowich was ready to fill the position himself.

These rumours seemed to be borne out when Wachowich

reached mandatory retirement age on January 30, 1999. Friedman had submitted his resignation effective February 28 and Wachowich was appointed coordinator on March 1.

Following the mediation meeting, Maloney and Maher made a settlement proposal. I would withdraw my application and Wachowich would withdraw his purported reassignment of me. I would retain my residence in Canmore subject to any ruling made by the Judicial Council, but I would sit as a regular member of the Calgary Criminal Division after October 1, 1999. I would receive $10,000 towards my legal costs, and make no public statement other than to acknowledge that a mutually agreeable settlement had been reached concerning the matters in dispute.

I was a little upset by the proposed $10,000 towards my legal fees. By that time they were about $50,000. Judge Maher had been very proactive in relation to judges' remuneration and had opposed Premier Klein's rollback of our salaries in 1994. I would have expected him to insist on full payment of my expenses because he was so adamant about reductions in judges' salaries being a violation of the financial security aspect of judicial independence. He was evidently not concerned about my experiencing what would amount to a rollback of some $40,000 in my salary that year.

The chief judge would not pay the amount personally, of course, because his expenses would be paid by the government. Their suggestion meant that I would either pay some $40,000 personally or that my lawyer wouldn't get paid. Neither of these options was satisfactory. I instructed Alan Hunter to accept the proposal subject to the payment of all of my costs and that the reassignment of October 1, 1999, could be shown to be necessary for the better administration of justice.

Hunter communicated my position to Tavender, who replied that neither the proposal contained in the September 21, 1998, letter from judges Maher and Maloney nor the modifications contained in Hunter's letter of September 24 were acceptable.

Tavender filed the notice of appeal on the same day we had the mediation meeting.

I spoke to Judge Maher about all this some time later. He said he had asked Wachowich if he would accept the proposal and his answer was, "I cannot." Whether this meant he was sticking to principle or he was under orders not to accept is a matter of debate.

❖ 16 ❖

MY OCTOBER CRISIS

On October 6, 1998, the pressure got to me. I will never know for sure if it was just anxiety or the mysterious power of Indian "bad medicine."

I was sitting in the court in Cochrane that day. It was a day the same as any other and I was feeling fine when I left for work. I took my customary route across the reserve, lamenting the last of the yellow leaves dropping from the trees and wondering about what the winter would be like. As usual I arrived in Cochrane early enough to stop by the Coffee Trader and get a cup of tea and the morning paper. Throughout my judicial career, I had always tried to get to court early so I could be relaxed and centred when I entered the courtroom. There is so much emotion attached to everything that happens in courtrooms that I felt it was my duty to keep the atmosphere as relaxed as possible.

I began court by reading the brief statement offering adjournments to anyone who was concerned about my judicial independence. I dealt with a few minor matters. I began to feel faint and short of breath, and I had pains in my chest that were like electrical impulses. I've since been told that this is not a typical symptom of a cardiac event. The real thing actually feels like a crushing pressure on the chest. The event was more frightening than painful, and I was afraid that something serious was going to happen, so I asked the clerk to call an adjournment and I went into my office and lay down on the couch.

In that particular courthouse, the judge enters from a door at the front of the room and walks up onto the bench. The door gave onto a hallway and across the hall was the door to the judge's office. The layout was such that if both doors were open, a person could see from the courtroom into the office, and could see the side of the couch I had gone to lie down on.

I must have looked like I was in some distress, because the clerk seemed to be in a bit of a panic, and as soon as I left the courtroom she went and called the paramedics. I lay down and loosened my collar and someone else loosened my belt as I panted, trying to catch my breath. Marjorie Powderface came and stood at the end of the couch. She prayed aloud but quietly in Stoney. The medics arrived and took my pulse and blood pressure. My blood pressure was 180 over 140 (normal would be 120 over 80) and my pulse was 140, when my normal resting rate would be about 60 and I would have to exercise vigorously to get it up to 140.

The medics hooked up their ECG. They said it did not indicate a problem, but that it was field equipment that was much less reliable than what would be in a hospital. They said the other symptoms were such that I should be taken to a hospital.

They suggested Foothills Hospital in Calgary, but the thought of being taken to that huge, impersonal institution was more frightening to me than my symptoms. I told them that if they insisted on taking me to a hospital, they could take me to Canmore. So that is what they did. They took me out to the ambulance on a stretcher, gave me oxygen and headed to Canmore. As I lay in the ambulance en route my heart rate began to settle down and my blood pressure returned to normal. When we came into the ambulance bay of the Canmore hospital, Dr. Catherine Hinds was waiting for me. She had blood tests and another ECG done. They showed no problem and I was discharged.

When I got home, Laura told me that Rose Auger had been at the house and waited for some time but then had had to leave. Laura said Rose wanted to see me, and I went out to the reserve the next morning. She and her son, Dale, were there, and so was Marjorie Powderface.

Marjorie told me that René Meatface, a fellow who had been charged with the brutal rape of Marjorie's 80-year-old mother, had used bad medicine against me. I hadn't paid attention to it at the time, but he had been in the Coffee Trader the day before the incident. He had walked around me, in a manner I now understand to be part of the cursing ritual. When he left the restaurant he spoke to me and said, "I don't want to appear before you again." On the day of this incident, he had come to court and sat in the front row, staring at me. This was something else I didn't notice at the time, but remembered it when Marjorie pointed it out. She told me she had placed herself at the side of the couch where I was lying to break the connection with Meatface, and she had prayed to counteract his medicine. By doing so, she had run the risk of it coming against her as well. She later attended a sweat to ask Rose and the grandmothers and grandfathers to pray for her and protect her.

I am an agnostic. I don't believe and I don't disbelieve in the power of the supernatural. I know that something accelerated my heart rate and elevated my blood pressure. I don't think it was the power of suggestion, because I hadn't even noticed René Meatface and didn't realize at the time who he was. I was certainly prepared to allow for the possibility that he was able to invoke evil spiritual forces against me, and that if it were so, the invocation of the good spiritual forces of the grandmothers and grandfathers would counteract that evil.

I spent the better part of that day on the reserve. When I returned home, Laura was a little put out with me. She had made an appointment for me to see our family doctor, Cindy Mylrea, and I had missed it. Laura is not as inclined to believe in the spiritual as I am, and she was very skeptical about the value of prayer over medical treatment.

I made another appointment with Dr. Mylrea, and this time I kept it. She told me not to go back to work until she had completed her diagnosis, which would include some outside consultation.

I felt fine. As I say, the incident was more frightening than painful, but I did not want it to happen again. There is no question that the litigation with the chief judge's office was a source of stress, and I often thought about the *Calgary Herald* article headlined "Controversial judge should get paid leave, says law professor." The story reported assertions by Chris Levy to the effect that some people could be uncomfortable appearing before Judge Reilly because they may perceive he is in a conflict of interest; that citizens want a judge who is independent from government but who is also independent from other pressures; and that generally speaking, a judge who gets into a fight with the system is put on leave of absence. It would seem that Chris Levy's opinion was not just good legal advice but seemed to be good medical advice as well.

Had this been a purely academic conflict, and had the chief judge been acting purely out of a motivation to protect the reputation of the court, I would very likely have been put on paid leave. I believe the real motive for both Wachowich and Stevenson was to ingratiate themselves with the justice minister. They would do that by punishing me for my judicial statements, not by giving me a paid holiday.

Dr. Mylrea arranged for me to see a cardiologist to determine if there was any problem with my heart, and a psychiatrist to find out whether I was suffering from clinical depression.

The cardiologist was Dr. Peter Nichol, a man I immediately liked. He is soft-spoken and gentle, and talks in layperson's terms that are easy to understand. He ordered a stress test and blood tests. He concluded that there was no obvious problem with my heart, but that occupational stress and my weight and cholesterol level were all cause for concern and I should take steps to ensure that problems did not develop. He gave me the choice of taking medication for the cholesterol or trying to reduce it through exercise. This was one of the other things I appreciated about Dr. Nichol: he didn't push pills. My preference was to use any alternative, so I chose exercise.

He had his assistant, Kelly Yurasec, give me a bit of coaching. I had to do something that would get my heart rate up to between 110 and 130 beats a minute for 20 minutes three times a week. I like hiking in the mountains, and I found that the walk up to Grassi Lakes would take me about 20 minutes and give me the desired heart rate. The road is a reasonably constant slope, with a height gain of about 300 metres over a distance of a little more than a kilometre. I still do this workout two or three times a week. I would estimate that in the last 15 years, I have done it about 2,000 times and I am always grateful to Kelly for getting me into this wonderful routine.

The psychiatrist was Dr. Douglas Watson. I enjoyed meeting with him. We had a very pleasant conversation, at the end of which he said it would not be necessary to see him again. His diagnosis was that I did not suffer from clinical depression, but he suggested I should learn meditation to deal with my occupational stress.

The final diagnosis regarding my difficulty of October 6, 1998, was that it was an acute anxiety attack brought on by occupational stress. The remedy was extended leave, at least until the litigation was finished.

It had been a matter of pride to me that in 20 years on the bench I had taken less than the total of 20 days sick leave. I now took the leave, except for days when I had matters for continuation. I did not return to full-time work until after Chief Judge Wachowich had reached mandatory retirement. I had hoped his replacement, the Honourable Ernest (Ernie) Walter, would allow for an improvement in my relationship with the chief judge's office. This was not to be the case.

❖ 17 ❖

THE JUDGES ASSOCIATION

October 6, 1998, was a Tuesday. The courts in Alberta were closed for the rest of that week to allow for the annual Alberta judges conference. And in that particular year, it was also Alberta's turn to host the annual meeting of the Canadian Association of Provincial Court Judges, in conjunction with the Alberta Provincial Court Judges Association meeting in Calgary. I missed the first day in order to attend the sweat that Rose Auger arranged for me. I missed the second day to keep my appointment with Dr. Mylrea.

I went to the dinner on the Friday and visited with a few of my colleagues. The incident in my Cochrane courtroom had obviously been a subject of conversation, and some of the judges expressed surprise that I was up and around. Like Mark Twain, I was able to assure them that rumours of my demise had been greatly exaggerated.

I recall a pleasant conversation with Judge Brosi Nutting, who only a few years before had been appointed chief judge of the Saskatchewan provincial courts. That province has a much larger percentage of Aboriginal people in its population than Alberta does, and I find the Saskatchewan judges seem generally more aware of the unique problems of Indigenous People. Judge Nutting is one of these, and he seemed very sympathetic to my situation. We discussed my litigation and my health, and when we parted his last comment was: "Take care of yourself. Remember, if you die, the chief wins."

It had been my intention to make a motion at the Alberta judges meeting that would be held on the Saturday morning. The motion was "that the Provincial Court Judges Association of Alberta accept liability for legal fees incurred by Judge John Reilly in his litigation with the Chief Judge." I had been working on my submission in support of that motion prior to the incident in Cochrane, and this probably contributed to the stress which caused the health problems.

Attending the meeting and making the motion was something I did not feel I would be able to do. I felt short of breath and my chest hurt just thinking about it, so I asked Judge Lynn Cook-Stanhope, of the Calgary Family and Youth Division, if she would make the motion for me. I don't recall why I asked her. She is a very knowledgeable and forceful individual, and she was probably just in the wrong place at the wrong time when I went looking for someone to do this for me. She said she would take care of it. She told me later that Judge Don Norheim, the resident judge in Jasper, made the motion, while she made a submission in support of it.

It may be just as well that I didn't deliver the submission I'd been working on. Had I read it to the meeting, it would have taken so long that even those who supported me might have voted against it. The text went on for seven pages. It set out the basic conflict over the chief judge's transfer order; summarized the arguments on jurisdiction; included the statement I'd been delivering upon opening each court session; and concluded with an extensive history of my education in relation to Aboriginal justice. I'm sure Judge Cook-Stanhope summarized it appropriately.

She told me later that while many of the judges were sympathetic to my situation, the consensus seemed to be that if the motion were put to a vote it would not pass. The association had raised the annual dues for membership by $1,000 or so per member in order to pay the legal fees it was incurring in its own litigation with the provincial government in relation to salaries.

Harry Gaede, the president of the judges association, told me the executive would not take a side in the dispute between me and the chief judge, but that they would support the judicial independence aspect if there were one. Apparently it was not clear to him that the argument did in fact involve judicial independence. He also told me he had heard from at least one judge who had said he would resign from the association if it supported me.

I imagine there was more than one judge who felt that way. With the focus on salaries, there were probably quite a number of judges who saw the furor I was causing as jeopardizing the possibility of settling the remuneration issue with the provincial government. I would speculate further that there were a number of judges who just didn't feel my situation applied to them. They were comfortable with the status quo and not likely to ever upset it.

I also believe some judges actively opposed the Aboriginal justice initiatives I was promoting. They would say it goes against the basic principle of equality before the law to give any one group special consideration in the criminal justice system. My answer to this objection is that the system as it stands does not give Aboriginal people equality. For them it is a foreign system that has been imposed on them and that they do not understand. Making allowances for their unique difficulties does not treat them with favouritism. Quite the contrary, it reduces the inequality they have been facing in the system ever since they were first subjected to it.

There were a few judges who quietly told me they appreciated what I was doing, in relation to both Aboriginal justice and judicial independence, but I never received any official support from the association.

❖ 18 ❖

THE APPEAL RE JURISDICTION

The appeal from Justice Mason's ruling on jurisdiction was heard on November 9, 1998. When Mr. Tavender filed the appeal, however, he had failed to apply for a stay of his obligation to file the record, an obligation that was clearly stated in Justice Mason's first order.

When Alan Hunter had given Tavender my position on the settlement proposed by Maher and Maloney, his notice specified that if we did not have an agreement by noon on Monday, September 28, 1998, we would require immediate compliance with the order of Justice Mason requiring the filing of the record.

I personally didn't see the need to have the record. I thought the letters we had already filed would be sufficient to establish that the order was faulty. But Alan said there might be a number of items in the record that would be of importance and he was very anxious to see what those might be. After making several demands for the record, he suggested we seek to have the chief judge cited in contempt of court for withholding it. When Tavender made no mention of the record in his reply of September 24, Hunter filed the notice of motion to cite the chief judge in contempt.

Tavender then obtained a stay of his obligation to file the record pending the determination of his appeal. However, the order provided that if the appeal was unsuccessful, he was required to file within three days of the appeal judgment.

On the day of the hearing, since it was Tavender's appeal, he spoke first. He droned on for several hours, repeating all of the same arguments he had made before Justice Mason. The court listened patiently, and when he was finished they took a short adjournment. The court then reconvened, told Hunter he did not have to respond, and dismissed Tavender's appeal.

I would have taken more satisfaction from this, but I don't think Tavender cared. He would still submit his bill for his hours and the government would pay it without question. In my opinion, the chief judge's position was indefensible, but Tavender's real job was to make it as difficult as possible for me to establish that.

Had it not been for Alan Hunter's altruistic dedication to justice, both for me and for the Aboriginal people I had tried to serve, I would have had to give up, because the costs would have been beyond my means. But giving up would have meant I accepted that my judgments in relation to Aboriginal people were wrong, that the chief judge had the power to punish me for such errors, and that he could do so without a hearing and without being subject to review.

❖ 19 ❖

THE RECORD

As mentioned earlier, if Mr. Tavender's appeal from Justice Mason's ruling on jurisdiction proved unsuccessful, he was required to disclose the record to us within three days of the appeal date. The Court of Appeal ruled on November 9, 1998, and thus the record was required by November 12, which happened to be a Thursday. We agreed that Monday the 16th would be sufficient if we received it by November 13. I received it on Friday the 13th.

It filled two large looseleaf binders. There were 650 pages, divided into 102 tabs: 130 pages of correspondence; 120 pages of newspaper articles; the initial *Hunter* judgment (by which I had ordered the investigation); drafts of the *Hunter* sentencing judgment; the filed judgment; my judgments in *Twoyoungmen* and *McKay*; Justice LoVecchio's judgment in *Hunter* (allowing the investigation into conditions on the Stoney reserve but limiting it); and transcripts of proceedings in *Hunter*, *Goodstoney* and other cases. There was also a memo by Judge Delong on contempt of court relating to Premier Klein's comments in the press about the appeal of my order for the investigation.

I found the very existence of this file disturbing. This was the first time I realized that ever since my order for the investigation in June of 1997 I had been the subject of ongoing scrutiny and investigation myself.

It also became apparent to me that Stevenson had been on a campaign to discredit me with the chief judge. I don't know why he did this, but I suspected it was because he wanted to be appointed chief judge. There was no question the Minister of Justice was angry towards me for ordering the investigation, and if Stevenson were instrumental in having me removed he would gain the favour of the minister.

The record contained a couple of things that upset me but explained what was happening. One was a letter in which Stevenson sent Wachowich a copy of my draft judgment with the comment: "My impression is that while he has toned down the rhetoric from the first draft, he has still gone quite some distance beyond the issue before him. In particular, his reliance on newspaper articles is most troubling."

I had given Stevenson the draft as a colleague and a friend. I would not have done so had I realized he would be forwarding it to Wachowich.

I thought it was amusing that he commented on my reliance on newspaper articles, when there were 120 pages of newspaper articles in the record. There is no question that a judge using a newspaper article as evidence in a trial would be making a serious mistake of law, because it would be hearsay. But in my view there is a difference between evidence in the trial and background information that would be relevant in a sentencing hearing.

I had ordered the investigation to get information on "the circumstances of the Aboriginal offender," and specifically information about the social conditions at Morley. The reduced scope of the investigation did not give that information, but the investigative reporting done by the *Calgary Herald* provided a great deal of reliable information about those social conditions. So I had provided the Court of Appeal with those articles in the hope that the judges would read them and acquire a bit of appreciation of those conditions.

In his letter to me of April 3, 1998, Wachowich said my judgment in *Hunter* and others were the most atrocious judgments he had seen as chief judge of the Provincial Court. He gave as an example "making findings of fact when there is no evidence." I wondered where that allegation came from. I speculate that it was based on Stevenson's reference to newspaper articles.

Stevenson went on to comment on the bail hearing in which I had re-released Christopher Goodstoney, who had breached his initial bail conditions. Stevenson said he had no concern about the re-release, but said he found comments of mine about it reported in the local paper *Cochrane This Week* to be disturbing. He volunteered that he had ordered a transcript of the proceedings "to check the accuracy of the press reports" and that he would report to Wachowich on that. The fact that he was actively investigating me and reporting negatively to the chief judge was upsetting.

What I had said to the paper was this: "One of the most culpable elements of the original horrible accident is that an 18-year-old was given a cheque for $40,000. He goes on a party, gets a new car, gets roaring drunk and kills four people. It is irresponsible to give people a big chunk of money with no training and no help on how to plan."

There is no question that my language reflected my frustration with the Department of Indian Affairs. Serious accidents, including fatal ones, were a common occurrence on the reserve at Morley following 18th birthdays. When the reserve was enjoying large oil and gas revenues, money was paid out in per capita distributions. Every man, woman and child on the reserve would receive as much as $500 every two weeks. For those under 18, half of the money went to the parents and half went into trust for the child. On a person's 18th birthday, they would receive a cheque for the accumulated amount. This could vary from nothing to as much as $100,000, depending on the amount of the revenues accrued during the 18 years of the child's life. Indian Affairs would pay that money out to young people without any effort to guide them in using it. Most of them had never had a significant sum of money in their lives. Their friends expected a party and anyone who refused to throw one might be subject to physical violence. Christopher Goodstoney had received his money from Indian Affairs, bought a truck, and bought a lot of alcohol for his friends. He was driving drunk when he caused the fatal collision.

The accident took the lives of four young people: Amber Lynn Keuben, 20; her sister Brandy, 14; Stephanie Lynn Smith, 14; and Craig Douglas Powell, 27. I felt tremendous sympathy for the families of the deceased young people, but nothing I could do would bring them back or make the loss any easier.

Goodstoney was ultimately sentenced to five years imprisonment. In my view the responsibility should have been shared by the Department of Indian Affairs and the tribal government. The department had written him a cheque without any provision for counselling in how to use the money. The tribal government was aware of the disastrous consequences of these payments and also did nothing about it.

Stevenson's letter also criticized the fact that I had been the keynote speaker at a seminar at the Banff Centre, "Building Aboriginal Community-Controlled Justice Systems," without informing him. The keynote was in the evening, so I was attending on my own time. I hadn't told him, because I didn't see any reason to. He said he was concerned I was being less than forthright with him on the extent of my involvement with the seminar.

After a number of additional comments, the letter concluded: "When you have had an opportunity to review and consider these matters I would appreciate discussing an appropriate course of action with you at your convenience."

Stevenson wrote this letter on November 27. It was six days later, December 3, that he wrote the letter referred to in chapter 4, in which he assured me that any changes on my circuit would be made on the basis of cost saving alone and I would be notified before any final recommendations were made.

Another interesting item in the record was a letter of March 30, 1998, in which Stevenson forwarded to Wachowich a copy of a ruling I had made, and commented: "Its contents continue an apparent obsession of Judge Reilly to subjugate the law to his perception of unjust social conditions on the Stoney First Nation reserve at Morley."

These same words were in the letter of May 25 by which Wachowich gave me the order to transfer to Calgary. This gave me the impression that it really wasn't Wachowich who was doing this to me, it was Stevenson.

He continued:

> While his approach may be well-intentioned, it is not, in my view, in conformity with his obligations [sic] as a jurist, which is to apply appropriate legal considerations to applications before him. I can only conclude from his comments on pages 9 and 10 of his ruling that when matters before him involve Aboriginal persons, he does not intend to act objectively, judicially or in accordance with Canadian law. The last paragraph of his ruling indicates a prejudgment attitude that would clearly, in my view, support an application to disqualify him from presiding over any case, on the basis of bias.

Stevenson then gave some information about monitoring my circuit and a conversation he had had with Mr. Paul, the court manager, and suggests that they could save $173,900 per year by moving me and closing the base point. He concluded with:

> I appreciate that the changes I am recommending may be interpreted in some quarters as being directed in a punitive way against Judge Reilly for his actions in the *Hunter* case and other matters involving Aboriginals. While it will be

impossible to prevent such interpretations from arising, the simple fact is that the changes, if approved, will not occur as a result of any government initiative; it [sic] will occur as a result of a judicial initiative.

The third upsetting item in the record was the memo from Laurie Herron to Wachowich referred to earlier, at the end of chapter 10. Herron had told me she didn't know what the March 26 meeting was about, but her memo made it clear that she did.

After scanning the return and reading the above letters, I spoke to Alan Hunter by phone. I couldn't tell whether he was upset or excited, but as always he was passionate. "What do think?" he asked.

"I am really upset to see Stevenson's been lying to me, he tells me he's my friend, talks to me about Wachowich as if Wachowich is the enemy, and all the time he's manipulating Wachowich to get him to transfer me. He's a backstabbing liar."

"John, they're both liars. Look at Wachowich's letter of April 9. He's telling Stevenson to create an exchange of correspondence to cover up the true reason for their action against you."

The letter of April 9 said:

Re Judge Reilly/Canmore–Banff base point

Thank you for your letter of March 30, 1998, on the above subject. I have given serious thought to this matter and I agree with you that the base point in Canmore be closed, Judge Reilly be moved to Calgary and the circuit be serviced from Calgary. This will be a cost-saving measure which is further justified by our desire to preserve the good reputation of the provincial judiciary.

Section 13(1) and (2) [sic] of the Provincial Courts Act [sic] have been declared to be of no force and effect by Justice McDonald's decision in R. v. Campbell (confirmed by the

Supreme Court of Canada in its September 18, 1997, decision *Ref. Re Public Sector Pay Reduction Act (PEI)* [sic]. Justice McDonald's decision which is now the law says [sic] that "decisions to designate the place at which a judge shall have his residence and the days on which court will hold sittings are 'administrative decisions that bear directly and immediately on the exercise of judicial function.'" On this issue McDonald J. also observed at page 579:

> The chief judge's and assistant chief judges' ability to combine flexibility with cost-efficiency and other relevant considerations (such as avoiding travel fatigue, providing the community with a diversity of judges, enhancing collegiality and consistency within the court) must not be fettered.
>
> I therefore suggest that you make a formal request to me to move Judge Reilly to Calgary, close the Canmore base point and convert it into a circuit point, with your reasons showing how you arrived at a cost saving. I will order the closure of that base point, move Judge Reilly to Calgary and forward the matter to the Minister to take appropriate action regarding financial and administrative matters in accordance with their procedures. ...

After we had discussed the record, I felt a lot of anger toward Stevenson, and my impulse to expose his deception was strong. But what was even stronger was Alan Hunter's oft-repeated advice to "take the high road."

There was no question that the errors established by the record would result in the litigation being decided in my favour, but Alan had other concerns. In his opinion the record established improper conduct that should be the subject of complaint to the Judicial Council. He was also very concerned about the damage it would do to the reputation of the court if the record were made public.

He asked me to instruct him to tell Tavender he did not have to file the record if he would just get the chief judge to withdraw his order and pay my costs. I did so, and Alan sent a letter to Tavender to that effect, dated November 16. That letter was then emailed to all of the provincial judges in Alberta.

On November 18, during my extended leave of absence, Judge James came to sit in Canmore. I went down to the courthouse to visit with him. He told me that "the spin" Stevenson was putting on my effort to avoid having the record filed was that I didn't want the material made public because it would be embarrassing to me.

It made me sad to reflect on how little respect he had for the truth.

It also made me sad to see in the file a memo by Wachowich dated October 25, 1997, in which he said:

> Phoned ACJ Brian Stevenson, told him ... that if Judge Reilly released the judgment it could mean his job and definitely he would be before the Judicial Council. I suggested to Brian that he and some of the level-headed judges i.e. Cioni etc. meet with Reilly and point out his mistakes. (See chapter 4.)

Whether Cioni knew he was acting on the chief judge's suggestion or not, I don't know.

I had not been completely deaf to the criticisms and comments I was receiving. After receiving Stevenson's letter commenting on the first draft of my judgment in *Hunter*, I rewrote it to "tone down the rhetoric," and this may have saved me from criticism by the Court of Appeal. If they had made critical comments, it might have made it much more difficult for me to successfully oppose the transfer order.

In any event, after all of the legal manoeuvring by the chief judge's lawyer to avoid disclosing the record, we now had it and could proceed to the actual hearing on the merits of my original application.

❖ 20 ❖

THE HEARING ON THE MERITS

The hearing took two full days: December 17 and 18, 1998. This was the proceeding I had naïvely thought, back in July, was going to take just a couple of hours.

Justice Mason began by asking if counsel were now agreed that he had jurisdiction to hear the matter. Mr. Tavender confirmed that he did and commented that his appeal of Mason's initial ruling had not been "one of [his] better days in court." He tried to make a joke of it. I didn't think it was the least bit funny.

Alan Hunter argued that the impugned decision was an unconstitutional interference with my adjudicative independence and that the decision to close the Canmore base point was merely a convenient excuse to justify the transfer.

Tavender's position was that the chief judge was not attempting to, and did not, interfere with my adjudicative independence, but that I had to be dealt with both from an administrative and a disciplinary standpoint because I had lost my objectivity and impartiality regarding Aboriginal people. He also argued that the transfer decision was made in conjunction with a valid cost-saving administrative decision to close the Canmore base point.

Tavender began by stating that neither he nor the chief judge questioned the sincerity of the views I had expressed on and off the bench. He stated that the chief judge did not interfere with my adjudicative independence. His argument consisted of five submissions:

1. He argued that the real issue was how and under what

circumstances I should be held accountable to my chief judge in respect of the perception that I had lost my objectivity. He argued that this was a concern of judicial conduct in a proper area of responsibility of the chief judge.

2. He admitted there were two reasons for the move. The primary one was my loss of objectivity. The second was the administrative cost-saving consideration.

3. He spoke of the role of the chief judge, the Judicial Council and the Court of Appeal and argued that the contents of judgments are matters that can be dealt with not only by the Court of Appeal but by the fact that judges are responsible to their chief judge for judicial conduct both on and off the bench. He argued my loss of objectivity was improper judicial conduct properly dealt with by the chief judge, and that the court of Queen's Bench should protect the institutional independence of the office of the chief judge by not interfering with what was done.

4. He then pointed to a number of matters which he said demonstrated my bias and lack of impartiality. These were:

    1. my interest in sentencing circles and other restorative justice initiatives;
    2. the *Hunter* presentencing decision;
    3. the *Hunter* sentencing decision;
    4. my having been the keynote speaker at a seminar;
    5. the *Goodstoney* decision;
    6. my concern over a potential Aboriginal court for the Tsuu T'ina and Stoney reserves;
    7. the *Twoyoungmen* decision (which he referred to as "the last straw");
    8. my request to conduct the Tsuu T'ina inquiry;
    9. the public and media reactions; and
    10. the complaint by Corporal Young.

5. He argued that, legally, the Provincial Court Judges Act gave

the chief judge the power to order me to move, and that rules of natural justice do not apply to such a decision. He again argued that the proper forum for this dispute was the Judicial Council and that the discretion the Ministry of Justice has in a judicial review application should be used to disallow the relief I was seeking.

Hunter divided his argument into nine basic submissions:

1. The true character of the impugned decision was punitive and disciplinary, that it was designed to punish and discipline me for the way I had decided the cases before me. This was not the prerogative of administrative judges. Only the Court of Appeal is empowered to rule on the quality of judgments. He further argued that the decision had already been made on April 3, 1998, and that after that date all documents and correspondence were merely a cover story for the real reason for moving me.

2. He argued authority and constitutionality: that there was no statutory authority for the chief judge to make the impugned decision, and that the decision was impermissible constitutionally for violating my adjudicative judicial independence.

3. In answer to Tavender's argument that the proper forum was the Judicial Council, Hunter argued that the council did not have the power to grant the remedy I was seeking. I wanted the impugned order declared invalid, and the council did not have the authority to make that declaration. The authority the Judicial Council does have is to review the conduct of a judge, but not to make rulings on the constitutionality of the judge's decisions.

4. He argued the appropriateness of the judicial review proceedings, and that there was no other adequate alternative remedy.

5. He made submissions in relation to the off-bench conduct the chief judge criticized and argued that the chief judge's

prosecution, investigation, conviction, sanction and punishment of me without a hearing was invalid procedure.

6. He made submissions in relation to the return and to the irony of Stevenson criticizing me for my references to newspaper clippings when there were such a large number of them contained in the record returned.

7. He argued that where Justice Mason had discretion, he should exercise it in my favour because of the unfavourable manner in which the chief judge had made his decision against me.

8. He made general comments on the standard of review in the proceedings before the court.

9. He argued that the lack of procedural fairness in making the decision against me should in itself invalidate the decision.

At the conclusion of these arguments Justice Mason thanked both counsel for their exhaustive research and submissions and said it would take him some time to go through it all and render a judgment. So I was once again on hold. We did not know when the judgment would be issued and we could only wait.

❖ 21 ❖

MY COMPLAINT

When we received and reviewed the record back in November of 1998, Alan Hunter had said to me that the conduct of Wachowich and Stevenson disclosed in that record should absolutely be the subject of review by the Judicial Council. He very passionately recounted the fact that the record showed they had lied to me, lied to the deputy minister and collaborated with each other to produce an exchange of correspondence that would hide their true motive for making the order for transfer. However, Alan had also said he did not want me to file a complaint before the judicial review hearing was over.

Following the hearing, we again discussed filing a complaint. Hunter said he would ideally like to wait until Justice Mason had delivered his judgment, but he was afraid Wachowich's impending mandatory retirement might mean the Judicial Council would not have jurisdiction to deal with the matter.

Hunter's motivation was an altruistic desire to preserve the integrity of the court and the judicial system. Mine was anger, not only for the action they had taken against me but also for the lack of support for my efforts to improve the delivery of justice to the Stoney people. Had I been supported, I might have accomplished something significant on the reserve at Morley. As it is, I have been given credit for some improvements, and I believe the media attention I generated added at least a little to public awareness of the plight of Aboriginal people. For the most part, though, not much has changed.

In any event, on December 21, 1998, I forwarded the following document to the Honourable Catherine Fraser, the Chief Justice of Alberta. The wording was largely that of Alan Hunter, QC:

Complaint respecting
The Honourable Edward R. Wachowich,
Chief Judge, Provincial Court of Alberta,
and
The Honourable Brian Stevenson,
Assistant Chief Judge, Provincial Court of Alberta

Please accept the within as a formal complaint against the Honourable Edward R. Wachowich, Chief Judge, Provincial Court of Alberta, and the Honourable Brian Stevenson, Assistant Chief Judge, Provincial Court of Alberta.

At a meeting in the office of ACJ Stevenson on May 26, 1998, CJ Wachowich and ACJ Stevenson advised me of a decision that they had made to reassign me from my sittings as the resident Provincial Court judge for Canmore/Banff/Cochrane to Calgary, and directing me to move my residence from Canmore to Calgary. All of this to be effective by September 1, 1998.

This decision is the subject of a judicial review in the Court of Queen's Bench of Alberta, Judicial District of Calgary, action #9801-08707.

The record in the Queen's Bench proceeding shows that CJ Wachowich and ACJ Stevenson acted together in this matter and documents the basis of my complaint, which is as follows:

1. The decision was an abuse of their administrative authority in that it was made for the purpose of controlling my judicial adjudicative function and was therefore constitutionally impermissible as a violation of my judicial independence.

2. They accorded me no procedural fairness and made the impugned decision without notice and without a hearing.

3. They deliberately misinformed me as to the purpose of the meeting, and deliberately withheld from me their intentions respecting their arbitrary and punitive decision. They misinformed the Deputy Minister of Justice as to their reasons, and they created an exchange of correspondence to disguise the true reason for their decision and characterize it as a "cost saving" measure, when the record is clear that the reason for their decision was their disapproval of a number of judgments that I had rendered in relation to Aboriginal offenders.

Given the infringements on my judicial adjudicative independence and the vital importance of the public right to be tried by an independent court, I respectfully request that a Board of Inquiry be established under the Judicature Act for the purpose of reviewing the conduct of CJ Wachowich and ACJ Stevenson in this matter.

Respectfully yours,
John Reilly, PCJ

On January 4, 1999, I received a letter from the office of the Chief Justice which simply acknowledged receipt of my complaint without further comment.

On January 14 Tavender filed a notice of motion in the judicial review application before Justice Mason to adduce additional evidence. He would argue that my filing of the complaint was an admission on my part that the Judicial Council was the proper forum for the hearing of the whole matter.

January 31, 1999, was Edward R. Wachowich's 70th birthday and marked his mandatory retirement as chief judge.

On February 5 I received a letter from Chief Justice Fraser. It said the following:

> I am writing on behalf of the Provincial Judicial Council. The letter which you directed to the Provincial Judicial Council and sent to my attention dated December 21, 1998, was discussed at a meeting of the Judicial Council held January 28, 1999. Your letter raises a number of issues requiring further consideration by the Council. We will be in contact with you once these have been addressed.

No action was ever taken on my complaint. I expected that the dishonesty disclosed by the record would motivate some action against Stevenson and Wachowich. I subsequently formed the impression that the judicial establishment of the Province of Alberta was more concerned about preserving the status quo, and that many were probably in agreement with the action that had been taken against me.

❖ 22 ❖

AT LONG LAST, THE RULING
ON THE MERITS

Justice Mason's ruling on the substance of the case was issued April 26, 1999. It was almost an anticlimax for me after the Supreme Court of Canada decision in *R. v. Gladue*. Like *Gladue*, it was better than I expected.

He gave his rulings in the first couple of pages of the 76-page text and then went on to set out the issues, the relevant facts, the arguments of counsel, his analysis and his conclusions. He stated the issues as:

1. Does the Court of Queen's Bench have jurisdiction to review?

2. What is the standard of review?

3. Does the chief judge of the Provincial Court have statutory or constitutional authority to order a judge to change his residence?

4. If the chief judge has that authority, was it properly exercised?

5. Is the chief judge required to follow procedural fairness, and if so did he meet the standard?

Justice Mason found that his court did have jurisdiction to review, because the concept of judicial independence was vital to the case. He quoted a remark by Supreme Court Justice John Sopinka (1933–1997) that judicial independence means "even if the government doesn't like your decisions, you still have a job."

He said the true character of the decision to relocate me was disciplinary "in spite of collaboration between the Chief Judge and Assistant Chief Judge Stevenson" to tie it to a cost-saving initiative, which would be administrative. He characterized that effort as "a mere subterfuge to cast the decision in an administrative context in an effort to disguise that disciplinary action was being meted out."

With respect to statutory authority to order my transfer Justice Mason said there was nothing in the Provincial Court Judges Act that gives the chief judge authority to transfer a judge from his designated circuit or residence. He also said that giving the chief judge any statutory or constitutional power to discipline a judge with whom the chief judge disagreed with respect to judgments rendered would threaten the judge's impartiality and create an apprehension of bias in that such authority could be used to punish judges whose decisions do not conform with the personal jurisprudence of the chief judge or, for that matter, to reward those whose judgments do so.

Justice Mason found that even if the chief judge had the authority, it was not properly exercised. It was clear from the record that the chief judge's reason was a disagreement with my judgments, and that was the purview of courts of appeal, not the chief judge. Justice Mason added that he was particularly disturbed by the chief judge's frequent references to decisions of mine that he obviously had problems with, along with comments as to their partiality or bias. Those decisions had proceeded through the court process in a normal fashion, and once the normal court process is over, the matter is closed.

As to procedural fairness, he said that even if he had found that the chief judge had the authority to make the impugned decision, he would have found that I was entitled to procedural fairness, that I did not receive the required level of procedural fairness, and that on this ground alone he would quash the chief judge's decision.

Unfortunately Justice Mason would make no comment on the bias or lack thereof in my judgments. In this regard he said:

> Because I find in these reasons that the chief judge did not have the statutory or constitutional authority to make the impugned decision, I need not, and will not, address the question of bias and loss of impartiality. Judge Reilly's conduct is not part of this judicial review.

This left the propriety of my statements unresolved. I would have liked a ruling that said there was no bias in any of my judgments or statements and that they were a proper application of the law. Still, it was only what I had expected. In my view the battle had already been won when Chief Judge Wachowich was forced to disclose the record. I don't know why he would have carried on after that. It must've been hugely embarrassing for him and it should have been totally obvious that he could not win. My suspicion is that he had no control over what was happening – that it was the government that was directing the proceedings against me, and that Tavender was really acting for the government, probably with instructions to draw the matter out for as long as he could, even if he couldn't win.

I had commented to Alan Hunter, when he was preparing for the December hearing, that I admired his ability to keep on fighting when the battle was already over. It soon became obvious that the fight was not over.

❖ 23 ❖

JUDGE WALTER

I had met the Honourable Judge Ernest E.J. (Ernie) Walter at a judges conference in Victoria in 1993. My good friend Judge Dave Tilley and his wife, Judy, and Laura and I were going out for dinner and Dave invited him to join us. My impression of him was that he was humourless. The only thing I remember him saying is that he wanted to be the chief judge.

My next recollection of him is at a judges conference in Red Deer sometime in 1997 or 1998. I was having breakfast in the dining room with a few other judges and expounding on my new-found interest in Aboriginal justice. Walter caught the gist of what I was saying and commented, "I get really tired of people trying to make me feel guilty for what my ancestors did to the Indians."

I wanted to say to him, "You are still enjoying what your ancestors took from the Indians. You should feel some responsibility for repairing the harm that your ancestors did to them." However, I chose not to create unpleasantness and said nothing. In my subsequent dealings with Judge Walter, though, I came to believe that his comment disclosed an attitude that coloured his relationship with me.

When Chief Judge Wachowich reached mandatory retirement age on January 30, 1999, Walter was named acting chief judge.

The Minister of Justice and Attorney General, Jon Havelock, did not want to make a permanent appointment at that time, because the government was amending the Provincial Court

Judges Act to provide for term appointments for the chief judge and assistant chief judges. Whereas Wachowich had been appointed for life, which meant mandatory retirement at 70, his replacement would only be appointed for a seven-year term.

By a letter dated March 1, 1999, Acting Chief Judge Walter announced the retirement of Judge S.A. Friedman, and that the now retired Chief Judge Wachowich was assuming Judge Friedman's duties as coordinator of the justice of the peace program.

This seemed to confirm Judge Phil Ketchum's information that Judge Friedman had taken the appointment from Wachowich on the condition that he step down when Wachowich was ready to take the job himself (see p. 90).

On May 7, 1999, Judge Walter visited Calgary and I met with him briefly in the judges lounge in the Provincial Court building. I had hoped that with the changing of the guard in the chief judge's office things might improve for me, and I asked him if we could discuss the litigation in *Reilly v. Wachowich*. He indicated he was not at liberty to do so. I said that as the acting chief judge he was now the ex officio respondent in the action, and that as parties to the lawsuit we should be able to talk about it. He told me it was much more complicated than that. It has always been my suspicion, as mentioned earlier, that the complication was that neither he nor Wachowich had control over the litigation – that the real control was in the Department of Justice and its minister, Jon Havelock.

When the new legislation was proclaimed in force, Walter was confirmed as chief judge. On June 1, 1999, I wrote to him to congratulate him and again asked if we could talk.

On June 2 Tavender filed a notice of appeal. Since Wachowich was no longer the chief judge, it should have been Walter's decision to file, or not to file, that appeal. I had asked him who would make the decision and he replied he could not say. Why wouldn't he tell me? This all confirmed my suspicion that Tavender was really taking his instructions from the Department of Justice and not from the chief judge.

On June 4 I received Walter's reply to my letter of June 1. It speculated that I now knew a notice of appeal had been filed, and that the essential question of whether the order to reassign and relocate me to Calgary would ultimately be quashed or upheld was now before the court. He went on to say he agreed there were outstanding issues between us, but that he believed

> ... matters have progressed to the stage where there must be greater clarity as to how supervisory, administrative and disciplinary powers of a chief judge may be exercised in both your and analogous circumstances. These matters go to the core of what I understand will be raised before the Court of Appeal and it seems to me that until there is a final decision of the courts on these matters I cannot effectively discuss them with you.

Sometimes I didn't know whether Walter was being deliberately obtuse or if he was just mentally slow. His reference to the appeal made it sound as if he didn't have anything to do with it.

His comment that supervisory, administrative and disciplinary powers of a chief judge were at the core of what would be raised in the Court of Appeal was clearly wrong, for Justice Mason's ruling had plainly said: "Defining the range of a chief judge's powers is beyond the scope of this judgment."

This total unwillingness to communicate, which often appeared to me as a total inability on Walter's part to understand what was being said to him, would be a feature of my life for the next seven years.

❖ 24 ❖

THE CHIEF JUDGE'S APPEAL

Subsequent to the filing of the notice of appeal, the lawyers filed the appeal books. These contain all of the evidence and prior rulings in the case, including the record and all of the pleadings that had been filed. They constituted five bound volumes totalling 905 pages.

Also filed were joint books of authorities: four additional bound volumes totalling 1,286 pages. These were filed on December 9, 1999.

The urgency with which the initial hearings had been scheduled had passed. The appeal was heard on February 3 and 4, 2000, by a panel made up of justices Willis O'Leary, Constance Hunt and Adelle Fruman.

The arguments were a rehash of those that had been made before Justice Mason. I would have to wait until September 5, 2000 (seven months), for the judgment. When I received it, I was delighted with its content. It was a unanimous decision. Madam Justice Hunt wrote the reasons, and justices O'Leary and Fruman concurred.

The judgment was contained in the first paragraph: "In the circumstances of this case, the chief judge did not have the jurisdiction to make the impugned decision, and the appeal must be dismissed."

Justice Hunt set out the facts in a way that I felt approved of my conduct and criticized Wachowich and Stevenson. She recited my efforts in Aboriginal justice, case management, sentencing circles and family group conferencing, along with my concerns about the impact of the judicial system on the Stoney Indians at Morley.

She spoke of the inquiry I ordered, that I had indicated I was making the order to comply with s. 718.2(e) of the Criminal Code, and that it set in motion the events that eventually led to the appeal.

She spoke of the media interest the order generated, of the narrowing of the scope of the order on the appeal heard by Justice LoVecchio, and of his comment that it had been inappropriate for me to impute criminal conduct to individuals who were not before the court.

She mentioned that I had given a copy of my draft sentencing judgment to Stevenson "as a colleague and friend" and that he had sent a copy with his own comments to the chief judge (the appellant), who communicated his view that "if Judge Reilly releases this judgment it could mean his job and definitely he would be before the Judicial Council."

She noted that the sentence I had imposed in *Hunter* had been increased by 18 months imprisonment on appeal, but she added that although the Court of Appeal stated that s. 718.2(e) of the Criminal Code was but one of several principles to be considered in fixing a fit sentence, the court had made no comments about the general tone of my sentencing decision.

I was particularly gratified by this remark because I thought Wachowich and Stevenson were in a very tenuous position criticizing my conduct when it was not in their jurisdiction, especially when the court that did have jurisdiction made no comment.

Justice Hunt referred to the November 27 letter Stevenson wrote to Wachowich (referred to above in chapter 19) in which he expressed concern about the tone of the *Hunter* sentencing draft, about remarks attributed to me in newspapers, and about the fact that without his knowledge I had agreed to deliver the keynote speech at a conference on Aboriginal justice systems. She then quoted the following paragraph:

> I have come to believe that Judge Reilly enjoys the notoriety he now possesses due to the extensive media coverage of the Stoney problems. Additionally, his position as the "resident judge" has, I fear, given him the impression that the justice system is "his" system, and that he can run it the way he wants. I also fear that his apparent obsession with the Morley/Stoney situation (and John Snow in particular) together with his increasing readiness to excuse criminal conduct on the basis of the political leadership that is presently in place there gives rise to a clear appearance of bias and legitimate public concern. I further fear that if the Crown made an application to prohibit him from hearing any criminal charge involving a Stoney person because of the public perception of bias, it would succeed.

She outlined an exchange I had with the chief judge in which I asked to be appointed to hear an inquiry at Tsuu T'ina. Wachowich said my request was almost conduct unbecoming a judge, and when I answered in a "conciliatory tone" (Justice Hunt's words), he replied with his letter of April 3, from which she quoted:

> I applaud you for your conversion on the road to Damascus and the help you are prepared to accord the Aboriginal people but I strongly object to how you are improperly abusing your judicial position to achieve this end. Your judgments in *Hunter* and others recently are the most atrocious judgments that I have seen as chief judge of the Provincial Court. An example is making findings of fact when there is no evidence before you and there are many others. You want to justify your actions under 718.2(e) which is an interpretation of that section by

yourself whereby you have greatly exceeded your jurisdiction. You should pay attention to what was said by Justice Levechio [sic] in the *Hunter* appeal. In short your recent handling of native matters before you is in my humble opinion an embarrassment to our court.

Justice Hunt summarized the *Twoyoungmen* decision in which I had refused a Crown application for an adjournment when the complainant, an Aboriginal woman, failed to appear to testify in the trial and the prosecutor had not prepared her for court. I stated that in future I would refuse to grant adjournments when the Crown had not prepared its witnesses.

In summarizing this case Justice Hunt said: "He underscored the difficulties that Aboriginal people have with the justice system, quoting at length from the Royal Commission on Aboriginal Peoples and the Cawsey Report (which concerned the impact of the Alberta justice system on Aboriginal people)."

She then referred to Stevenson's letter to Wachowich of March 30, 1998, by which he forwarded the *Twoyoungmen* decision and observed that

> ... its content continues an apparent obsession by Judge Reilly to subjugate the law to his perception of unjust social conditions on the Stoney First Nation Reserve at Morley. ...
>
> I can only conclude from his comments ... that when matters before him involve Aboriginal persons, he does not intend to act objectively, judicially or in accordance with Canadian law. The last paragraph of his ruling indicates a prejudgment attitude that would clearly, in my view, support an application to disqualify him from presiding over any case on the basis of bias.
>
> For these reasons alone it is my recommendation that Judge Reilly be reassigned to preside in a legal environment

other than the circuit where he now resides. [Emphasis added by Justice Hunt.]

(Apropos of *Twoyoungmen*, the Crown in fact successfully appealed my decision in the case and the matter was again set for trial, scheduled for a day when I was presiding. I advised the Crown prosecutor, Gary Belecke, that I had already dismissed this charge, and asked if he would like me to disqualify myself. He indicated he was quite content to have me hear it. The matter proceeded and the young Aboriginal woman was called as a witness. She failed to answer any of the questions put to her, and Mr. Belecke invited me to again dismiss the charge, which I did.)

In her continuing description of the facts, Justice Hunt referred to Wachowich's note of April 3, 1998, asking his legal counsel to advise on the procedure for moving me. (This was the date held to be the actual date of the decision to relocate me, a decision I was not informed of until the meeting of May 26.)

Justice Hunt also set out the content of the April 9 letter in which Wachowich informed Stevenson that he agreed with Stevenson's recommendation to move me and quoted Justice McDonald's judgment in *R. v. Campbell* as his authority for his power to designate a judge's place of residence. This is the letter that most interested Alan Hunter when we received the record. He saw it as the deliberate cover-up of their true motive for moving me. The letter is transcribed in chapter 19.

The appeal court further noted that I was asked to meet with the chief judge and assistant chief judge on May 26 but was not told the nature or purpose of the meeting. Justice Hunt cited my affidavit recounting that when I had asked about the subject of the meeting, Assistant Chief Judge Stevenson advised that he did not know (even though several weeks earlier he had seen drafts of the letters to be delivered at that meeting). She included Wachowich's notes of the meeting, which confirmed I was being moved because I had lost my objectivity and was not acting judiciously.

The appeal reasons went on to set out the history of the judicial proceedings, Justice Mason's chambers decision quashing the order for transfer, and the relevant legislation.

In dealing with the error Wachowich and Stevenson made in relying on the *Campbell* case as their authority to transfer me, Justice Hunt referred to the scc ruling on the appeal in that case and three others, which she pointed out was released several months before Wachowich's decision. She noted that the scc determined that s. 13(1)(*a*) and (*b*) of the Provincial Court Judges Act were unconstitutional because they conferred powers on the Attorney General and Minister of Justice to make decisions that infringed on the administrative independence of the Alberta Provincial Court, namely, to designate a judge's place of residence at any time... and that this "creates the reasonable apprehension that it could be used to punish judges whose decisions do not favour the government, or alternatively, to favour judges whose decisions benefit the government."

She confirmed that the scc decision in *Campbell* did not consider the role of a chief judge in selecting the place of residence of a judge, and explained why removing an unconstitutional power from the Attorney General did not give it to the chief judge. She further pointed out that when I had requested the transfer to Canmore in the first place, Wachowich appeared to have assumed that, as chief judge, he lacked the power to designate a judge's residence, because he had sought approval from the Attorney General.

I was especially pleased that Justice Hunt said the scc's "disquiet about the executive's power to transfer a judge applies equally to a chief judge's exercise of the same power. If unconstrained, such a power reposed in a chief judge could also engender concerns about the use of the power for punishment or reward." In my view, that paragraph was the whole judgment. There was no question in my mind that Wachowich, having erroneously assumed he had the power, attempted to use it in order to punish me for judgments he didn't like.

The judgment went on for another 50 paragraphs disposing of other arguments.

One of Tavender's submissions was that if the chief judge didn't have the power to redesignate my residence, he did have the power to reassign me, and the court should allow the reassignment to Calgary. The appeal court held that the redesignation of the residence and the reassignment had been inextricably joined by the way Wachowich had made his order, and that the court would not change it in a way he had not initially contemplated.

I was quite relieved by this ruling, because in my view the chief judge's powers would have allowed him to simply reassign me. If his real motive had been to take just Aboriginal cases away from me because he did not feel I was fit to hear them, he could have done so by assigning me two courts in Calgary instead of the one in Cochrane on Cochrane court days. Had he done that, I do not think I could have successfully objected. There would still have been the constitutional argument that he was punishing me for making decisions he didn't like, but there would be no jurisdictional dispute about his authority to make the reassignment.

The fact that he attempted to redesignate my residence confirms my view that there was an attempt to punish me. There is no question that being required to move from Canmore would have been a very painful thing for me and my family. I believe this is what the government wanted because of the anger that was generated by my attempts to force them to look at the terrible conditions on the Stoney reserve at Morley.

Other arguments raised by Tavender were as follows:

Section 16(1) of the Provincial Court Judges Act (1981) provided that no action could be brought against a judge for any act done or omitted to be done in the execution of the judge's duty. Tavender had argued that this should preclude my action for judicial review. The court held that the section did not apply.

Tavender argued that the Nova Scotia case *MacKeigan v. Hickman* gave the chief judge an immunity that should preclude my action. In *MacKeigan* the Supreme Court of Canada said a chief judge could not be compelled to testify, before a Royal Commission reviewing the conviction of Donald Marshall, as to why he assigned a particular judge to the panel. The court found that the case did not apply.

Tavender had again asserted that judicial review should not apply because the Judicial Council was an appropriate alternative remedy. The court ruled that the Judicial Council did not have jurisdiction to quash the order for transfer and therefore was not an alternative.

Tavender even argued that I should not receive an award of costs. Wachowich might be personally liable for the payment thereof. In my view, this argument was specious. I have no doubt that all of Wachowich's legal bills were paid by the government without question and that any bills he submitted on my behalf would have been paid in the same way. The fact that they argued against my being indemnified for a matter that was decided in my favour on the basis of constitutionality was, in my opinion, simply an example of their vindictiveness towards me.

The court confirmed the award of costs in my favour.

❖ 25 ❖

THE GOVERNMENT RESPONDS
LEGISLATIVELY

Following my litigation, the Justice Statutes Amendment Act 2000 added a provision to the Provincial Court Act (s. 21.1(7)) exempting from judicial review any reasonable administrative actions by the chief judge. Today the identical wording forms s. 9.1(7) of the Provincial Court Act. Other current provisions governing the powers of the chief judge and the designation of a judge's place of residence are in ss. 9.1(5) and (6) and 9.42 of the latter Act:

> 9.1... (5) Subject to section 9.42, the chief judge has the power and duty to supervise the judges in the performance of their duties, including the power and duty to
>
> > (a) designate a particular case or other matter or class of cases or matters in respect of which a particular judge is to act;
> > (b) designate which court facilities shall be used by particular judges;
> > (c) assign duties to judges;
> > (d) exercise any other powers and perform any other duties prescribed by the Lieutenant Governor in Council.
>
> (6) The Chief Judge in consultation with the Assistant Chief Judges may designate the sittings of the Court.
>
> (7) Where the Chief Judge makes any decision or takes

any action with respect to a matter referred to in subsection (5) or (6) or any other matter relating to the administration of the Court, that decision or action is not subject to any type of judicial review by a superior court unless that decision or action is, in the opinion of a superior court, patently unreasonable or not within the powers, duties or jurisdiction of the Chief Judge.

Judge's residence

9.42(1) The Minister of Justice and Solicitor General or a person authorized by that Minister may, on the appointment of a judge, designate the place at which the judge is to reside.

(2) Where a designation is made under subsection (1), any subsequent change in designation may only be made by the Judicial Council at the request of the Chief Judge and only if, in the opinion of the Judicial Council, the change in residence is required for the better administration of the Court.

I don't think there can be much dispute that s. 21.1(7), now called s. 9.1(7), of the Provincial Court Act, was the government's response to my successful application for judicial review of Wachowich's attempt to transfer me. I don't have any doubt that the real adversary in my litigation was the government and that the chief judge did not have control. It must have been humiliating for Judge Wachowich to have the record of his errors made public in the course of the proceedings, but when Judge Maher asked him if he would agree to the settlement, his answer was "I cannot." From Judge Walter's comments he didn't seem to be involved. He couldn't talk to me about it. He couldn't tell me who it was that decided to appeal, and he didn't seem to know what the appeal was about.

So when it was over, and the government lost, they passed legislation to make it more difficult for a judge in my position to ever beat them again. I believe this is an egregious example of politicians trying to control the judiciary. They don't seem to understand that independent judges are the prime protector of the rights of the individual. If the government can tell the judges how to act, we do not have a free society, we have a police state.

The very reasoned judgment of Justice Blair Mason documented the constitutional problem here. The specific issue of the designation of a judge's residence has been dealt with. Section 9.42(1) was the Alberta government's answer to the Supreme Court of Canada declaring the former section unconstitutional, but s. 9.1(7) purports to increase the power of a chief judge over judges, and that was their response to a situation that was found to infringe on judicial independence.

In my view a government that was truly interested in preserving the constitutionally protected rights of its citizens would have addressed the problem of constitutionality head on and would have passed legislation that would limit the powers of a chief judge.

I suggest that a provision that would comply with the law as set out in *Reilly v. Wachowich* would read as follows:

> All decisions of the chief judge which may be perceived to impinge on the individual adjudicative independence of any judge shall be subject to judicial review and if reviewed shall be reviewed on the basis that the fundamental principle of individual adjudicative independence requires that any such decision shall be made according to the highest standards of reasonableness, openness and strict adherence to jurisdiction.

I further suggest that in order to prevent a repetition of the error that was made, a fair-minded Minister of Justice and Attorney General might have suggested legislation that would set out procedural safeguards for the exercise of the chief judge's powers under subsections (5) and (6).

I am hopeful that a more democratic government or perhaps a constitutionally-minded MLA who reads this book might be sufficiently concerned about what happened to me to propose corrective legislation.

❖ 26 ❖

THE JUDICIAL RAILROAD

The appeal in *Reilly v. Wachowich* was filed June 2, 1999. The matter was argued April 3 and 4, 2000, and judgment was issued on September 5, 2000. During that time, I was having ongoing trouble with Judge Stevenson, who I felt was using his administrative authority to make my life difficult. I wrote to Judge Walter a number of times and he was of no assistance to me.

I wrote to the Chief Justice of Alberta, Catherine Fraser, to inquire as to the status of my complaint against Wachowich and Stevenson. On September 10, 1999, she informed me that my complaint had been referred to the Judicial Council and I would be hearing from Chief Judge Walter. This was very little comfort, as I believed Judge Walter was part of the opposing team. In fact, as the successor to Judge Wachowich he was the ex officio respondent in my judicial review application.

On October 21, 1999, Walter informed me that with respect to my complaint of December 21, 1998, "the Judicial Council will be constrained to hold it in abeyance until the legal action instituted by you against Chief Judge Wachowich (which involves Assistant Chief Judge Stevenson also) is disposed of by the courts. It would not only be inappropriate for the Judicial Council to discuss a matter which is *sub judice*, it might amount to contempt of court."

It rankled me that he spoke of "the legal action instituted by you against Chief Judge Wachowich." Judgment had been issued in my favour on April 26, 1999. The appeal from that judgment was filed June 2, 1999. But Walter had become the acting chief judge on January 31, 1999, and as such, it should have been his decision whether or not to file an appeal. (As mentioned earlier, I believe the Minister of Justice directed the appeal, but it should have been Walter's decision.) Therefore it was not my legal action that was the holdup, it was his appeal.

His suggestion that for the council to even discuss it might be a contempt of court for violating the *sub judice* rule was totally wrong. The *sub judice* rule prohibits making public statements about a matter in litigation that might influence a court decision. An example might be Premier Klein's public comments about my order in *R. v. Hunter* for the investigation into conditions on the reserve at Morley when that matter was before the courts. Those statements might well have put pressure on the judge to decide the way Klein wanted it decided.

In point of fact there may have been some merit to the position that the Judicial Council could not deal with the matter until the litigation was concluded, but nevertheless I saw Walter's reply as a refusal to deal with my difficulties.

By letter of October 28, 1999, Walter informed me that he had received a copy of a complaint against me from the Stoney tribal administration, signed by the three Chiefs – Darcy Dixon of the Bearspaw Band, Paul Chiniquay of the Chiniki and John Snow of the Wesley – related to comments I had made in the matter of the fatality inquiry into the death of Sherman Labelle.

By letter of November 1, Walter sent me a copy of a statutory declaration by Ernest Hunter dated September 10, 1999, which Walter had received by a letter dated October 21, 1999. The contents were as follows:

I, Ernest Vernon Hunter, of the town of Morley, in the Province of Alberta, do solemnly declare that:

1. On January 2, 1997, I was charged with domestic assault.

2. After my preliminary hearing, I met Judge Reilly in the hallway of the Cochrane courthouse. I told him that I did not have any transportation into Cochrane for my next appearance at the Provincial Court (Cochrane).

3. Judge Reilly told me to meet him at the Morley turnoff on Highway 1A at 9:30 am on the day of my hearing. He said to me that he always comes from Canmore to Cochrane on Highway 1A and could give me a ride.

4. On May 27, 1997, Judge Reilly picked me up on the 1A highway and drove me to the courthouse in a small brown station wagon type of vehicle.

5. On the ride into Cochrane, Judge Reilly asked me many questions about the conditions on the Stoney reserve. He also asked me many questions about Chief John Snow.

6. Judge Reilly told me that I would become famous for helping my people.

7. Judge Reilly told me that if I helped him, I would be remanded and I would not go to jail.

8. I pleaded guilty to the charge on May 27, 1997.

9. On June 26, 1997, Judge Reilly again picked me up on Highway 1A at the Morley turnoff. Judge Reilly again promised me that I would not go to jail and I would be on probation. Judge Reilly again asked me many questions about the living conditions on the Stoney Reserve.

10. On our way to the courthouse, Judge Reilly told me to meet him in a private office in the Cochrane courthouse.

11. In the private office, Judge Reilly promised me that I would not go to jail and that I would be on probation.

12. My lawyer, James Ogle, was not with me when I met with Judge Reilly.

13. My mother told me, and I believed it to be true, that sometime before June 26, 1997, Judge Reilly phoned my mother's house wanting to talk to me. I was not there at the time.

14. Prior to June 26, 1997, I was in Canmore and Judge Reilly came up to me outside the Sundance Inn and hugged me and thanked me for helping him. I was with Olive Holloway and another Stoney lady who both witnessed this event.

15. Judge Reilly has not contacted me since June 26, 1997.

Since I had Walter's letter to me of October 21 telling me that nothing would be done with my complaint against Wachowich and Stevenson until the Court of Appeal proceedings were concluded, I assumed nothing would be done with the complaints against me until then either.

In my view, the steps Walter took were not just indicative of his bias towards me, they were proof of his vindictiveness against me.

Under the Judicature Act a chief judge receiving a complaint against a judge could do one or more of the following:

(a) reprimand the judge
(b) take corrective measures
(c) refer the matter to the Judicial Council
(d) determine that no further action be taken

The decision to refer to the Judicial Council was the most onerous measure Walter could take against me, and he did it without ever asking me for input. Admittedly he had told me he had received the complaints, but since the *Hunter* case was the reason for the litigation, I thought it was reasonable to assume that this would all be held in abeyance.

I had been required to appear before the Judicial Council in the 1980s because of some injudicious comments I had made that were reported in the *Calgary Sun*. (See the section on Justice Herb Laycraft in Appendix A.) On that occasion, Chief Judge Con Kosowan had me come to his office to inform me of his intention to refer the matter to the Judicial Council and gave me the opportunity to speak to him about it. It seemed obvious to me that he had made up his mind, but he gave me the courtesy of making submissions to him before he did so. I was then informed of the date on which the Judicial Council would hear the matter and I was given the opportunity to retain counsel and appear to make submissions.

The Judicial Council on reviewing a complaint can, under the Judicature Act, do one or more of the following:

(a) reprimand the judge
(b) take corrective measures
(c) refer the complaint for a judicial inquiry
(d) dismiss the complaint if it is frivolous or vexatious or is not a matter in respect of which a complaint may be made
(e) determine that no further action need be taken

Again, the most onerous decision they could make against me would be to refer the matter to a judicial inquiry board, and that is what they did, without giving me notice, without a hearing and without the benefit of counsel.

By letter of January 14, 2000, Walter advised me that the Judicial Council had met and considered the complaints. They had dismissed the complaint from the three Chiefs of the Stoney tribal administration, but had ordered a judicial inquiry in relation to the Hunter complaint.

The council did this without even interviewing Hunter to

assess his credibility. They simply took the statutory declaration at face value and said it created a prima facie case that, if true, would show conduct unbecoming a judge by fraternizing with an accused and promising no jail in exchange for information on conditions on the Stoney reserve, and that it would also show disregard of the law pertaining to sentencing for extralegal considerations.

So the council had agreed that, if true, these allegations could bring the administration of justice into disrepute and put Judge Reilly in jeopardy. These allegations must therefore be inquired into. They apparently did this on the basis of a COPY of the declaration. They didn't even have the original.

My first reaction on seeing this was to wonder why Hunter's declaration was dated September 10 and forwarded by letter dated October 21. In preparing for the judicial inquiry, Alan and I learned that Hunter had burned the original. The copy was forwarded at the direction of the Rev. Dr. Chief John Snow, who, as it turned out, had been instrumental in its creation.

The council established a judicial inquiry board consisting of Justice E.P. MacCallum of the Court of Queen's Bench; Assistant Chief Judge B.E. Scott of the Provincial Court, Civil Division, Calgary; and Assistant Chief Judge D.L. Crowe of the Provincial Court, Red Deer.

I suppose I should have been upset by the fact that I would be the subject of a judicial inquiry. I hadn't taken the complaints very seriously because I didn't think any reasonable person would pay any attention to them, and I assumed nothing would be done until the litigation in *Reilly v. Wachowich* was concluded.

By letter of January 18, 2000, I told Walter I expected the Judicial Council would not deal with the complaints while the *Reilly v. Wachowich* appeal was outstanding. I asked him who sat on the Judicial Council, and whether he had disqualified himself in view of the fact that as chief judge he was now a party to my litigation.

By letter of February 23, 2000, Walter replied that the Hunter complaint was not related in any way to *Reilly v. Wachowich*, that my query as to who sat on the council was improper, and that he was not required to recuse himself because the matters were not related to the litigation.

I have no doubt that if I had been dealing with a fair-minded person who had informed himself about was going on, and had a basic appreciation of procedural fairness, things would have been different.

Walter was ex officio the opposite party in my litigation. Even if he was friendly towards me, he should have disqualified himself from any dealings with me because of this.

If he had read the file on *Reilly v. Wachowich* he would have known that the whole matter centred around my judgment in the *Hunter* matter.

Both his decision to refer the matter to the Judicial Council, and the decision of the council to refer it in turn to a judicial inquiry board, were decisions that required procedural fairness. If Walter had read Justice Mason's judgment in *Reilly v. Wachowich*, he would have seen the ruling that Wachowich's failure to give me a hearing violated the rules of procedural fairness, and that on that ground alone his order would have been quashed.

Walter's most outrageous position was that it was improper for me to ask who the members of the panel were that had made the decision against me. In England in the 15th century there was a court that sat at the Royal Palace of Westminster in a room called the Star Chamber. Court sessions were held in secret and there were no indictments and no witnesses. Over time this evolved into a political weapon, a symbol of the misuse and abuse of power by the English monarchy. The term Star Chamber is now synonymous with injustice, and Walter was reverting to that type of procedure.

By letter dated March 6, 2000, Alan Hunter set out reasons why Judge Walter should recuse himself: that, as the new chief judge, he must have had a part in the decision to appeal *Reilly v. Wachowich* and also in the non-payment of the costs that had been ordered against his office; and that he had not addressed my ongoing difficulties with Assistant Chief Judge Stevenson. Alan also objected to the administrative judges who had been assigned to the judicial inquiry board and asked that copies of his letter be forwarded to the members of the council, since Judge Walter would not tell us who they were.

Walter confirmed that he had forwarded copies of Alan's letter to all members of the Judicial Council that had "unanimously" decided to refer the matter to a judicial inquiry board. He also said the assertion that he lacked impartiality was unfounded and offensive as was the reference to the lack of impartiality of administrative judges. He added that since the appointment of the judicial inquiry board he had no role in the proceedings and neither had any member of the Judicial Council, and further that either he nor the Judicial Council had any jurisdiction to withdraw the decision constituting a judicial inquiry board.

That latter statement also proved to be incorrect, at least to the extent that a reconstituted council subsequently changed the members of the judicial inquiry board. Assistant chief judges Scott and Crow were replaced by judges Donnelly and Hope.

By letter dated April 6 Justice John B. Dea of the Court of Queen's Bench invited me to make submissions, which were to be directed to Justice J.E. Côté.

By letter of April 15, I made lengthy submissions.

I said that I took the request for submissions to indicate a willingness to reconsider their decision and thanked them for that.

I confirmed that I had instructed my counsel to apply for

judicial review of both Chief Judge Walter's initial referral to the council and the decision of the Judicial Council to refer the complaint to the judicial inquiry board.

I said I did not feel the chief judge had dealt with the original complaint by Hunter in a fair and impartial manner, and that if he had discussed it with me he might well have decided to dismiss the complaint without a referral.

I advised that the complainant, Hunter, was the same person as the accused in the case in which I ordered the investigation at Morley on June 26, 1997, and that Judge Walter apparently did not know this.

I said I had not made any comment to Walter about the complaint because I assumed the matter would be held in abeyance until the completion of the litigation, just as my complaint against former Chief Judge Wachowich and Assistant Chief Judge Stevenson was being held in abeyance.

I went into detail about my initiatives in relation to s. 718.2(e) of the Criminal Code as well as my efforts to expose abuses on the reserve and the fact that in doing so I had angered various political figures, including John Snow.

I stated that I had come to know many people on the reserve who provided me with reliable information about the conditions there, and that I would not have jeopardized my career by improper dealings with an unemployed alcoholic with over 40 criminal convictions.

I outlined information which indicated that John Snow was involved in the complaint by Hunter, and suggested there should be an inquiry as to why Hunter's statutory declaration was sworn on September 10, 1999, and forwarded on October 21, 1999.

I denied all of the allegations made by Hunter, but admitted I had given him a ride on June 26, 1997, the day I made the order for the investigation, but that I did not recognize him until he had entered my vehicle. I explained that his allegation that I had promised not to send him to jail was a statement I had made in open court, and quoted the transcript (which I also enclosed).

I suggested Hunter's credibility was suspect and that some assessment should have been made before the matter proceeded. I said that if I had been given an opportunity to talk to the chief judge I would have asked him to speak to Hunter or have an investigator or lawyer speak to him to make an assessment of his credibility and perhaps determine why the statutory declaration is dated October 21, 1999. I pointed out that I doubted this had been done, given that the declaration was forwarded October 21 and the chief judge's letter informing me he was sending it to the Judicial Council was dated November 1.

In summary, I said that if I had been dealing with an impartial decision maker who would have discussed this matter with me and with potential witnesses, who would have met with the complainant and assessed his credibility, and who would have made a fair and reasoned decision, the matter would not have been referred to the Judicial Council.

I said I should have had a similar opportunity at the hearing of the Judicial Council and that the appointment of the judicial inquiry board was a very onerous step which was unwarranted by the quality of the complaint against me, damaging to my reputation, and would cause me to incur further liability for legal services.

With regard to the appointment of assistant chief judges Crowe and Scott to the judicial inquiry board, I said that I considered them friends, but that they were part of the court administration with which I was in conflict and I was therefore concerned about the possibility of bias.

My submission was answered in a letter from Justice Dea addressed to Chief Darcy Dixon, Chief Paul Chiniquay, Chief John Snow, Mr. Ernest Hunter, Judge J.D. Reilly and A.D. Hunter, QC.

Justice Dea said the council had in no way judged who was telling the truth and that a hearing was in the best interests of the public and of both the complainant and the judge concerned.

I found little reassurance in the fact that the council had determined to cause a judge to submit to an inquiry on the written allegations of a disgruntled accused without ever having heard from him directly or done anything to assess his credibility.

Alan Hunter wrote to Justice Dea and inquired as to why the letter had been sent to the three Chiefs. Justice Côté answered in the absence of Justice Dea. He told us the complaint made by Ernest Hunter had come to the Judicial Council from two sources. It was contained in the material filed by the three Chiefs in a letter dated October 6, 1999. Subsequently the same complaint was provided to the Judicial Council in a letter dated October 21, 1999, by Ernest Hunter himself. Because of that, the letter of May 1, 2000, was sent to the three Chiefs in addition to the other persons indicated.

Justice Côté also informed us that the composition of the Judicial Council which first decided to refer the matter was Chief Judge Walter, justices Côté and Dea and Messrs. T. Claxton, A.F. Kiernan and R. King.

The council that reconsidered was composed of justices Côté and Dea, Alan Macleod, QC, and Messrs. A.F. Kiernan and R. King.

It was little comfort to me that four of the original members of the council were still there when the matter was reconsidered. There was no question in my mind that Walter was seriously biased against me. He had participated in the first meeting and that meeting had unanimously decided to refer to a judicial inquiry board.

Because of my challenge to his impartiality, Walter didn't participate in the subsequent discussion. But he presumably spoke to the first meeting. Côté, Dea, Kiernan and King had agreed with him the first time around, and they constituted a majority the second time around. There was no one to argue on my behalf, and they simply "rubber-stamped" what they had done in the first place, with the adjustment in relation to the makeup of the judicial inquiry board.

The difference between the handling of the complaint against me and the treatment of the complaint I filed is interesting. I had documentary evidence showing that Wachowich and Stevenson had lied to me and to the deputy minister and had collaborated with each other to create an exchange of correspondence to cover up their motive. This was confirmed by Justice Mason's written reasons for judgment, in which he termed their conduct "mere subterfuge."

I was a judge with 20 years of service and nothing was done with my complaint. But a man with 40 criminal convictions sends a copy of a false statutory declaration to Judge Walter, in a covering letter that is dated six weeks after the declaration is sworn, and Walter rushes it through a meeting of the Judicial Council, and they order a judicial inquiry.

By letter dated May 15, 2000, Alan Hunter requested a copy of the enclosures included with the complaint of the three Chiefs. He repeated his request on June 1, June 8 and July 5. He had filed an originating notice for a judicial review and this material would determine whether or not we would proceed.

I was pretty sure John Snow had caused Ernest Hunter to make the statutory declaration and had probably paid him for so doing. Alan and I were anxious to see what was in that package. By letter dated August 8, 2000, Justice Dea sent us three enclosures:

(a) a bundle of newspaper clippings;
(b) the fatality report of September 16, 1999; and
(c) the sentencing decision in *R. v. Hunter.*

His letter now claimed that "further investigation" had "disclosed that the Ernest Hunter complaint was not attached" to the letter from the three Chiefs, and that earlier suggestions that it may have been attached arose from the way the material was photocopied when it was sent to the Judicial Council.

Alan was angered by the reply. "John, I think they're lying to us."

"Oh come on, Alan, surely the members of the Judicial Council wouldn't do that."

"Well, they tell us in one letter that they received the Hunter complaint in the materials from the Chiefs, and now they say it didn't come in those materials. *And* it took them three months to answer my request."

"I'm sure John Snow put Hunter up to it. I'm pretty sure he doesn't like me very much." I laughed: "I wonder if this is how the Indians feel when they appear in our courts."

"There is no question their decision to refer this to a judicial inquiry is bad, for their failure to give you a proper hearing. It will be set aside on the judicial review, just like Wachowich's decision was."

"I'm sure you're right, and I'm sure the Court of Appeal is going to find in our favour, but I don't think I have the energy for another judicial review application. It's more than two years since we started the one with Wachowich. God knows how much longer that's going to take. Thank God you kept me out of the Judicial Council. From the way they've railroaded me on this, we would have been dead in the water."

"I think MacCallum's okay. What do you know about judges Donnelly and Hope?"

"I don't know either of them very well, but they both strike me as quite reasonable people. Neither of them comes across as an Indian-hating redneck."

"What do you think Hunter will be like as a witness?"

"I think any reasonable judge who listens to him for a few minutes will be totally unimpressed. If Walter had just interviewed him or had him interviewed, I'm sure this wouldn't be happening."

"My advice is that we just go ahead with the judicial inquiry board. We may even be able to have the inquiry subject to our right to have a review of the Judicial Council's decision to refer it to a judicial inquiry."

So we decided to accept a hearing before the judicial inquiry board, and it was set for two weeks in October of 2000.

❖ 27 ❖

THE JUDICIAL INQUIRY

The first order of business for the judicial inquiry board was to appoint their counsel, a lawyer who would interview witnesses, present them at the hearing and generally act as counsel to the board. The board appointed William H. Hurlburt, QC.

He was a gentleman and in my view the epitome of the dispassionate prosecutor. He had no interest in the outcome of the proceedings. He simply had the job of gathering and presenting evidence to the board. I agreed to be interviewed by him, and he was one of the first people, other than Alan Hunter, who actually listened to me and seemed genuinely interested in what I had to say. After all of the actions that had been taken against me without ever giving me a chance to speak on my own behalf, this was a delightful change.

As mentioned earlier, I didn't take Ernest Hunter's declaration seriously when I first saw it. I was sure anyone who took a hard look at it would see it was nonsense. But Judge Walter didn't see it that way, and now that I was the subject of a judicial inquiry, Alan Hunter and I took it very seriously as well. If there were any possibility that Ernest Hunter's allegations would be believed, then every possible piece of evidence to the contrary would have to be called to refute them.

My defence would involve three parts. First, I would testify to deny any impropriety in my dealings with Ernest Hunter. Then I would call evidence to support my statements. And finally, I would call evidence to establish John Snow's complicity in the creation of the statutory declaration and the payoff Ernest Hunter received for making it.

I couldn't categorically deny everything, because there were a few elements of truth in the story. His assertion that I had called his mother wanting to speak to him was a fabrication, but his mother had in fact given me her phone number. I had chatted with her at the wake of Tina Fox's husband, Kent.

Hunter's story that I had met him in the parking lot of the Sundance Inn in Canmore before June 26, 1997, and that I had thanked him for helping me was false. I did meet him there once, but that was after the Court of Appeal had added the term of imprisonment to his sentence, and I told him he should contact his lawyer about that.

Hunter's claims that I had met with him in the courthouse and arranged to give him rides to court were a fabrication, but I did in fact give him a ride to court on June 26, 1997, the day I ordered the investigation. As mentioned earlier, I had made it a practice to pick up hitchhikers on the reserve. This was as a result of case management meetings which had shown there were an inordinate number of adjournments at Cochrane. The Indigenous court worker, Marjorie Powderface, would regularly apply for them because her clients could not get transportation. I had even inquired about the possibility of getting a school bus driver to make a run to Cochrane on court days. Roy Pennoyer, the chief of the Stoney tribal police, wrote me a letter saying this could be done if the court would pay for it. I was pretty sure that wasn't going to happen, and nothing further was done in this regard, so I started picking up hitchhikers on my way to court in Cochrane.

I started doing this one day after I'd passed Hiram Kootenay trying to get a ride. I knew Hiram because he was a frequent attender at the Cochrane court, usually charged with minor, alcohol-related offences. At the end of the court session, his name was called and I was asked to issue a warrant for his arrest for his failure to appear. I said in open court that I was hesitant to issue the warrant, because I had seen him trying to get a ride. Instead, I adjourned the matter for a week with a "warrant to hold," a procedure that meant that the court's jurisdiction was maintained but the accused would not be arrested so long as he made the next appearance.

After that I made a practice of picking up hitchhikers on my way to court. Word went around the reserve that I was doing this, and I think it helped make the foreign system of justice I represented seem a little less foreign.

I picked up Hiram a number of times. On one occasion he told me he was taking a course to become a heavy equipment operator. Another time, I picked up his twin brother, Clive. They were so similar looking that I couldn't tell them apart and I asked if he had been able to get employment as a heavy equipment operator. He looked at me a little strangely and said, "This is Clive." They also had a cousin Clyde. They all looked so alike that it was rumoured they had actually done time (served prison sentences) for each other.

On another occasion, there were three young Stoneys hitchhiking on a bitterly cold day. I wondered about picking up this group, but they weren't dressed for the cold and I couldn't just leave them on the road. They recognized me when they got in the car and confirmed I was going to the courthouse in Cochrane. The one who took the front seat told me he was charged with attempted murder. I told him I couldn't talk about his case, but he volunteered that it was a "chickenshit" charge.

When I got to Cochrane, Clare Jarman, the probation officer, came into my office. She too lives in Canmore and had been driving behind me when I picked up the hitchhikers. She had become a good friend and had no reservations about criticizing me.

"Don't you think it was stupid to pick up those three kids?"

"Clare, it's 30 below and they weren't dressed for it. I wasn't going to leave them on the road."

"What if they were charged with something really serious."

"The boy in the front seat told me he was charged with attempted murder."

"There, you see?" she said somewhat triumphantly.

"Relax, Clare. He told me it was a chickenshit charge."

THE PROPOSED SUPPORTING EVIDENCE

In order to corroborate my evidence that I never met with Ernest Hunter in the courthouse, neither in the hallway nor in my private office, I gave Mr. Hurlburt the names of the clerks who had been working on all of the days Ernest Hunter had been in court: Jackie Rosko, Jennifer Woods and Gail Kazimer; the Cochrane RCMP liaison officer, Jodi Guertin; and the Canmore court administrator, Cheryl Dubuc.

I expected they would all say it would be highly unusual for me to speak to an accused person in the hallway or in a private office, and that if it did happen it would be so unusual that they would remember it. They could then say they had no such recollection.

I would call evidence to establish that I enjoyed the confidence and support of many people in the Stoney community, including Elders and members of tribal council, which evidence would be tendered to discredit the allegation of Ernest Hunter that I would make a career-threatening arrangement with a habitual criminal to get a little information about John Snow and the reserve. These witnesses would be the following:

1. Tina Fox, who had been the Indigenous court worker when I sat in Cochrane in the '80s. I didn't get to know her then but I remembered her. She was in her sixth term on the tribal council. She had given me a tremendous amount of information

before I ordered the investigation and publicly supported my order when it generated media interest.

2. Greg Twoyoungmen, also a member of the tribal council, and a long-time critic of Chief John Snow.

3. Warren Harbeck, a newspaper columnist and linguist who had come to Morley in 1965 in association with Wycliffe Bible Translators to assist the Stoney community in developing a writing system for their language and consult with them on translating the Bible into Stoney. Harbeck later severed ties with Wycliffe but had learned to speak Stoney and worked directly with John Snow for a number of years.

4. Rick Butler, who was the band administrator at the time I ordered the investigation. He told me he had come to see the truth in everything I had said about the reserve and would testify on my behalf.

5. Lawrence Twoyoungmen, a Stoney Elder who had been justice liaison for the Stoney and in that position had become friends with the late chief Crown prosecutor Jerry Salinger and had been one of the speakers at his funeral.

6. Bill McLean, Bearspaw Elder and son of the late Chief Walking Buffalo.

7. Bert Wildman, Chiniki Elder and former manager of the Star Ranch on the Stoney reserve.

8. John Robinson Twoyoungmen, Elder, retired teacher, former member of the tribal council.

9. Watson Kaquitts, former member of tribal council.

10. Alice Kaquitts, who has a university degree in social work and is co-founder of Nakoda Solutions, a healing program for Stoney people.

11. Tom Snow, John Snow's brother, co-founder of Nakoda Solutions.

Evidence of John Snow's complicity in the statutory declaration

My greatest concern in this matter was that John Snow had caused Ernest Hunter to make the statutory declaration. I wanted to show his involvement in order to discredit Ernest Hunter's evidence, and also in the hope that I might cause charges to be laid against him as a party to what was clearly a criminal offence by Hunter. The witnesses in this regard were to be these:

1. Tina Fox would testify that Hunter had told her he had been hired by John Snow to keep an eye on people at the administration building.

2. Greg Twoyoungmen would testify that Gardiner Poucette had given Hunter a garbage collection job that should have been publicly posted but was given to Hunter at the direction of Chief Snow.

3. Lawrence Twoyoungmen would testify that he spoke to John Snow and suggested he back off on his efforts to get rid of me and that Snow had gotten very angry at the suggestion.

4. Bill McLean would testify that John Snow had had a petition taken to have me removed, and that when they asked McLean to sign it he refused and had others who had signed it take their names off.

Bill Hurlburt set up at Nakoda Lodge to interview all of these potential witnesses. He also interviewed John Snow and Snow's so-called "litigation consultant," Terry Munro. In his interview with Snow, Hurlburt asked the Chief what he thought of me. Snow's reply was to the effect of "what would you think of someone who compared you to the dictator of a banana republic?" It gave me some satisfaction to know that my words had had an effect on him. At the same time, I was dismayed at his sense of entitlement. He knew he was exploiting his people and he saw nothing wrong with it.

From Hurlburt's notes and the other information I received, I was able to piece together what I believe is an accurate history.

The fact that I didn't sentence Ernest Hunter to a period of imprisonment was common knowledge on the reserve and evidently the subject of considerable comment. Hunter had been telling people I had not sent him to jail because he was helping me get information about the reserve and John Snow. After the Court of Appeal decision, however, he was arrested and incarcerated. He served 12 of the 18 months and was released on parole in September of 1999.

John Snow became aware of Ernest Hunter's claims and contacted him on his release. Together they decided to take action against me. Snow took him to the offices of Munro & Associates. There, Ernest Hunter, with John Snow and Terry Munro, composed the content of the statutory declaration, and Hunter signed it in the presence of Tibor Osvath, a lawyer who did some work for the Stoneys. The statutory declaration was then left with Hunter for him to forward to the chief judge.

It was also from Hurlburt's notes that I got the answer to my question about the differing dates on the statutory declaration and the covering letter. Ernest Hunter had reiterated his story to John Snow and signed the statutory declaration but he didn't send it. He burned the original. He knew it wasn't true.

Somehow John Snow found out it had not been sent. On October 21, 1999, he had Terry Munro take a copy of the statutory declaration and the covering letter to Ernest Hunter. Hunter signed the letter, and then either he or Munro mailed those two documents to the chief judge's office.

I surmise that it was through communication with the Judicial Council that Snow found out Hunter had not sent the declaration, but neither I nor my lawyer was given disclosure of that communication.

In our criminal justice system every accused has the right to see all the material that leads to a criminal charge, no matter how minor the charge. A judge in Alberta apparently does not have this right.

Alan Hunter and I were confident that both the referral from Walter to the Judicial Council and the referral from the Judicial Council to the judicial inquiry board were decisions we could successfully challenge on judicial review. They had both been made without procedural fairness and with the appearance of bias on the part of Judge Walter, and in our opinion this was sufficient to taint both decisions by the Judicial Council.

Alan explained our position to Bill Hurlburt and Hurlburt agreed to conduct the hearing before the judicial inquiry board with the proviso that it would be subject to our right to challenge the referral if we didn't like the outcome. This meant we would accept a ruling in our favour but could challenge the board's jurisdiction if it went against us.

On Monday, October 16, 2000, we attended for the hearing. The first witness was to be Ernest Hunter. He didn't show up. There were discussions amongst the board and the lawyers as to procedure and what to do about the non-appearance. A private investigator was called to give evidence as to prior contact with Ernest Hunter. He outlined several difficulties in getting him to attend at Nakoda Lodge for an interview with Hurlburt. In the end Hunter had come to Nakoda Lodge to pick up his subpoena and a cheque for conduct money. There seemed to be an inference that it was the conduct money that motivated him to come to the lodge. The board issued a warrant for Hunter's attendance and adjourned the hearing to Wednesday morning to allow for his attendance.

On Wednesday morning Ernest Hunter was in custody and would be brought in to testify. There was again discussion as to procedure and the board agreed to proceed on the proviso that I would be able to challenge the referral by the chief judge depending on the finding of the board.

When Hunter testified, he did not repeat his allegations of meetings in the courthouse hallway or a private office. He said his lawyer had met with me. He said it was his lawyer who said he would become famous for helping his people. He maintained that I had picked him up twice and that on the first ride I told him I would pick him up again. He was very indefinite on the dates but he seemed to be referring to the May 27 and June 26 appearances. He said we discussed his charges but he did not say I promised him no jail in exchange for information. He made no reference to the phone call to his mother. He did say we had met at the Sundance Inn, and that I had thanked him for helping me, in the presence of the two Stoney women who were with him.

At the end of Mr. Hurlburt's examination in chief, the board adjourned for lunch. When we reconvened, Alan Hunter was going to cross-examine the witness, but this became unnecessary. Hurlburt advised the board that in his view there was no case to be met. He filed the notes he had made in his prehearing interview with Ernest Hunter and he told the board that the "story changes in highly material aspects on every occasion."

Alan Hunter indicated that in view of Mr. Hurlburt's comments he had no cross-examination of Ernest Hunter. Both lawyers agreed that all of the collateral evidence that was going to be called had become unnecessary and that I would be the only remaining witness.

Justice MacCallum inquired as to why I would be called. Alan Hunter's reply demonstrated his ongoing passion, even though it was almost whispered through his voice amplifier because of his chronic larynx problem. His answer was:

> Because of the possible inference that Judge Reilly didn't, say, address this statutory declaration. What has to be

remembered here is that when the complaint went to the chief judge, he didn't inquire of Judge Reilly. He didn't tell him about it. He didn't ask for his views. He made no attempt to contact the complainant to see if there was any basis to it. He made a decision to refer to the Judicial Council, and he chaired the Judicial Council. And again, no notice to Judge Reilly, no "what have you got to say about this?" And no effort to inquire of Mr. Hunter. Just bingo: judicial inquiry board and all of these things.

So that you shouldn't be guessing about Judge Reilly's evidence here, which will be that he denies everything except that he picked Hunter up once, and he wants to explain to you what is involved in that. So this has been a long history and a very difficult thing to deal with, and it's Judge Reilly's desire to acquaint you with that.

So I testified, going through each of the allegations. Since Ernest Hunter had not repeated most of the content of the statutory declaration, most of this was unnecessary. We wanted it on the record partly to show how wrong the chief judge and the Judicial Council were in making the referral in the first place. We were hopeful that we might persuade the judicial inquiry board to make critical comment on the procedure followed by both the chief judge and the Judicial Council.

I rambled at some length about my efforts at Morley. I was a little concerned that my practice of picking up hitchhikers might substantiate the criticism of the Judicial Council of fraternizing with accused persons. I don't apologize for this. I believe it was helpful in getting a few accused people to court and thereby reducing the number of warrants. Most importantly it allowed the Stoney community to see a judge of the Provincial Court who wanted to help them and who was not an instrument of their oppression.

The report of the inquiry board was released in early November. It briefly reviewed the mandate and jurisdiction of the board, the background regarding Ernest Hunter's complaint, and the evidence. It confirmed that while the testimony of Ernest Hunter was such that there was no case to meet, they had heard my testimony anyway because "[Judge Reilly was] anxious to refute the very serious allegations made against him by Ernest Hunter in the statutory declaration, particularly in view of the fact that he had not been granted a right of audience before either Chief Judge Walter or the Judicial Council."

Regarding John Snow they said:

> Ernest Hunter testified that upon his release from prison he complained to Chief Snow that Judge Reilly had promised him he would not go to jail but in fact he did. He said that Chief Snow suggested to him that he should make a complaint and that Chief Snow would help him out.
>
> The question of motive for the complaint and the part played by Chief John Snow in the affair might have been important in judging credibility had the board found it necessary to continue the inquiry by hearing all of the proposed witnesses. As matters developed, however, the complaint was seen to be groundless based on Ernest Hunter's evidence alone. Accordingly neither John Snow nor any other witness from the reserve was called, so the board considers that it would not only be unfair to third parties to discuss motive, it is no longer necessary to the resolution of the inquiry.

The board concluded the report with their findings:

> In our discussion of paragraph 9 of the statutory declaration we noted Judge Reilly's testimony that he regularly picked up people as he crossed the reserve, in the interests of getting

them to court as well as showing empathy. While Judge Reilly is to be commended for his spirit of co-operation and helpfulness, the imprudence of a judge giving rides to people who might well be appearing before him as accused or witnesses must be obvious to him. That said, the board does not find it to be conduct unbecoming a judge.

We agree with counsel William Hurlburt that Ernest Hunter's statutory declaration, his inquiry evidence and the statements he made to Mr. Hurlburt on October 4, 2000, are materially inconsistent. Ernest Hunter is a witness who is not worthy of belief and the inquiry might have closed at the conclusion of his evidence. Judge Reilly, however, wanted to testify under oath to repudiate the serious allegations which threatened his reputation as a judge and as a dedicated advocate for the sensitive delivery of justice to the native people. His counsel, Alan Hunter, agrees with Mr. Hurlburt that there was no case to meet at the inquiry and says that in fact there never was a case to meet. He argues that this would have been obvious to both the chief judge of the Provincial Court and then to the Judicial Council had Ernest Hunter at least been interviewed, and had a right of audience been given to Judge Reilly. Because it was not, he says that an elementary principle of law was overlooked and that this should be emphasized by us in our report.

Under section 32.6(1) of the Judicature Act we are obliged to find the facts and find whether or not there was a basis for the complaint. We have stated our findings of fact and it is our conclusion that there was no basis for the complaint. We have fulfilled our fundamental statutory obligations. To go further by way of commenting upon lack of procedural fairness on the part of either the chief judge of the Provincial Court or the Judicial Council, or upon their alleged failure to review or inquire into the complaint before referring it to this inquiry board, would be, in our view, to indulge in a form of judicial review which is beyond our mandate.

The costs of the parties to the inquiry are beyond our jurisdiction to set, but Mr. Alan Hunter has suggested that we could recommend that Judge Reilly's costs be met on a solicitor/client basis. Not only has the matter been expensive and protracted for him, it is a question of judicial independence. A judge just should not have to face financial hardship as a result of complaints made about the performance of his duties. Under section 32.8 of the Judicature Act:

> The Judicial Council, on the conclusion of any hearing, may make an order regarding costs as it considers just, including costs relating to the judicial inquiry board.

In the circumstances of this case we have no hesitation in recommending to the Judicial Council that, with respect to Judge Reilly's costs relating to the judicial inquiry board, they be met on a solicitor/client basis.

❖ 28 ❖

MY COURT COSTS

In civil proceedings, as opposed to criminal matters, the unsuccessful party usually is ordered to pay "costs" to the successful party. But these costs, referred to as party and party costs, will usually amount to something less than the lawyer's actual bill. It is only in exceptional cases that the unsuccessful party will be directed to pay the amount the successful party has in fact been billed for by his lawyer. This is referred to as solicitor/client costs or costs on an indemnity basis.

Solicitor/client costs may be awarded where:

1. There is blameworthiness on the part of the unsuccessful party. This might involve hindering, delaying or confusing the litigation; requiring a lengthy, expensive proceeding where there is no serious issue of fact; showing contempt for the aggrieved party; attempting to deceive the court and defeat justice; or any conduct that should be deterred and penalized beyond the ordinary order of costs.

2. Justice can only be done by complete indemnity to the successful party.

My case was exceptional for a number of reasons. One is judicial independence. Judges deal with contentious issues in almost everything they do. If they had to be concerned about losing money on every case they decided, the merits of the case before them might become a secondary consideration to their own financial security. The parties before them would therefore not be obtaining a decision made by an "independent and impartial tribunal."

The frustrating thing for me was that I had been told that other judges who had been required to retain counsel in relation to actions taken against them had simply had their legal bills paid by the chief judge's office. The office just submitted them to the Department of Justice for payment. I believe that if I had been dealing with people of goodwill, who just legitimately held an opposing legal opinion, my bills would have been paid immediately upon receipt.

After the filing of the decision of Justice Mason, Alan Hunter sent me his bill for services rendered in *Reilly v. Wachowich*. His fee was a flat $125,000, which disbursements and taxes brought to $137,609.82.

I forwarded the bill to the chief judge's office in my letter of June 1, 1999, in which I congratulated Judge Walter on the confirmation of his appointment as chief judge and asked to meet with him.

In his reply on June 4, 1999, he said:

> I do not, on the face of it, see any express provision in the Provincial Court Judges Act which would cover this, but it is possible that a submission could be made on your behalf to the provincial government for reimbursement. If you would provide my office with authorities and the statement of the principles supporting your request for reimbursement, I would be prepared to consider this matter further. I await your reply.

During all the years of conflict with the chief judge's office, I don't think I ever felt any anger towards Ed Wachowich. I always felt he was either the victim of Brian Stevenson's manipulation or the puppet of the government or both. This was not the case with the Honourable Ernest E.J. (Ernie) Walter. His comment that the notice of appeal had been filed, as if he didn't have anything to do with it, and his request for submissions and authorities on the payment of my account so that he could consider the matter further, made me angry.

I believe he could simply have sent the account to the provincial government for payment and that would have been the end of it. When the matter first began, Judge Gary Cioni had told me that when he once had been required to retain counsel in relation to his judicial duties, his legal bills were paid without a problem, and he understood that legal services incurred by judges in the course of their employment were routinely paid by the chief judge's office. I discussed the matter with Alan Hunter and he suggested we should proceed with an application for costs before Justice Mason.

We proceeded with the hearing, and again the matter required briefs of argument and books of authorities. Alan filed 30 pages of the one and 143 pages of the other. His brief recited the fact that the matter involved a constitutionally impermissible infringement of judicial independence; that I had been denied procedural fairness; and that the effort to characterize the order of transfer as administrative had been found to be "mere subterfuge" in order to disguise disciplinary action. It recited also that every step of the procedure was challenged, thereby protracting the litigation.

Alan further argued that the case involved rare and exceptional circumstances and a matter of public interest and was brought to uphold the constitutional right of the public to a hearing by an independent and impartial tribunal.

Tavender's brief of argument was uncharacteristically short: only eight pages, supported by a 56-page book of authorities. In it he argued that Wachowich acted as a tribunal in making the impugned decision and that the general rule is that no costs are awarded against a tribunal. Costs are only awarded where the tribunal loses jurisdiction through capricious, arbitrary or other bad-faith conduct. Even if such bad faith is found in the loss of jurisdiction, costs should only be awarded on a party and party basis.

Tavender also argued that since the application was against the named respondent, Edward R. Wachowich, Chief Judge, he would be personally liable for payment and this would be a breach of his judicial independence, just as I had argued that being responsible for my costs would be an infringement on mine.

He attached Walter's letter of June 4, 1999, as an exhibit and stated that the current chief judge was prepared to treat the submissions in my brief as a statement of authorities and principles supporting my request for reimbursement for legal fees so that, independent of the court, an application could be made to the provincial government.

Tavender further asserted that since the cases said costs should only be awarded where there is reprehensible, scandalous or outrageous conduct deserving of chastisement, my case did not require an award of costs. He commented on the court's finding that the chief judge's administrative rationale for the impugned decision was "mere subterfuge" and re-argued that it was administrative, but that the disciplinary rationale was relied on for the decision as well.

In my view, the argument that Wachowich would be personally liable was disingenuous to say the least. I thought it was outright dishonest. I don't think there was ever any question whether the government would pay the chief judge's bill, and I believe my costs would have been paid immediately had the chief judge so directed.

I was a little embarrassed when I read in the factum that I had not answered Walter's letter. I had in fact written a 13-page letter in which I had asked him to consider that Wachowich and Stevenson had been incompetent, self-serving and dishonest in their dealing with me, and I had pleaded with him not to support the appeal. I had discussed this letter with Alan, however, and he had advised me not to send it. Alan pretty much wrote the reply which basically apologized for not answering his letter of June 4, 1999, and thanked him for his suggestion respecting payment of Mr. Hunter's account. The letter concluded with:

> I expect you will have received and considered the brief of argument on costs that has been filed on my behalf. I rely on the principles set out in that brief, particularly the infringement of financial independence and my duty to uphold the constitutional guarantee of judicial independence and impartiality.
>
> I understand the payment of Mr. Hunter's account is under discussion between Mr. Hunter and Mr. Tavender. It seems to me that the account should be paid out of the same fund as that from which Wachowich's account is paid. If this cannot be done by agreement we will be proceeding with our application for costs on Monday, July 5.

The application for costs was argued on July 5, 1999. On August 16 Justice Mason issued a 19-page judgment in which he summarized the arguments of both counsel, the cases referred him to, and stated his conclusion:

> In this case, the unilateral action of the chief judge, beyond his statutory jurisdiction and outside of the constitutional framework, with respect to a discipline issue, does amount to rare and exceptional circumstances.... I find ... that the Respondent elected to take the course of action that he did, that he instituted it without procedural fairness and, in so doing, struck at the very core of judicial independence ... Although there may have been statutory grounds for believing that the Respondent had the requisite jurisdiction to make disciplinary decisions of this nature, I find that the Respondent stepped well outside the boundaries of his jurisdiction in this instance.

> For the above reasons I order that the Applicant is entitled
> to his costs on an indemnification basis.

The front page of the *Calgary Herald* for August 19 carried an article by Bob Beaty headlined "Public to pay judge's legal bill: Reilly fight costs $300,000." The article stated that "the ruling from Queen's Bench Justice Blair Mason effectively forces the Alberta government to pay all of Reilly's $136,000 legal bill for his fight against former Provincial Court Chief Judge Ed Wachowich."

The article also said the province acknowledged it had already covered Wachowich's bill, and that Alberta Justice spokesman Bob Scott had said that until the appeal of Justice Mason's fundamental decision was heard, the provincial government wouldn't be paying Reilly's.

Alan Hunter didn't usually speak to the press, but he talked to Beaty: "'I think it is very unfair,' Hunter said of the government's decision to withhold payment to Reilly until the appeal court decision. 'It's just part of hanging people out to dry,' Hunter said of the general government attitude toward its judiciary."

Liberal critic Barb Olsen, MLA for Edmonton Norwood, said the legal bills for Wachowich and Reilly would easily add up to $300,000. I would have liked to have told her that it would probably be a lot more than that. When I was attempting to get support from the Alberta Provincial Court Judges Association a year earlier, before the hearing on the merits, Alan Hunter had calculated his fees to that date to be $35,000. At that time, Judge Cheryl Daniels told me that someone in the Milner Fenerty firm had told her Tavender had already billed the government over $100,000. If that proportion were maintained, his fees would be $600,000 when mine were $200,000. Given the costs of the judges and court staff involved, my estimate is that the ultimate cost was likely in excess of $1-million.

The bill for preparation and argument on the matter of costs was $15,000, and with disbursements and taxes it totalled $17,227.46. Hunter and Tavender agreed that the decision on costs could be added to the substantive appeal, which was set for February 3 and 4, 2000.

This time, Tavender filed a book of authorities on costs that included 25 references in 180 pages. Hunter's contained four references in 55 pages.

When the appeal was dismissed there was another bill added to my total that was eventually paid by the provincial government. The total of my fees was:

All steps in the litigation with Chief Judge Wachowich up to the order of April 26, 1999, quashing the order to transfer: $125,000

The taxation of my account, which included a chambers application and judgment: $15,000

All of the steps in the appeal, including filing the factums and argument in court: $50,000

With disbursements the total came to $205,726.86. It was not paid until November of 2000, even though the first $150,000 was payable at the time of Justice Mason's order of August 16, 1999, and the $50,000 was payable when the Court of Appeal order was made on September 5, 2000. The provincial government paid an additional $11,000 in judgment interest because of their late payment.

There was a further bill for $20,000 for services rendered in relation to our dealings with the Judicial Council. This included fees for the judicial review of Chief Judge Walter's referral of Ernest Hunter's complaint to the Judicial Council. Walter's lawyer, Rod McLennan, agreed that on the withdrawal of the originating notice, the fees I owed in that regard would be paid.

Finally, on the conclusion of the hearing by the judicial inquiry board I received an account for fees of $30,000 plus another $3,048 in disbursements. This too was paid by the provincial government, bringing the total to over $270,000.

Even though Alan Hunter had told me he would not pursue me for payment of these fees, they were a source of considerable anxiety for me, and it was an equally considerable relief when they were paid.

❖ 29 ❖

AFTER THE INQUIRY

When Chief John Snow walked out of the March 21, 1997, Cochrane case management and Stoney justice initiatives meeting, I took it personally. I was offering to help him and his people and he blew me off. The brief exchange I had with him was enough to convince me that I didn't like him.

From all of the interview notes William Hurlburt gave us, I was of the opinion they contained evidence which would establish that John Snow was a party to the criminal fabrication of evidence against me.

Alan Hunter agreed there should be a criminal investigation relating to the preparation of Ernest Hunter's statutory declaration. He suggested, with a quiet little laugh, that I should send it back to Chief Judge Walter and have him request the investigation in view of the fact that he was so misled by it. I pointed out that Chief Judge Walter had refused to take any action on a number of complaints I had made to him, and I didn't expect he would do anything with this either.

We decided that Alan would forward the report of the judicial inquiry board directly to Assistant Commissioner D.N. (Don) McDermid, the commanding officer of K Division of the RCMP. I had met McDermid in connection with my interest in family group conferencing, and I spoke to him about the matter. He told me to forward a copy to him and to the acting chief Crown prosecutor, Harold Hagglund. McDermid would refer it to his chief superintendent of operations, Rick Bovey, who would work with the prosecutor's office in determining the appropriate action. This was in October 2000.

In due course Sgt. Ken Chatel was assigned to the investigation. In June of 2001 Chatel contacted me to say he had spoken to William Hurlburt about getting his interview notes but had been unsuccessful because the judicial inquiry board had sealed them. I provided him with a letter supporting an application to unseal the documents and consenting to their release. His affidavit in support of the application was sworn in June of 2003. Evidently my "in" with the RCMP assistant commissioner had not resulted in a priority status for this investigation.

On August 19, 2003, a Queen's Bench order was issued directing William Hurlburt, QC, to turn over all relevant documents to the RCMP. Sgt. Chatel reviewed all of them and asked me if I had anything further. On completion of his review, he determined there was sufficient evidence to charge Ernest Hunter with an attempt to obstruct justice contrary to s. 139(2) of the Criminal Code. This offence carries a maximum penalty of 10 years imprisonment. Chatel was unable to proceed against either John Snow or Terry Munro, because even though there was substantial evidence that they were involved in the preparation of the statutory declaration, he had no way of proving they knew Ernest Hunter's statements in that declaration were false.

Hunter pleaded guilty on his first appearance, May 18, 2004. The matter was put over for sentencing. I was asked to provide a victim impact statement.

Victim impact statements had been introduced through amendments to the Criminal Code in the 1990s. All victims are to be asked to make such a statement, and judges are required to invite the victim to read their statement in open court. If the victim does not wish to read it, the judge is required to read it. These statements allow the victim to be heard and they provide additional material on which the judge can assess the seriousness of the crime.

Victim impact statements are not intended to allow the victim to make submissions on sentence, however, and this distinction between the victim speaking about the impact of the crime on them individually and the making of submissions on sentence is sometimes difficult to control. Submissions on appropriate sentence are the purview of the Crown. A judge will sentence on the basis of the seriousness of the offence. There is no provision for considering the vindictiveness or the forgivingness of the particular victim.

In the first paragraphs of my victim impact statement I said that the matter had caused me significant anxiety; that it had resulted in a judicial inquiry board hearing for which my lawyer and I had spent many hours in preparation; and that I incurred legal fees in excess of $30,000, which were ultimately paid by the government.

I went on for another three pages basically pleading for leniency for Ernest Hunter. I referred to his original charge of domestic assault. I said I had used it as a test case in relation to s. 718.2(e) of the Criminal Code, and this had caused the proceedings to be unusually protracted. My efforts to use a restorative justice sentence had resulted in a much more difficult process for Hunter. He was ultimately sentenced to 18 months by the Court of Appeal, and the notoriety the case received had made his hard time even harder, including getting beaten up while in prison. I concluded by setting out my suspicions that the real player in the action against me was Chief John Snow. I didn't attend the sentencing hearing, and I don't know what effect my victim impact statement had on the sentencing judge.

By letter dated December 20, 2004, the prosecutor, Sheila Brown, gave me a final report. Ernest Hunter was sentenced on December 16, 2004. The sentence was six months incarceration, consecutive to time he was already serving. (He had committed other offences and was doing time for those when he was sentenced on the obstruction charge.) Ms. Brown said Hunter was scheduled to begin day parole, and that the date would not be affected by the additional six months. It would only affect him if he breached his parole, in which case his release date would be later.

In the sentencing hearing an agreed statement of facts was put before the court that included the suggestion that Chief John Snow had manipulated Mr. Hunter into proceeding with the complaint. Hunter's sentence was based on his role as more of a pawn than the driving force behind the complaint.

Prosecutor Brown and Sgt. Chatel reviewed the matter and decided there would never be sufficient evidence to pursue charges against Chief Snow or anyone else who may have played a part in bringing the complaint. Brown told me that Hunter had confided in his counsel that Chief Snow had put him up to making the complaint, but there would always be the problem that he would not be considered a credible witness.

In the meantime, Chief Snow had gone back to the Judicial Council. By letter dated October 25, 2000, he complained about statements I had made in the judgments in *R. v. Hunter* (June 26 and November 28, 1997), and about comments in a *Herald* article of September 3, 1997. The article was said to be an "exclusive interview" and was headlined "Expose Stoney injustices, says Reilly."

That article had in fact caused me considerable anxiety, because I did not realize a photo shoot was being treated as an interview. Kim Lunman, who wrote the piece, had met me outside the courthouse that morning and asked if she could have her photographer take some pictures so they would have them on file. I agreed and we chatted. I thought we were just having casual conversation, but I suppose there is no such thing when you are talking to a newspaper reporter.

I had said to Lunman that it was time to expose years of hidden injustice on the Stoney reserve, injustice that had been allowed to happen because it had been kept hidden. I told her about the armed occupation of the band office by protesters back in the 1970s over allegations of financial corruption. That episode had led to an investigation by Indian Affairs. I spoke of similar accusations by band members in the '80s. I told her there had been a flurry of activity both times but that nothing ever came of it, and that I was hoping what I had started would keep going until something changed. That interview came on the eve of the hearing by Justice LoVecchio into my jurisdiction to order the investigation at Morley.

If anything I did in the course of all the controversy could have been found to be conduct unbecoming a judge, it was giving that interview (which, as I say, I didn't realize was an interview). The gist of the *sub judice* rule is that public statements made with the intent of influencing a judicial proceeding can be found to be a contempt of court. That article on the front page of the City section, campaigning for the exposure of injustices, could well have been found to be such a statement.

Fortunately, it seems that Justice Dea and the other members of the Judicial Council were unfamiliar with Judge Manfred Delong's research into the matter – research that was contained in the chief judge's record in *Reilly v. Wachowich*.

Delong had volunteered the brief on the *sub judice* rule in response to statements that had been made by Justice Minister Havelock and Premier Klein publicly criticizing my alleged lack of jurisdiction to order the investigation at Morley. The suggestion was that the comments by the minister and the premier may have been breaches of the rule, and therefore contempt of court.

If it had been argued that the Lunman article was a contempt of court for breach of the *sub judice* rule, and therefore conduct unbecoming a judge, my only defence would be that I did not consider the conversation an interview and did not realize the content would be published. The possibility that this would not be believed was very frightening to me.

John Snow's problem with it was a little less academic. He highlighted a paragraph that said: "Reilly pointed criticism at Chief John Snow in the ruling and likened the reserve to a dictatorship of a banana republic." In any event, the Judicial Council said my comments were insufficient to sustain the complaint. By letter dated March 23, Justice Dea advised Snow that the council had unanimously determined that no further action need be taken.

It was frustrating for me that I couldn't get anything to stick against John Snow, but it must have been even more frustrating for him. He had wielded almost absolute power on that reserve for almost 30 years. Then he lost an election in 1992, and after he got re-elected in 1996 I severely limited his power. Following my order for the investigation, the Department of Indian Affairs and Northern Development put the reserve under third-party management, thereby removing Snow's power to deal with the money. He organized the complaint made by the three Chiefs. He got Ernest Hunter to make his complaint.

He also prepared a petition by the Elders to have me removed from hearing Stoney cases. Elder Bill McLean told me that when he was asked to sign the petition, he not only refused but went to some of the Elders who had already signed it and had them remove their names, thereby terminating that action against me.

Snow's last attack on me was a motion before the Stoney tribal council calling for me to make a public apology for the comments I had made about the reserve.

I took some satisfaction from an article in the May 20, 2000, issue of the *Canmore Leader* headlined "Stoney council rejects apology call." It reported the motion was defeated by a vote of 13 to 2. Only Snow and councillor Jerry Powderface had voted in favour of it. This meant that the other two Chiefs who had signed the letter of complaint, dated October 6, 1999, had voted against the motion.

Greg Twoyoungmen was quoted in the article as saying that "John Snow should apologize to Judge Reilly." Tina Fox told me she was the first to speak on the motion and she had said she wouldn't ask anyone to apologize for speaking the truth.

Considering that Snow had been virtually an autocrat for so long, it gave me some satisfaction to think I had been a part of reducing his power and affording the people a little more democracy.

❖ 30 ❖

MY COMPLAINT

The release of the report of the judicial inquiry board in early November of 2000, and the payment of all of my outstanding legal fees, was the end of almost three years of defending myself against attacks that I saw as dishonest, self-serving and unjustified. Now it was my turn to go on the offensive. I expected there would now be some action taken on my complaint of December 21, 1998, against Chief Judge Wachowich and Assistant Chief Judge Stevenson.

The Court of Appeal judgment just happened to be released the same week as the fall conference of the Alberta Provincial Court Judges Association. There was a dinner on Thursday, September 8, 2000. Laura and I attended and sat through a number of presentations that were made to those judges who had been active in the litigation involving judges' salaries. There was no mention of the developments in *Reilly v. Wachowich*.

After dinner Chief Judge Walter approached me and spoke about making peace in the court. He said there would likely not be an appeal to the Supreme Court of Canada, but he did not say there would not be. He told me I should make peace with Brian Stevenson. I told him he should ask Stevenson to resign in view of the fact that both the Queen's Bench and the Court of Appeal had confirmed his dishonesty.

Walter's concluding comment to me was: "You should think about these things and talk to your friends." Laura joined us and he made the same comment to her. Laura could be very feisty, and the years of litigation had not improved her humour. Her angry reply was: "What do you think we've been doing for the last three years?! We *have* been talking to our friends and thinking about this, and most of our friends are pretty f**ing disgusted by the way we've been f**ed around by your office!"

Apparently this was not the reaction Walter was expecting, and we didn't speak further that evening.

On the following Monday, September 11, 2000, I wrote to him and thanked him for approaching me and Laura after the APCJA dinner and told him I agreed there should be peace in our court. I said that the dinner might have been a bit early for discussion, as we had been under some stress for some time, but told him I would appreciate the opportunity to talk to him about my ongoing concerns and work with him in an effort to repair the harm that had been done to the reputation of the court as a result of the unfortunate litigation in *Reilly v. Wachowich*.

He replied by letter on September 18 saying he would be out of town until Monday the 25th, and would be in touch with me on his return.

I didn't hear anything from Walter for several weeks, and wrote again on October 10. I said that since I hadn't heard from him I would open discussion by telling him what my expectations were.

I said I expected any difficulty created by his dual role as both chairman of the Judicial Council and chief judge would be eliminated by his recusing himself from any council dealing with my complaints against Wachowich and Stevenson, and that he might then facilitate resolution of my difficulties with them. I told him I would like to begin that process by meeting with him to review the litigation in *Reilly v. Wachowich* and related matters so that he would have an understanding of my grievances.

By letter of November 1 he replied that he would get in touch after the *Reilly v. Wachowich* litigation was finally over.

That letter made me angry. The litigation was not officially over, because the time period for appealing to the Supreme Court of Canada had not yet expired, but he had said at the dinner that the ruling would probably not be appealed. I believed he was using this as an excuse for doing nothing.

Alan Hunter and I discussed the matter and decided to add Walter to my complaint against Wachowich and Stevenson and file the amended complaint with the Judicial Council.

I rewrote the complaint, providing 17 pages of particulars with another 150 pages of attachments. Much of it was just me venting after three years of conflict with my administrative judges. Alan's office photocopied and bound the documents and forwarded them to the Judicial Council.

With the benefit of hindsight, I can see that the complaint would have been much more effective had it been much shorter.

I alleged that Wachowich and Stevenson had engaged in a course of conduct intended to prevent me from performing my duties as a judge according to my conscience and my understanding of the law and the Constitution of Canada, and that it was my apprehension that they did so for the purpose of obtaining political favour with the government of Alberta.

I alleged against Walter that he had been deliberately blind to the wrongdoing of Wachowich and Stevenson and was derelict in his duty as chief judge in that he refused to speak to me, refused to deal with my concerns about Stevenson's continuing and improper actions against me, refused to deal with defamatory statements in the media, and acted improperly in referring the false complaint about me to the Judicial Council and in chairing a meeting of the Judicial Council which referred a false complaint to a judicial inquiry board.

I then went on to set out particulars of my complaints, supported by materials from the chief judge's record in *Reilly v. Wachowich*.

I attached 60 pieces of correspondence. I included the

announcements of Judge Friedman's resignation and Wachowich's appointment as coordinator of the justice of the peace program, in support of my allegation that Wachowich had used his position as chief judge for personal gain by making an arrangement to keep this position available to himself on his retirement.

I included Stevenson's memo of October 9, 1998, confirming that he was a candidate for the position of chief judge, to corroborate my allegation that he had political motivation for the action he took against me.

I included the correspondence related to Walter's referral to the Judicial Council of the complaint by Ernest Hunter, and his chairing the Judicial Council that made the referral to the judicial inquiry board.

I believed it was outrageous that Walter would deal with complaints against me when he, as chief judge, was ex officio the respondent in the action I had taken against the former chief judge. That he persisted in so acting, and chaired a meeting of the Judicial Council in relation to the complaints against me, was, in my view, either vindictiveness or complete incompetence.

I also included a page from Alberta Hansard recording the words of Justice Minister Jon Havelock speaking to Bill 25, the Justice Statutes Amendment Act, 1998: "The chief judge also wanted to be able to change a judge's residence based on his own decision. We, however, went with the provision where the chief judge would recommend to the Judicial Council for their consideration that a particular residence of a judge be changed."

This was April 20, 1998, a month before I was given the order to relocate. I saw it as showing that the chief judge knew he didn't have the power to make the transfer order, but made it anyway.

I believed that the materials I filed constituted a strong case of judicial misconduct against all three of the respondents. However, being a strong advocate of restorative justice, I suggested to Chief Judge Walter that we convene a meeting to mediate my complaint.

❖ 31 ❖

MEDIATION

This finally seemed to get Judge Walter's attention. He agreed through his counsel, Rod McLennan, to meet with me to discuss our differences. On January 12, 2001, Walter flew down to Calgary and I met him in the dining room of the airport hotel at about 10:30. We talked, had lunch, and talked some more. In all, the meeting lasted nearly four hours.

Before lunch we just talked about what I wanted from him. I wanted Walter to produce a protocol that would protect other judges from what had happened to me.

To start, Wachowich and Stevenson had exchanged correspondence in which they discussed me, but they did not inform me of those discussions. I wanted a protocol that would provide that any correspondence between any administrative judge and anyone else that relates to a sitting judge should be copied to that judge.

Wachowich and Stevenson had decided to relocate me, and Walter had chosen to refer the Hunter complaint to the Judicial Council. Both of these decisions were made without notice to me and without an opportunity for me to be heard. I asked for a protocol that would provide for notice to and an opportunity to be heard for any judge in relation to whom any decision of consequence is considered.

I told Walter I thought the judicial inquiry that came out of the Hunter complaint had been a waste of time and that it all could have been avoided if there had just been some preliminary work done before the decision was made. I wanted a protocol which would provide that before the Judicial Council made any decision of consequence in relation to a judge, the judge would have notice and an opportunity to be heard.

I told him the financial cost of the litigation had been a huge source of anxiety for me. I asked for a protocol that would provide that any judge requiring legal services in the course of their duties would have counsel provided to them at the expense of the chief judge's office or the government.

I told him the litigation itself had been a result of Wachowich and Stevenson failing to understand that their authority as administrative judges did not include any authority over the judicial function of a sitting judge. I asked for a protocol that would make it absolutely clear that administrative judges have no authority over a judge's judicial function.

I referred to the amendment to the Provincial Court Act (limiting judicial review), mentioned at page 139 above, and suggested he might submit my proposed alternative to Alberta Justice.

We covered all of this ground before lunch. Walter indicated he would discuss the proposal with his lawyer and he seemed amenable to preparing a document such as I suggested.

We had a pleasant lunch making small talk and when we had finished he asked if this would satisfy me. I told him it would satisfy me in relation to my complaint against him, but not against Wachowich and Stevenson. I told him I thought their conduct against me was morally wrong, and that they should both resign as a result.

We then got into a bit more delicate conversation about Wachowich and Stevenson. Walter made no concessions but he seemed to change expression in relation to a few of the things I said. I told him of our attempts to terminate the litigation after the mediation effort by Maher and Maloney, and again after the record was produced but before it was filed. He seemed impressed by this information.

I told him that Justice Fruman, in the course of the appeal, had referred to Wachowich's letter of April 3, 1998, in which he told me he didn't know of any corrective measures he could take, and his memo of the same date to Vijay Bhardwaj asking for the procedure to transfer me. Justice Fruman had asked Mr. Tavender in open court: "Isn't that deceptive?"

I referred Walter to Stevenson's letter of December 3, 1997, in which he assured me no changes would be made to my circuit without notice to me and input from me, while at the same time he was manipulating Wachowich into moving me. I told Walter I expected him to be outraged at the breach of undertaking and the dishonesty in their dealings with me.

Walter said there was no way they would consider resigning. I told him I would listen to any proposal that would repair the harm they had done. He said he would get back to me, that his lawyer would be in touch with my lawyer.

Rod McLennan and Alan Hunter then arranged a mediation meeting. Wachowich, Stevenson, Walter and I would meet with a panel consisting of former Chief Justice of Alberta Herb Laycraft, retired Court of Appeal Justice Milt Harradence and Provincial Court Judge Percy Marshall. The meeting was set for March 29, 2001, in a private room at the Ranchmen's Club. I was delighted with the panel that was to preside.

THE MEDIATION HEARING

I attended in a room with the three jurists for whom I had the greatest respect and admiration, and with three for whom I felt significant contempt. I was totally focused on what I saw as the dishonesty of Wachowich and Stevenson, and the abuse of authority and lack of procedural fairness by them and Walter.

Prior to the meeting, I had been asked to provide an agenda. In my usual habit of saying way too much, I produced a 10-page document which set out seven questions and suggested a disposition.

The questions were:

1. Was the order for transfer a misconduct by Wachowich and Stevenson?
2. Was the letter of December 3, 1997, from Stevenson an undertaking by him? By Wachowich? Did they breach that undertaking?
3. Were the letters between Stevenson and Wachowich a deliberate cover-up?
4. Was there deliberate deception by Wachowich and Stevenson?
5. Was there deliberate intimidation?
6. Was the litigation in *Reilly v. Wachowich* unnecessarily prolonged?
7. Had Chief Judge Walter been derelict in his duty as chief judge in his conduct towards me.

The 10 pages were filled with my submissions indicating positive answers to all of my own questions. My suggestion as to disposition was that Wachowich would resign as chairman of the justice of the peace program, Stevenson would resign as assistant chief judge, and Walter would publish a protocol setting out procedures that would protect all other judges from the situation I had faced in the preceding years.

Each respondent made a written reply to my agenda.

Walter

The chief judge submitted a one-page document in which he set out the receipt of the Ernest Hunter complaint, the referral to the Judicial Council and the Judicial Council's referral to a judicial inquiry board because "they considered that the fairest way to deal with it."

He didn't comment on my complaints about the lack of

procedural fairness in the referral to the Judicial Council or in the council's referral to a judicial inquiry board.

Walter didn't confirm that he had chaired the first meeting of the council. He said I had "expressed concern" about the appointments to the board and his involvement. He said he referred these concerns to a subsequent meeting and recused himself from further dealings. He didn't volunteer that he had refused to disqualify himself on my objection, and that the recusal had come only after the objection was explained in detail by my lawyer. I didn't know whether he was deliberately ignoring the substance of my complaint or he just didn't understand it. I suspect it was the latter.

Both Justice Mason at Queen's Bench and the Court of Appeal panel had said the transfer order was faulty because of lack of procedural fairness, and that on that ground alone it would have been declared bad. One of the most frustrating aspects of the three years in litigation was that I obtained an important ruling, in my favour, and the chief judge just ignored it.

Wachowich

I was most impressed by the statement made by former Chief Judge Wachowich. He looked old and tired at the meeting, and I felt some compassion for him and guilt for what I was putting him through.

He said he was filing his response to a sad and appalling state of affairs affecting Judge Reilly and the Provincial Court of Alberta. He maintained he had attempted to deal effectively and internally with perceptions that he and others held of my judicial misconduct. He said he regretted that the whole matter remained unresolved, in large measure because, as the courts had held, he exceeded his jurisdiction in ordering me to relocate from the Canmore court circuit to Calgary. While he said he genuinely believed he was acting properly and within his powers as chief judge, the courts had told him he was wrong, and for that he apologized to me and to all concerned.

He also said it was appalling to him that a judge of the Provincial Court would file complaints with the Judicial Council that levelled unsupported and unfair allegations against him and other senior members of the Provincial Court. Allegations of this sort can do nothing but damage relationships and the reputation of the Provincial Court of Alberta. To the extent that his actions contributed to this appalling situation, he apologized.

He went on to say that acting on the information and advice of Assistant Chief Judge Stevenson and of his own solicitor, the late Vijay Bhardwaj, and on his own review, he had concluded that in statements both on and off the bench, I had demonstrated a loss of objectivity and impartiality with respect to Aboriginal matters which constituted judicial misconduct requiring sanction. He maintained he took this action solely in accordance with his understanding of his duties and responsibilities in order to remove me from what he called at the time "harm's way." In his view the proper administration of justice meant that I could not preside over a court circuit where there was a high preponderance of Aboriginal cases.

He described his reasons for his belief that I had lost my impartiality in relation to Aboriginal cases and why I should therefore be removed from hearing them. This was of course our fundamental disagreement. I believed I was dealing with Aboriginal cases with a knowledge and sensitivity to their circumstances as was required by the law. He saw it differently.

He said he resented and denied the allegations and innuendo that he used intimidation or deception or in any way acted under an improper or personal motive. He said he thought he had acted in a manner that best protected my interests by removing me from the court circuit where my loss of impartiality would most frequently collide with Aboriginal cases, and that because he was mistaken about his jurisdiction, the issue of my accountability for my misconduct was unresolved.

He commented that he and Assistant Chief Judge Stevenson had both apologized, but he was unaware of any apology from me for my role in all these matters.

He concluded by saying he welcomed this mediation and invited everyone to look for solutions that would put this sorry matter behind us without diminishing the overall administration of justice in the Provincial Court of Alberta.

While we would never resolve our fundamental disagreement – Wachowich maintaining I had lost my impartiality, I maintaining I was dealing with these cases knowledgeably as required by law – I was prepared to believe that what he said was true. I believed Stevenson had influenced Wachowich in doing what he did, and I wasn't so ready to believe Stevenson was sincere in his submission.

Stevenson

Assistant Chief Judge Stevenson began his statement by acknowledging that the order to transfer me was wrong, that he was a party to that attempt and that in view of the courts' ruling he apologized. However, he continued by justifying the action taken by him and Wachowich on the basis of their belief that as a result of my actions and conduct at the time, and more particularly as displayed in my judgment in the *Hunter* case, I had lost my objectivity and impartiality with respect to Aboriginal matters both on and off the bench. Furthermore, they were both concerned that I might be asked by litigants appearing before me to recuse myself due to a reasonable apprehension of bias in such matters.

In addition he said he was concerned that several of my comments concerning the elected leadership of the Stoney First Nation might result in civil action against me for libel, slander and/or defamation.

He said that in hindsight the proper course of action might

have been to refer my conduct directly to the Judicial Council for their review, but rather than do that, he and Wachowich had decided that a practical solution to their apprehensions of judicial bias would be to remove me from the environment where those potential bias accusations might arise. He said he remained of the view that I had continued to display injudicial conduct with respect to Aboriginal matters and issues that exist on First Nations reserves, both within and outside of Alberta.

Stevenson went on for a couple of pages setting out my lack of impartiality and his criticisms of my handling of the *Hunter* case, and talked about the concern over my having to disqualify myself on cases on the basis of bias. In fact, there never was an application to have me recuse myself from a case, other than that by Cpl. Young. There is no question that if any member of the tribal government had appeared before me, charged with an offence, I would have had to disqualify myself, and I would have done that on my own motion. The Aboriginal people who were almost exclusively charged with criminal offences were the poor, and in my view, a part of the circumstances I was required to consider in sentencing them was the political system that kept them poor and dysfunctional. However, the mediation meeting never got into the merits of our opposing judicial philosophies.

I had been confident that the panel would all be offended by the dishonesty and lack of procedural fairness to which I had been subjected. That wasn't quite the way they saw it. I ranted on, and then the members of the panel spoke.

The Panel

Herb Laycraft was sitting at the head of the table. He said that in his view the Judicial Council did not have jurisdiction to deal with the complaint against Wachowich, because of his retirement. He said he himself had been on a federal Judicial Council which had made that ruling in relation to another matter. He went on to say that in his experience as a chief justice he would have thought some action was necessary to control the unfortunate controversy which I had generated and which was attracting so much media attention. He pointed out that the errors in the method used had been corrected in litigation and told me that by pressing my complaints I was doing the court further harm.

Percy Marshall was sitting next to me and he quietly said to me, "John, you should just let this go."

Milt Harradence was sitting across the table from me, next to Stevenson and Wachowich. He commented on the fact that Stevenson and I had been friends, that we had all been friends and that I should try and get back to that.

Walter, Wachowich and Stevenson hardly spoke. It seemed to become a matter of me and the three jurists I so admired. Laycraft telling me to let it go for the good of the court. Harradence telling me to let it go in the interest of friendship. Percy Marshall telling me to let it go just for goodness sake.

So I told the meeting I would let it go. I would withdraw my complaint and would so advise the Judicial Council. I didn't feel it had been resolved, but it was hopeless to press it any further. What was apparent to me was that everyone concerned was anxious that the whole matter would just go away.

❖ 32 ❖

AFTER THE MEDIATION

I was emotionally exhausted. I had been an advocate of restorative justice and forgiveness for over five years, but when it came to my own matters I was disappointed there would be no repercussions for my adversaries.

Still, I swallowed my pride and wrote to the Judicial Council advising them that as a result of the mediation meeting, I was withdrawing my complaint. I called Alan Hunter to tell him I had agreed to withdraw the complaint. He sounded disappointed. It was as if I had given up. I told him the exchange I had with Herb Laycraft made me see things a little less self-righteously.

I even wrote a letter of apology to my three adversaries, Walter, Wachowich and Stevenson. I told them that as a result of the input from Herb Laycraft and Milt Harradence I saw my own conduct in this entire matter a little less self-righteously than I had prior to the meeting. I said Ed's suggestion that I should apologize angered me at first, but that I did not enjoy seeing his discomfiture at the meeting, and I apologized for having been the cause of that and for causing all of the other difficulties I had caused for him over the last several years.

I went on to say:

> I took the position throughout that I did what was right in the performance of my judicial duty and that those who criticized me were wrong. I now concede that my conduct was the cause of legitimate concern that gave rise to the action taken against me. I do ask that you understand that I was

overwhelmed by the suffering and social injustice that I saw when I engaged in my quest to learn about and understand the Stoney people. I had no other motivation in embarking on that quest, other than the proper performance of my judicial duties. I can see that I pushed the envelope of my judicial function to the limit and then some. While I have received credit for being the cause of significant changes for the better at Morley, and even across Canada, I can see that my methods offend traditional jurists. Even though I will start my 25th year on the bench this summer, I concede I am not a traditional jurist.

I ask Brian to reconsider his view that my conduct continues to be injudicial. While I accept that I have erred in my efforts to improve the delivery of justice to the Stoney people, I believe that overall I have demonstrated a willingness to learn about this community and to apply the law in a manner which is sensitive to their unique circumstances. I believe that this is in keeping with the current state of the law. As to indicating that I was pleased with the results of the tribal election, I cannot apologize. The man who was elected, when he was Chief from 1992 to 1996, created an education program that had 150 Stoney adults upgrading their education. The man who was defeated last year cancelled that program when he came back into office in 1997. I believe the new administration will be better for the people, and I make no apology for being pleased about that or for saying so. I believe the comment is allowable by item D6 of *Ethical Principles for Judges*. I am also mindful of the preface to that item that "restraint" is the watchword, and I will bear that in mind in the future.

Concern was expressed at the meeting that this would really be over. Brian was going to say something about what he had heard from "four judges" when Herb cut him off. I acknowledge that I have said many negative things about Ed and Brian over the last several years. I felt that I had been treated dishonestly and I said so.

I have now withdrawn my formal complaint and with that I should stop my informal complaining as well. I give each of you my firm undertaking that I will make no further negative comments. If asked about the matter, I will simply say that I withdrew my complaint because Milt Harradence asked me to, and now that the matter is over, I am inclined to the view that I was not easy to deal with, and that in the circumstances everyone did the best they could.

In relation to Brian's offer to have my circuit administered by another ACJ, I will accept whatever decision is made, but I asked him to reconsider this as well. Whether or not the change is seen as my fault or Brian's, it will have to be seen as a sign of continuing discord, and that will not do the court any good.

The proposal was at my request and had some appeal to me. The prospect of being able to travel a little farther than Calgary when I have occasion to do an exchange has appeal, and I was inclined to take some vindictive satisfaction from the fact that Brian would be seen as unable to continue to administer my circuit. On consideration, I would like the opportunity to rise above that vindictiveness. If Brian is willing to postpone that change indefinitely, perhaps it will become unnecessary. We might simply agree about the day-to-day scheduling continuing as is, and if there is ever a matter of contention, any such contentious matter will be delegated to the chief judge or to another CJ.

Finally, Laura would like me to tell you all that she is very disappointed that I did not at least obtain some statement of future policy that will answer the issues of procedural fairness. I recognize that I may have received that concession from Ernie, and lost it by insisting on action against Ed and Brian. I can now only request that Ernie still consider the creation of a policy that will address the concerns that were raised.

Walter replied and thanked me for "your very gracious and kind letter of April 2." He agreed with my suggestion that my circuit continue to be administered by Brian and expressed the hope that things would turn out well if Brian and I worked on it. He said nothing about creating a policy to answer the issues of procedural fairness. Neither Ed Wachowich nor Brian Stevenson acknowledged the letter.

On May 2, 2001, I received a letter from the Judicial Council advising that they had convened on April 27, 2001, to inquire into my complaint. They informed me that after considering my letter of March 29, 2001, the council unanimously determined that no further action need be taken.

I had actually thought they might have done something more than that.

In criminal prosecutions, it often happens that a victim reports an alleged offence but then has a change of heart and does not wish to proceed. However, once the information is before the court, it is up to the Crown, not the victim, to decide whether the matter proceeds, and it often happens that matters will proceed in spite of a request by the victim to withdraw. In my view, the Judicial Council could have decided to inquire further in spite of my letter withdrawing my complaint.

They still had all of the material I had filed, which in my opinion established serious judicial misconduct, but still they determined that no further action was needed. The message I got from this was that they just didn't want to deal with it, and so they didn't. I didn't really care one way or the other now. I hoped that the withdrawal of my complaint might be the end of the conflict.

Such was not to be the case, and unfortunately the message that the Alberta judiciary just didn't want to hear any more from me didn't sink in sufficiently to save me from subsequent difficulty and expense.

❖ 33 ❖

S/SGT. COHN INVESTIGATES
MY CONDUCT

Throughout my conflicts with the administrative judges, I had continued to visit people at Morley and convene case management meetings. At one such session in Canmore on April 5, 2002, the new RCMP officer in charge of the Canmore detachment, Staff Sergeant D.C. Cohn, was in attendance. He described himself as an "old school bureaucrat." In front of a meeting of about 20 people he criticized me for my relaxed courtroom manner. I didn't bother to point out to him that it was only because of my relaxed manner that a police officer could speak to me as he was doing.

I also visited the Morley school regularly to talk to the Elders on the education committee and to Yvonne DePeel, the superintendent of schools for the Stoney Education Authority. I regarded Yvonne as an ally in my efforts at Morley. She was concerned about violence in the community and was dealing with it at the school level. As part of her effort she arranged a workshop for all of her teachers, including those from the schools at Eden Valley and Big Horn. The workshop was conducted by Diane Gossen, author of *Restitution: Restructuring School Discipline*, who had done extensive work in the schools and in the prison system in Saskatchewan. Laura and I both attended the workshop, and she was so impressed with it that she asked me to get copies of Gossen's book for the principals of each of the schools in Canmore.

Yvonne got the books for me and on October 8, 2002, I dropped in to pick them up and pay her for them. When I arrived she was in a meeting with Tom Snow and Alice Kaquitts about some trouble their son was having as a student at Canmore Collegiate High School.

I knew Tom and Alice because of a program they had created called Nakoda Solutions, designed to help Stoney people deal with the dysfunction in their community through traditional Indigenous spiritualism. Tom was Chief John Snow's brother, and he had run against John in the 1992 band election. This split the Snow family vote, enabling Ernest Wesley to become Chief.

Tom and Alice told me about an incident at the school in Canmore in which their son was involved in a conflict with another boy and there was an allegation that he had threatened to use a knife.

Yvonne wondered if there was anything I could do to resolve the situation for them. I wanted to help them and it seemed like an ideal opportunity to introduce a restorative justice process at the school. Since I was planning to visit there anyway to give the principal a copy of Diane Gossen's book, I volunteered to talk to her about the possibility of resolving the situation by way of a community justice forum. I called to make an appointment, and looked forward to a meeting in which I saw myself as a volunteer offering to help implement new ideas in school discipline that had been employed with great success in Saskatchewan.

The greeting I received from the principal and vice-principal was not what I had anticipated. I thought I was coming to have an academic discussion with educators and believed I would be welcomed. What I encountered was two people in their role as administrators who saw me as challenging their jurisdiction.

I handed the principal her copy of the Gossen book and told her I had spoken to the parents of one of the boys involved in the recent incident. I asked her if she would consider dealing with the matter by way of a community justice forum or healing circle type of meeting and volunteered to facilitate this if she would agree. I told them I had been using this type of hearing in resolving conflicts on the reserve and that Yvonne DePeel and Diane Gossen had been using it with success in their schools. I suggested it would be a worthwhile exercise in cross-cultural relations.

The principal and vice-principal told me they had some 600 students in the school and that they did not intend to treat one group differently than any other.

This is where the conversation really went sideways. I explained that one of the big lessons I had learned in my efforts to understand Aboriginal culture was what the Cawsey Report had said about systemic discrimination: that when you treat people who are not the same as if they are the same, you in fact discriminate against them and that this is a type of racism.

The vice-principal challenged this comment, asking me if I was calling him a racist. I was still in the mindset that I was having an academic discussion with an educator, and my reply was something like, "Well, in that sense, yes. Refusing to deal with their different traditions and treating them the same as everyone else is a form of racism." That comment would come back to haunt me.

The simple answer they could have given me was that the matter was a *fait accompli*, but they were limited in what they could say by virtue of school confidentiality relating to students. I now believe that the process at the school had been completed and the boys involved had already been expelled. Tom and Alice may have been deliberately vague on this. I had understood that everything was still pending, but I now believe I was wrong.

In any event, I pressed on, not realizing the anger I was generating. The principal and vice-principal told me there had also been police involvement in the incident and that the investigating officer was Cst. Barry Beales. I asked if they would be willing to participate in a community justice forum if this could be arranged. They seemed to agree to this and I left the school.

I called Cst. Beales and inquired about the possibility of dealing with the matter by way of a community justice forum, and he seemed to be in favour of this.

I didn't hear anything further until November 6. I arrived at the courthouse in Canmore that morning at about 8:30 to read the mail and review the docket for the day. The mail contained a 33-page packet from Assistant Chief Judge Brian Stevenson. Page 1 was the covering letter from Stevenson saying he had "received the enclosed concerns relating to an investigation and charges involving two young persons who are being prosecuted in Canmore."

Page 2 was a letter from S/Sgt. Cohn to Stevenson headed "Alleged Improprieties of Judge Reilly." Paragraph 1 said: "As a follow-up to our meeting of the 24 inst. and the conversation we had, please find enclosed statements from the principal and vice-principal of the Canmore Collegiate High School, my constable and myself."

Page 3 was an RCMP briefing note. Under the heading "Type of incident" it said "Improper interference by Provincial Court judge in the investigation of an assault." The balance of the contents were the witness statements of the principal, the vice-principal, Cst. Beales and S/Sgt. Cohn.

Seeing this file caused me to have an anxiety attack similar to the one I had in October of 1998. I could hardly breathe, my chest hurt and I felt like I might pass out. Fortunately, the years of stress during all of the litigation had allowed me to think I knew the difference between an anxiety attack and cardiac arrest. I sat at my desk and worked to control my breathing. I managed to settle down sufficiently to conduct the business of the court, but it was exceedingly difficult to focus.

I didn't feel I had done anything wrong. The principal's

statement said she thought I had come to organize restorative justice, which was exactly what I wanted to do. Unfortunately, my suggestion that Aboriginal people might be treated differently than others, as I was trying to do in my own field, gave offence. The remarks I made on racism, which I had meant as academic comment only, were taken as a direct allegation of racism. This, together with a self-described "old school bureaucrat" policeman who didn't like my relaxed courtroom manner, and an assistant chief judge who must have been humiliated by the exposure he had suffered in my litigation, seemed to stack the cards against me.

Nothing further came of the investigation into my "improprieties." I wrote a letter of apology to the principal, with a copy to the vice-principal, and tried to explain that I did not wish to interfere but rather to help. I explained that my reference to racism was meant to be academic, and was sorry that it had been taken personally. I repeated my offer to speak at the school should they wish to have me speak on justice matters. I was never asked.

A few days after I wrote the apology to the Canmore Collegiate principal, I received a letter from the chair of the board of trustees of the Canadian Rockies School Division telling me it was the impression of the school administrators that I was intending to exert influence with the intent of getting the administrators not to carry forward with their duties under the School Act. In conclusion it requested that I limit my intervention in school matters to those granted me as a parent. I wrote another letter of apology in reply, again offering to speak at the school and asking if we could discuss the matter further. I gave the school board chair my direct phone number, but never heard from him.

REACHING OUT TO JUDGE STEVENSON

While I was writing apology letters, I even wrote one to Brian Stevenson that I titled "Reconciliation." I told him I had listened to the Rev. Dale Lang, whose son had been murdered at the Taber,

Alberta, high school. Lang is a crusader against school violence and an outspoken advocate for forgiveness.

I told Brian I was bitter about the S/Sgt. Cohn matter, that I saw his handling of the Canmore school affair as a deliberate act of meanness, but that I forgave him for it and suggested we move on.

I also told him I had said some unpleasant things about him in a meeting with Chief Judge Walter and that I was sending Walter a copy of the letter to put that right.

If Brian had just said "thank you" reconciliation might have been possible, but on January 3, 2003, he replied with a three-page letter that made me angry. I cooled off for a few months and then sent him a seven-page rant that he probably never read and that I probably shouldn't have sent.

Nevertheless I think it is important to set out excerpts from the exchange because it so demonstrates the difference between our views of justice. We are not very different in age, but he is typical of many old-school judges and I am the maverick. He wants to preserve the justice system he knows and I want it to change.

I write this book to demonstrate the difficulties of Aboriginal people in the justice system, and I see a major difficulty to be the refusal of people like Brian Stevenson to accept their own errors and those of their system.

He said he was aware of comments I had made and he viewed them as a personal vendetta and campaign against him and his reputation, and he forgave me for that.

Unfortunately this comment too annoyed me. I didn't think I had done anything to be forgiven for. Perhaps this is my own intransigence coming through. He lied to me and I told people he had lied to me. I make no apology for telling the truth, and I don't ask forgiveness for doing so.

I said:

... it was you, not I, who conducted the campaign. You attacked my reputation as a judge; discredited my judgments; diagnosed me as suffering from "judicial isolation syndrome"; accused me of bias, a prejudgment attitude and a loss of objectivity; and generally established, to the former chief judge's satisfaction, that I was not competent to fulfill the duties of my office.

I still do not know why you acted as you did. At the September judges conference in 1997 (three months after I made the much publicized order for the investigation at Morley) you praised me for "making friends for the court" and you criticized Harry Gaede for telling you that you should control your judges.

I believe that your attitude towards me changed when you learned about Jon Havelock's anger towards me. He was angry because of my comments on the government's failure to do anything about corruption in tribal governments. I believe you saw this as an opportunity to further some agenda of your own. Whether it was to ingratiate yourself with him to further your ambition to be chief judge, or simply because you didn't want me moved here in 1993 and saw my loss of favour with the Minister of Justice as a way of moving me back, I don't know.

What I do know (and the chief judge's record clearly documents this) is that you embarked on a course of action designed to discredit me and to convince the then chief judge that he had the authority to move me. You made your derogatory and defamatory comments to the former chief judge without the courtesy of copies to me. Your campaign against me lasted from October 1997 to May 1998, and was conducted with no opportunity for me to answer.

He said his actions in 1998 were part of his duty to report conduct that in his opinion transgressed the boundaries of judicial ethics.

I said:

> I correctly interpreted and applied the law. Your perception was wrong. Your attempt to use your administrative authority to correct what you incorrectly perceived was my error was a violation of judicial independence. This is clearly set out in *Reilly v. Wachowich.*
>
> For you to speak about your 1998 perceptions as if they are a justification, in my view, shows contempt for the judicial process and a denial of the truth.

He said: "... it was my perception that several of your comments from the bench were inappropriate and were, at least in part, based on hearsay and not on evidence presented to you in court."

I said:

> ... I made extensive comments about the social and political conditions on the Stoney Indian reserve at Morley for which I did not have evidence. It was my considered opinion that *R. v. McDonnell* (a Supreme Court of Canada case that said a judge's knowledge of his community is relevant in sentencing) allowed me to rely on my knowledge of the community in determining a fit sentence without direct evidence. This was my view at the time and it still is.

He said: "Your ability to take judicial notice of such hearsay evidence is inappropriate."

I said:

> ... I was confirmed by the scc in *R. v. Gladue*:
>
>> ... in all instances it will be necessary for the judge

to take judicial notice of the systemic and background
factors ... relevant to Aboriginal offenders.

He said: "I expressed concerns to you following your request
that I review a draft of your judgment in the *Hunter* case."
I said:

> ... Your assertion that I requested your review of the draft
> in *Hunter* is a misstatement. Your written comments which
> are in your letter of October 21, 1997, were gratuitous. That
> letter begins with the words "Thank you for providing me with
> draft #2 of your sentencing decision in the *Hunter* matter. I
> presume that by doing so you invite comment ..." I provided
> you with the draft, in confidence, at your request that I give
> you notice of anything that might attract media attention.

He said he regretted not advising me in advance of the
intended purpose of the "transfer" meeting. "In retrospect, I was
wrong and the fact that I was wrong was the subject of comment
in the review of the subsequent proceedings taken by you against
Judge Wachowich. For my action in keeping you in the dark, I
apologize."
I said:

> This [apology] offends me for what it does not say. It does
> not admit that you instigated the unconstitutional attempt to
> transfer me. It doesn't apologize for the years of civil litigation,
> the years in which Laura and I didn't know whether we would
> be able to keep our home here in Canmore, the years of anx-
> iety over the debt we would have if we were unsuccessful. It
> doesn't apologize for the stress that was so severe it caused
> an anxiety attack that resulted in my having to be taken from
> the court by ambulance, and prevented me from working for
> three months. It doesn't apologize for the reputation I have
> among many of our fellow judges, who I believe see me as a

well-intentioned troublemaker because of your subtle defamatory comments, and because of my litigation with the former chief judge, which would not have happened but for your dishonest manipulation.

Not only does your letter not apologize for the unfair aspersions you have cast on my reputation as a judge, it repeats them. Not only does it not apologize for the litigation, it ignores its rulings....

Wachowich was wrong in his criticism of my interpretation of 718.2(e). My judgments said that a different treatment was called for in regard to Aboriginal offenders. This was ultimately confirmed by the SCC in *R. v. Gladue*:

> In our view, s 718.2(e) is <u>more</u> than simply a
> reaffirmation of existing sentencing principles. The
> remedial component of the provision consists not only in
> the fact that it codifies a principle of sentencing, but, far
> more importantly, in its direction to sentencing judges to
> undertake the process of sentencing Aboriginal offenders
> differently, in order to achieve a truly fit and proper
> sentence in the particular case.

... *Reilly v. Wachowich* was The Constitution v. The Status Quo. The Constitution won. You were on the wrong side. Why can you not just admit that you were wrong? Your continuing denial and justification continues to damage my reputation, that of the court and your own.

He said: "In and around that time you were having virtually daily meetings with members of the media about your perception of First Nations issues, particularly at Morley, and I was concerned that the transfer proposal would simply become another headline and inflame an already volatile situation."

I said:

> Your allegation that I was having virtually daily meetings is
> false. I had no such meetings. It is true that the media were
> calling me on a regular basis. For the most part I politely
> explained to them that I could not speak to them.
>
> I was invited to be on a number of talk shows, which I
> refused. I would have loved to have gone on national tele-
> vision and talked about the self-serving, dishonest assistant
> chief judge who instigated the order for my transfer, to shut
> me up, in order to ingratiate himself with the politicians who
> did not want the injustices to Aboriginal people made public.
> I had this opportunity more than once, but did not take it,
> because of my concern for the reputation of the court. You
> should be grateful for what I did not say.

He said: "I greatly admire your interest in First Nations history
and issues. I have no doubt whatsoever that the views on those
issues you have expressed publicly are strongly held and sincere.
I am not in a position to dispute their veracity; they may all be
true. ...."

I said:

> Your comments "strongly held and sincere" and "they may
> all be true" damn with faint praise. I say that virtually every-
> thing I said has been confirmed in fact and in law. I am given
> credit by Aboriginal people and others, across Canada, for sig-
> nificantly improving justice and governance on reserves. I did
> this by properly requiring the Crown to give me information
> about the circumstances of Aboriginal offenders.

I also said: "The law changed with the amendments in 1996. I
embraced this change because it applied directly to a large part of
my work. My judgments were controversial because the change
in the law was controversial. I believe that all the rulings I made,

and all of the facts on which I based my rulings, have subsequently been shown to be correct, both in fact and in law ..."

He said: "... The only concern I have is what limits exist in your role as a judge to express them in a manner chosen by you to do so. Obviously, on that issue, you and I disagree. ..."

I said:

> I have properly expressed my views in my judgments. Outside of court I have explained those judgments, and the changes in the law, when asked about them. I say that is specifically approved, and mandated, by the Canadian Judicial Council in its handbook *Ethical Principles for Judges* under the heading Contributions to the Administration of Justice Generally:
>
> > 13. Judges ... may contribute to the administration of justice by ... taking part in ... activities to make the law and the legal process more understandable and accessible to the public.

I also said: "I believe that the first attribute of a judge should be absolute honesty. If we have this, then fairness, equality, impartiality and everything else we seek in the law will occur. If we do not have this, then everything we do is futile. I say that honesty has been lacking in all of your dealings with me for the last six years and it continues to be lacking in your letter of January 6, 2003."

He said: "I believe that great care must be taken about public support for causes where the advocacy for those causes could be misinterpreted by the public we serve as creating a bias. I further maintain that a judge must not express an advocacy interest in any proceeding, either before or after charges are laid."

I said:

Your comment that "a judge must not express an advocacy..." insinuates that I do.

In relation to Aboriginal justice generally, I say I am not an advocate for Aboriginal rights. I have correctly interpreted a change in the law that prescribes a different treatment of Aboriginal offenders, and applied the law accordingly.

In relation to the incident at the Canmore school, I was not there as an advocate for the boys involved. I went there to inquire about the possibility of using a community justice forum to deal with the matter involving Aboriginal young people who were in difficulty at the school. I was simply proposing a process and offering to assist in its implementation.

...

You make very high-sounding statements about the need for the perception of impartiality. I say that I, John Reilly, a judge of the Provincial Court of Alberta for 25 years, am also entitled to the perception of impartiality in any matter raised against me. I say that, given the constitutional sanctity of judicial independence, I should be entitled to the highest level of impartiality in relation to any investigation, prosecution and adjudication which relates to me.

I do not believe that you are capable of dealing with me in an impartial manner. I believe that your dealings in relation to the impugned transfer were malicious and dishonest. I believe that by standing up to your dishonest manipulation, I exposed you for the dishonest manipulator that you are. I became the instrument of your humiliation when both the Court of Appeal and the national media commented on your conduct.

He said:

I am pleased that you have "let go" of the bitter feelings you held toward me. I assure you that at no time did I ever wish our professional disagreement to become personal, confrontational and vindictive in the way that you have perceived it to be, nor, in my view, have I ever conducted myself in that manner and I regret that you have interpreted my actions in that way and responded as you have both publicly and privately. However, in keeping with Reverend Lang's message, I forgive you.

I said: "I believe you would do anything you thought you could get away with in order to discredit me, to in some way vindicate yourself for the wrongful actions you have taken against me in the past. I therefore demand that you recuse yourself in any future matter which might involve me."

The letter unfortunately erased the beneficial effect of Rev. Lang's talk. I had gone through three years of litigation anxiety because Brian Stevenson did not like my judgments and convinced Chief Judge Wachowich to transfer me. I had successfully defended my position. The Supreme Court of Canada, in the *Gladue* case, had confirmed my views and Stevenson was forgiving me.

Stevenson never acknowledged receipt of the letter and that was probably a good thing. I had vented at length and there wasn't any more to be said. We never talked after that, other than to exchange pleasantries when we passed in the hall at the courthouse.

❖ 34 ❖

CAUX

My last fight with the chief judge's office was over a conference I attended in Caux, Switzerland.

My efforts at Morley were the cause of a lot of aggravation, both for me and for those who tried to control me. What made it all worthwhile was my conviction that I was doing something worthwhile, much more worthwhile than just meting out standard penalties for standard offences, and also getting to know the Stoneys, especially the Elders.

One of those Elders was Bill McLean. He had been the Chief of the Bearspaw band and certainly deserved the title of Elder in his own right, but his main claim to fame was being the son of George McLean.

A former Lieutenant Governor of Alberta, Grant MacEwan, wrote a book about George McLean, *Tatanga Mani: Walking Buffalo of the Stonies.* It is the story of a man born in 1872, just five years before the signing of Treaty 7. As a child he was carried on a travois on the reserve at Morley. In his old age he travelled around the world by airplane.

In 1934 he met Frank Buchman at the Banff Springs Hotel. Buchman was the leader of the Oxford Group, a movement that preached a message of change in the world in order to achieve world peace. At this meeting McLean inducted Buchman into the Stoney Nation and gave him the name Ao-Zan-Zan-Tonga, meaning Great Light out of Darkness.

When Buchman celebrated his 80th birthday in 1958, at what

was by then called the Moral Rearmament Conference Centre on Mackinac Island, Michigan, George McLean attended as a guest.

Buchman had begun to gradually change the name of his movement to "Moral Rearmament" by the late 1930s and had continued to deliver a message aimed at world peace. After the First World War, he had said that if the world did not have a "moral rearmament" there would be another war. Unfortunately his prediction was fulfilled, but he continued to work tirelessly for world peace. His efforts resulted in the establishment of Mountain House in Caux, Switzerland, the Moral Rearmament World Conference Centre. This facility, originally built as a luxury hotel, was purchased by the Swiss government and made available as a gesture of thanksgiving by Switzerland for being spared the ravages of war. It was here that ministers of all the warring countries of Europe gathered to plan the post-war reconstruction of Europe. The Germans were not included at the first meeting, however, and Buchman said there could not be peace unless they were. He was a leader in French–German reconciliation and worked with French foreign minister Robert Schuman, who in 1950 developed the Schuman Plan that eventually led to the European Union.

As part of Buchman's birthday celebration, there was a presentation of the play The Crowning Experience, based on the life of Mary McLeod Bethune. Bethune was a child of former slaves who became educated and established a school for African American girls that is now Bethune Cookman University in Daytona Beach, Florida. Following the presentation on Mackinac Island, the play travelled to Washington, DC, and George McLean was invited to attend its opening there. He was given a seat in the presidential box and acknowledged by Washington dignitaries.

Prior to his experiences with Frank Buchman and Moral Rearmament, George McLean would freely admit that he hated white men. They had taken away the land and the way of life that his people had enjoyed for thousands of years and relegated them to a life of poverty on reserves. But he saw Buchman's message of forgiveness, peace and understanding as similar to his own Indian values and he embraced the philosophy, returned to Mackinac Island, then went on a world tour to preach those values to everyone who would listen. Millions of people around the world heard his message.

I met George's son, Bill, when the latter was in his late seventies. He loved to talk about his father and his own experience at Mackinac Island. He had attended the conference with his father in 1958 and would often talk about how it changed his life. He had been required to share a room with Jack Freebury, and he hated Jack because he was a white man. He didn't speak to him for the first several days. As Bill attended the sessions and listened to the messages, he began to see himself and to realize how bitterness had consumed him. After one of these sessions he went to his room and asked Jack to forgive him for hating him because he was a white man. Jack too apologized, for his insensitivity to Indigenous People, and they developed an understanding and became lifelong friends.

One day when I was writing this chapter, I went to a banquet at Morley. It is a Stoney custom to hold feasts to honour the deceased, and Tina Fox was hosting one to honour her late husband, Kent. Bill McLean was there and we had a pleasant visit. He turned 93 on December 1, 2013. He was using a walker but his eyes were still bright and he laughed and smiled easily. We talked about Caux and he repeated the story of his experience with Jack Freebury. He smiled and said that ever since then, he has been a friend to everybody.

The 40th anniversary of Chief Walking Buffalo's world tour with Moral Rearmament was in 2001. To commemorate the event, Bill McLean arranged for the three Chiefs of the Stoney reserve to attend a conference at Mountain House in Caux, and he invited me to join them.

The prospect of attending a week-long conference with the three Chiefs was very appealing to me. I was still promoting the concept of justice programs, but with limited success. The week might give me the opportunity of engaging the Chiefs in the concept and perhaps gaining their support.

Bill and I agreed that the division of the Stoneys into the three "bands" is a serious impediment to social development on the reserve. A community of about 4,500 people divided into three bands, each with a Chief, four councillors and a separate administration, absorbs hundreds of thousands of dollars in administration while the school, health services and healing programs are underfunded or don't have any money at all.

Bill was hopeful that the conference might effect the kind of conversion in the Chiefs that he had experienced on Mackinac Island. It is not only the cost of the three administrations, but conflicts among them that so hamper the progress of the Stoney community.

The conference was called Peace Building Initiatives and was mostly concerned with peace between nations, but there was a lot of valuable material that would apply to mediation and reconciliation. These were concepts that were being introduced to the Canadian criminal justice system by the 1996 amendments.

My only misgiving about attending the conference was my ongoing criticism of spending tribal moneys on travel. My concerns were answered. The cost of the Stoneys attending would be paid from a fund administered by Moral Rearmament. The fund had been established with a bequest by Evelyn Williston, a teacher at Morley who died in 1994.

THE PROFESSIONAL DEVELOPMENT FUND

I was quite willing to go at my own expense, but a conversation

I had with Nomi Whalen changed that. She thought my plan to go to Caux was wonderful and she suggested it was something the government should pay for. I didn't think the government would ever pay for anything I wanted to do with the Stoneys, but her remark gave me the idea that it would be an appropriate use of the professional development fund. This was an idea that ultimately became very expensive for me.

The professional development fund had been established on the basis of recommendations by the Judicial Compensation Commission in 2000. The idea had been submitted to the commission by Judge Manfred Delong.

Judge Delong was the former chief Crown prosecutor for Calgary, and he was a meticulous lawyer who would research every point of law he dealt with. His courtroom practice was similarly precise. I was at the opposite end of the spectrum from him. S/Sgt. Cohn may have had good reason for saying my courtroom practice was too relaxed for his liking. He would have liked Judge Delong's. If I was unsure of a point of law in the course of a trial, I would be more inclined to guess that the correct interpretation was the one that supported the outcome I wanted.

Judge Delong resigned from the judges association because he disagreed with the association making a joint submission with the Alberta government to the Compensation Commission. The reason why the Supreme Court of Canada had mandated the commission in the first place was to eliminate judges having to negotiate their salaries with government. In Delong's view, getting together with the government to make a joint submission was no different than negotiating directly with them. He is a very highly principled man, and it was on principle that he resigned.

Judge Delong's initial submission to the Compensation Commission was:

> It is recommended that each provincial judge be allocated

a non-taxable educational allowance of $2,500 per year for the purpose of furthering his or her education in the law by attending conferences and seminars, by buying books and materials, and by maintaining memberships in judicial and professional organizations. The recovery of this expenditure should be by expense account submitted through the chief judge's office.

The recommendation of the commission was: "Judges should be allowed an accountable (non-taxable) professional allowance of $2,500 per year, beginning April 1, 2000."

The provision creating the allowance is the following section of the Provincial Court Judges and Masters in Chambers Compensation Regulation [as it then read]:

4.1(1) On and after April 1, 2000, a judge other than a supernumerary judge is entitled to a professional allowance of $2500 per year to be used for the following purposes as authorized by the chief judge:

(a) the attendance at relevant conferences and seminars that are related to the carrying out of the duties and functions of a provincial court judge;

(b) the buying of books and journals that are related to the carrying out of the duties and functions of a provincial court judge;

(c) the maintenance of memberships in judicial and professional organizations;

(d) the purchase of security systems for a provincial court judge's home and the monthly service charges for those systems.

Neither the chief judge nor the judges association gave Judge Delong any support in making his submission. There was even some criticism of him for making it. Some of the judges were afraid it would detract from the main thrust of their submission relating to salary and pensions.

However, once the fund was established, the chief judge and the association became very involved in the administration of it. They drew up an extensive list of guidelines for its use and revised these several times.

I disagreed with the concept of guidelines and oversight by the chief judge. In my view, the intent of the fund was to support judicial independence by allowing individual judges to make their own choices as to what conferences, seminars, written materials and professional organizations would most benefit them in the exercise of their judicial function.

In my view, the legislation passed by the government, and in particular the phrase "as authorized by the chief judge," created a limitation on the fund that was not contemplated by Judge Delong's submission or the recommendation of the commission.

What security systems had to do with professional development was also a mystery to me. Apparently some judges were asking the government to pay for security systems they felt were necessary for their safety as judges. Making this an authorized use of the Professional Development Fund would of course save the government the extra cost of providing them.

Because of the litigation in *Reilly v. Wachowich*, I was very concerned about the chief judge's powers. I saw the authority given to the chief judge to approve the use of the fund as the government maintaining control of the use of the fund through the chief judge.

In my view, all of the rules that were established were contrary to the spirit of the original submission. I believed there was no limitation on use expressed by either Judge Delong in his submission or the Compensation Commission in its recommendation. Nevertheless, I attempted to comply.

MY REQUEST TO USE THE PROFESSIONAL DEVELOPMENT FUND

By a 10-page letter dated July 13, 2001, I requested authorization to use the fund toward the expenses of attending the Caux conference. The guideline required me to say why I thought the expenditure should be approved, and I explained this in extensive detail. Bill McLean was hopeful the three Chiefs might come to an agreement to work together in the atmosphere of peace and reconciliation that had been created at Mountain House in Caux. I saw it as an opportunity to gain insight into the problems plaguing the Stoney reserve and hopefully to get the three Chiefs to agree to work together on a justice program for their community.

Walter refused my request. He said he had reviewed it in detail and that my concerns for the welfare of the people of the Stoney Nation were expressed clearly and, he believed, sincerely. Unfortunately, he said, even if he stretched the boundaries for educational conferences and the guidelines the association had established for the professional allowance, my request would be beyond it. He also pointed out that if a conference is held outside of the country, ministerial approval is required, even when utilizing the professional allowance, and approval often takes at least a month to obtain.

In spite of this refusal, I attended the conference. When I returned, I sent a claim for expenses to the chief judge and asked him to reconsider his refusal.

I pointed to the emphasis on educating judges about judicial dispute resolution and mediation and suggested that the principles of communicating, developing understanding and pursuing mutually beneficial and accepted solutions were the same on an international scale as they are between parties to particular litigation, and that the lessons of Caux would contribute to my efforts in putting judicial dispute resolution into practice.

I further argued that the dictum in *R. v. Gladue* confirmed that a judge should learn about the Aboriginal community where he presides, and that the opportunity to spend a week with one of the Stoneys' most respected Elders and their three Chiefs was a significant contribution to my knowledge of this community. I also asserted that being able to decide matters in a culturally appropriate manner was a necessary part of my education.

As a final note, I told the chief judge I had spoken to Judge Delong about the refusal and he had expressed concern about ministerial approval being a violation of judicial independence.

By letter dated September 18, 2001, Chief Judge Walter replied that his opinion remained the same and he sent back my claim. He admitted he didn't like having to obtain ministerial approval either but it was something he had to do.

On October 31, 2001, I sent an email to all of the Provincial Court judges setting out my difficulty in relation to the Caux conference. I told them I viewed the conference as appropriate to my judicial education in that it related to mediation and judicial dispute resolution and that it was an excellent opportunity to get to know the Chiefs of the reserve in my jurisdiction and gain insights into their community.

I further argued that the purpose of the fund was to support judicial independence by allowing individual judges to choose the conferences they see as best assisting them in the perform- ance of their judicial duties, and that limitations on the use of the fund by the chief judge, the judges association or the minister are infringements on the judicial independence of the individual judge.

I raised this as a subject of discussion at a judges meeting on November 3, 2001. Following that discussion, I again wrote to

Walter requesting clarification of some of the points that were raised, namely:

1. There appeared to be a consensus that the matter of ministerial approval was inconsistent with judicial independence and that Walter had indicated he might just proceed without it in future.
2. Did he agree that approval or denial was in fact an exercise of his discretion?
3. Did he agree with the suggestion that since a judge had to give reasons why a request was appropriate, the chief judge should likewise give reasons for refusal?

By letter of December 18, 2001, Walter simply acknowledged my letter, and without answering any of my comments said he considered the matter closed and suggested I should too.

I was still having regular conversations with Alan Hunter around this time. He and I had become quite good friends. I now shake my head at how patient he was with my "rants." I went on at length, railing about Walter:

> Me: I don't think there can be any doubt about it. Walter doesn't like me and he doesn't like Indians. That comment he made in Red Deer about "I get goddamned tired of people trying to make me feel guilty about what my ancestors did to the Indians" just totally demonstrates his attitude. I'd like to do a judicial review of his decision and put the whole history of his actions against me before the court to show that his refusal is just part of a personal grudge.
>
> Alan: That might give you some personal satisfaction, but you should take the high road. There is a serious question of judicial independence here. He should not be able to

choose what conferences he thinks will be of benefit to you. That should be up to you.

Alan Hunter wrote to Walter on January 3, 2002, to advise that he had instructions from me to apply for judicial review of his refusal to pay my expenses. The letter referred to the six-month limitation period that governs the judicial review procedure, pointing out that if the date of the first refusal, July 20, 2001, were the effective date, we would be required to file notice by January 20, 2002. If we could take the date of his final refusal, December 18, 2001, as the effective date, we would not have to file until June 18, 2002. By letter of January 7 Walter graciously agreed that he would accept the effective date of his administrative decision as being December 18.

On September 27, 2003, I made the following motion at the annual general meeting of the Provincial Court Judges Association:

> That the association recommend to the chief judge that use of the professional development allowance be at the discretion of the individual judge and not require approval of the chief judge.

The motion was tabled to the meeting to be held in May 2004. Walter agreed not to rely on the limitation period if we filed by June 30, 2004. At the May meeting the motion was adjourned to September 2004. Walter agreed to extend to October 29, 2004. In September the motion was again adjourned, to May 2005, and Walter agreed to an extension to the end of June 2005.

At the meeting on May 20, 2005, there were two items on the agenda. One was a proposal by Judge Maloney and Judge Maher to establish a review process to assist in resolving disputes with respect to the use of the professional development allowance. The second item was my motion that use of the allowance be at the discretion of the individual judge and not require approval by the chief judge.

I made my submission very briefly. The power of the chief judge could be used to influence a judge and was therefore contrary to the principle of judicial independence. Judges should be trusted to make their own choices, and if a judge abused the fund it would be a matter of misconduct which could go before the Judicial Council.

I spoke from the floor of the meeting. Judge Walter spoke from a raised table at the front. He replied that control of the fund was necessary for proper administration of it. In answer to my suggestion that it be left to the discretion of individual judges and that those who abused it should be required to answer to the Judicial Council, he said it was not his style to put judges before the Judicial Council.

I wanted to stand up and tell him he was a liar, and speak of my personal experience of how he had chaired a meeting of the Judicial Council that ordered me to appear before a judicial inquiry board without even giving me a chance to reply. I didn't have the courage or the energy to argue further. My motion was put to a vote and defeated by about 40 to 1. Mine was the only vote in favour. A cousin of mine, Judge Syd Wood, had given me a proxy, so it could have been two votes for, but I didn't bother.

The motion by Maloney and Maher was carried by about the same number. There were no votes against. I abstained.

To give Maher and Maloney credit, they were always the mediators and their proposal was probably the best compromise they could see. On reflection, I should have taken the alternative they proposed and made my presentations to the review panel they proposed. I didn't do that.

REILLY V. WALTER

I asked Alan Hunter to proceed with the review application.

When we had first talked about it, I had drafted a 25-page affidavit setting out every complaint I had against Walter. I wanted to focus on his bias against me in order to attack his decision.

Alan maintained his usual position of "take the high road." He advised me not to make it a matter of personal conflict but to stick to the principle. In his view the case law, the dictums from the Supreme Court of Canada and the writings of prominent legal scholars all supported the principle that a chief judge is first among equals and that the limitations on his administrative authority do not allow him to enforce his opinion over that of an individual judge.

The notice and supporting affidavit were filed before the end of June. The affidavit simply set out that I had attended the conference, applied for reimbursement and been refused.

The actual amounts involved were never mentioned in the review. The total cost of travel and attendance at the conference was $2,267, of which $1,465 was airfare. I had used the professional development allowance to pay dues to the Alberta Provincial Court Judges Association and the Canadian Bar Association, both of which were included on the preapproved list. The balance of the year's allowance that was available for the Caux conference was $1,389.

Much was made of the fact that the conference was in Switzerland. After other expenses only $878 would have been available towards the airfare, an amount that can easily be spent travelling to conferences within Canada.

Justice Bonnie Rawlins heard the matter on March 10, 2006. Everett Bunnell appeared for the chief judge.

My case was unique. I was probably the only judge in Canada who had commenced legal action against his chief judge for the purpose of limiting the chief judge's authority. Because of this there were no precedent cases that could be argued in favour of one side or the other. Therefore both counsel used the writings of legal scholars to support their arguments.

My lawyer had the benefit of three such sources.

The first was *Judicial Conduct and Accountability*, by T. David Marshall of the Ontario Court of Justice and formerly of the Supreme Court of the Northwest Territories and Yukon. Justice Marshall (1939–2009) was also a physician and a professor of law.

He said the office of chief judge is a hybrid of both administrative and judicial roles and that the two may not sit well together. The traditional administrator is engaged to carry out the policies of their superior or employer, the executive arm of government. This is contrary to the maintenance of, and the traditional views of, judicial independence. It is also contrary to the more traditional doctrine that the administrative judge or chief is merely the one who sets the list – a job that someone must do. *Primus inter pares* – a first among equals.

The second work consulted was *A Place Apart: Judicial Independence and Accountability in Canada*, by University of Toronto emeritus law professor Martin L. Friedland. In addition to teaching law at Osgoode Hall, Friedland was a member of the Law Reform Commission of Canada and received a Canadian Association of Law Teachers/Law Reform Commission of Canada Award for Outstanding Contribution to Legal Research and Law Reform.

In a chapter titled "Chief Justices and Their Courts," professor Friedland quotes an address the same Justice Marshall gave at the Dalhousie School of Law: "The attribution of more and more power to chief judges may well have the effect of making the judicial ideology of the chief judge the only truly independent ideology on the court.... Every increase in power to a chief judge over others might be seen as a threat to judicial independence."

The third authority Alan cited was *The Independence of Provincial Court Judges: A Public Trust*, by Douglas A. Schmeiser, QC, and

W. Howard McConnell. Schmeiser served as dean and professor of law at the University of Saskatchewan and sat on several federal/provincial advisory councils, including for Meech Lake and the Charlottetown Accord. He chaired the Law Reform Commission of Saskatchewan and was a director of both the Saskatoon Bar Association and the Saskatoon Association on Human Rights.

McConnell was a well-known constitutional and international legal scholar. From 1959 to 1963 he served in the Judge Advocate General's office, advising the government and the Canadian Forces on military law. He was a professor emeritus at the University of Saskatchewan until his death in 2006.

Wrote Schmeiser and McConnell: "The administrative responsibilities of a chief judge, no matter how broadly defined, do not permit him or her to interfere in the exercise of judicial functions by a judge, whether directly or indirectly."

Everett Bunnell argued for the need for control by the chief judge. He referred to *Judicial Independence and Judicial Governance in the Provincial Courts*, a report by Peter J. McCormick.

McCormick is a political science professor at the University of Lethbridge who had graduated from the London School of Economics and Political Science in 1974.

In the introduction to his report, McCormick makes a sarcastic comment which no doubt refers to me: "The reassignment of a judge to a new courtroom 100 kilometres down the road can become a *cause célèbre* for months, the judge himself becoming an instant celebrity who is invited to speak at university campuses across the province."

Later in his text, the professor refers to me by name (along with Quebec jurist Andrée Ruffo):

The two major *causes célèbres* of chief judge/puisne judge

confrontation, Ruffo and Reilly, make the point. Both clearly pushed the limits of what judges on their court were supposed to do, and in the process annoyed a superior who simply wanted them to do their job the way (he thought) they were supposed to do it; but at the same time they were knowingly pushing the limits in the service of principles they thought were extremely important, and this is what judicial independence is supposed to be about.

In her reasons for judgment, Queen's Bench Justice Rawlins quoted the following from McCormick's report: "The obvious solution is neither to allow the chief judge so much discretionary power as to shadow the judicial independence of the puisne judges, nor to constrain the chief judge to the point that simple administration and 'crowd control' become problematic ..."

Generally speaking, when judges receive conflicting authorities they will assess them and follow the ones that have the most weight. It seemed to me that my position was supported by distinguished legal experts who all warned of the danger the powers of the chief judge present to judicial independence. It also seemed to me that the only authority that supported the chief judge was a political scientist who apparently had no experience or education in the law. I didn't see how I could possibly lose.

But I know that whenever I was deciding a case where the correct interpretation of the law was nebulous, I would go with the interpretation that gave the result I wanted. I think there was a consensus among the judiciary generally that Reilly fighting with the chief judge was bad for the court and that the best way to end it was for Reilly to lose.

Justice Rawlins concluded that "this matter does not touch upon Judge Reilly's adjudicative function."

She referred to the argument that the power of the chief judge to dole out or withhold opportunities for education could be used as reward or punishment to those in or out of favour with the chief judge, and said she was not prepared to find that this kind of speculative possibility is sufficient to constitute an affront to judicial independence. "The potential for misuse of an authority does not, without more, connote that there is no such authority," wrote Justice Rawlins.

She then said: "I hasten to add that there has been no such allegation against Chief Judge Walter and neither is there any basis in the evidence for such an allegation."

This comment made me wonder what difference it would have made had we set out all of the other difficulties I had had with Chief Judge Walter, but we had decided to limit the issue to the principle of judicial independence and avoid the matter of my personality conflict with Walter.

Justice Rawlins also commented on the length of the Caux conference and that it was held in Switzerland and said the reasonable person outside of the judiciary might view it not as an important educational opportunity for a judge, but rather as an adjunct and a contribution to his summer holiday: "I believe that an objective 'man on the street' would view this not as a public benefit but more of a personal benefit to Judge Reilly. As I have already determined, that is not the purpose of the professional allowance."

Again I wondered if it would have made a difference if Justice Rawlins had realized we were only dealing with $1,389.

In the result, she dismissed my application and awarded costs against me.

We were not giving up. We filed a notice of appeal. A court composed of justices Ellen Picard, Constance Hunt and Marina Paperny heard the appeal on January 15, 2008.

At one point during the appeal, Justice Paperny wondered aloud if a chief judge would approve a course in mechanics if she thought it would help her in her decision making. I wanted to interject that this was precisely the point: if she had an unusual number of mechanics coming before her, and felt she would gain helpful insights into those cases by taking a mechanics course, she should be able to do so without having to go hat in hand to her chief judge to justify her choice.

It seemed as if Justice Paperny was leaning in our favour, but Alan passed over the comment, and I of course could not say anything in those circumstances. I didn't think Alan was his old "sharp as a razor" self that day, but whatever the outcome of this case, I was deeply indebted to him for all he had done throughout the preceding ten years.

He and his wife, Ginny, had built a beautiful house in the Nicola Valley in BC and I visited them there several times. It was there that Alan told me he had been diagnosed with Alzheimer's disease, but in his usual self-confident mindset he resolved he would overcome it. He also told me that the diagnosis is only certain after the autopsy.

Alan Hunter died on April 6, 2010. The autopsy determined that he died of encephalitis.

Justice Paperny wrote the judgment, which was filed March 3, 2008. The court found there was no reversible error and dismissed the appeal. We then applied for leave to appeal to the Supreme Court of Canada. Leave was not granted.

Again I was ordered to pay court costs. These amounted to about $15,000, plus I paid Alan Hunter's firm a flat $20,000, which was just enough to cover their disbursements. So my $1,389 claim cost me $35,000. I think I was more upset by the fact that the judgment seemed to take the side of the political scientist over the learned experts in constitutional law than I was by the financial cost.

❖ 35 ❖

REFLECTIONS

As I said at the beginning of this book, I have come to see that I was a thorn in the side of the administrative judges who had to deal with me, but I do not apologize. They were acting on the prejudgment attitude that our justice system produces justice for all. When I saw Parliament's directive to rethink the application of the justice system in relation to Aboriginal peoples, I began to see that it was in fact producing some pretty severe injustices, and not just for Aboriginal people.

I think one of the most important lessons I learned as a judge is that "same" is not a synonym for "equal." As far back as 1991, the Cawsey Report had said that if you treat people who are unlike as if they are alike you are practising systemic discrimination. That lesson seemed so clear to me. My great frustration was that I could not get many of my fellow judges to understand it.

When Stevenson told me, "I take the position that a judge should apply the laws impartially and without bias in equal measure to all who appear before that judge," he wasn't acknowledging the distinction between same and equal. He was reverting to the pre-amendment position that had changed with s. 718.2(*e*) of the Criminal Code and the scc ruling in *R. v. Gladue*.

In the context of my conflict, I have come to believe that the words "objectivity" and "ignorance" are much more synonymous than "same" and "equal." I was accused of losing my objectivity. I say I lost my ignorance, but it amounts to the same thing. In the 1980s I knew nothing about Aboriginal people and it was easy to apply the law to them in the same way as I applied it to everyone else. But when I made an effort to learn about them and understand why they were so overrepresented in the judicial system, it became much more difficult to simply "apply the law" as I had done in the past.

What I have come to understand is that the history of the treatment of the Aboriginal peoples has left them with ongoing difficulties that put them in an unequal position to start with. When I picture the classic image of Lady Justice, I see her scales as weighted against the Aboriginal offender and in need of a counterpoise to bring them into balance.

The weights that go against the Aboriginal are all of the aspects of colonial history that affect only the Aboriginal. The Europeans brought their system here, and every immigrant from every other place who comes here voluntarily, by doing so, accepts the laws that are in place.

The difference with the Aboriginal peoples is that they were here and had flourishing cultures and well-developed economies long before the Europeans came and thrust this foreign law upon them. The first and worst characteristic of colonialism is the imposition of foreign law and government on a people without their consent.

The Aboriginal peoples never agreed to become subjects of the English Crown; they were allies. Further, they never agreed to be subject to the government of Canada. As the settler population grew and became dominant, the Canadian government just assumed the power to govern the Indigenous People without ever obtaining their consent. Assuming the power to govern then regressed to the policy of assimilation and the deliberate effort of successive Canadian governments, regardless of political party, to eliminate the Aboriginal cultures so that it would be as if tribal societies had never existed. As Sir John A. Macdonald himself put it in an 1880 letter to the Governor General of the day, the Marquess of Lorne:

> It is hoped that a system may be adopted which will have the effect of accustoming the Indians to the modes of government prevalent in the white communities surrounding them, and that it will thus tend to prepare them for earlier amalgamation with the general population of the country.

This effort included the residential school system with its stated intention of "taking the Indian out of the Indian child." I believe that the "evil" that the residential school system was designed to destroy was the family construct of the Aboriginal people, which was seen as contrary to Christian morality. So for a hundred years the children were "institutionalized" and the family structure of the people was decimated. The family is the building block of society, of course, and with the destruction of the family came the near-eradication of Aboriginal society.

My friend Austin Tootoosis, a Cree healer who works with Aboriginal people, speaks of the "disruption" – the coming of the white men and their attempts to change the Aboriginal people. He says there are five levels of assimilation. At level 1, there is no assimilation. Level 1 Aboriginals live according to their traditional customs and beliefs and most are mentally healthy and well adjusted and never come to the attention of the police. Level 5 are the Aboriginals who have been completely assimilated. They aren't really Indians anymore. They are white people who used to be Indians, but they have achieved a new identity and most are mentally healthy, well adjusted and never come to the attention of the police. Levels 2, 3 and 4 are the problem. These are the people who don't know who they are. They have no real identity and no sense of direction. Their lives are so confusing that they drink to escape a reality they don't understand.

For most non-Aboriginals – and many are sincerely concerned about the plight of the Aboriginal people – the solution is for everyone to get educated in the ways of the general population, get regular jobs and live happily ever after. For some this will be a solution. But what the promoters of this concept don't realize is that they are advocating the same assimilation that caused the problem in the first place. I think it is time that the general population accepted that there may be other answers and that Aboriginal people should be encouraged to look for them, and when they find them they should be supported in implementing them.

I don't purport to know what those solutions are. I have seen it as my task to educate anyone who will listen about the problem. I hope someone can find the solutions.

When a federal election was called on March 26, 2011, I resigned my position as a supernumerary judge in order to run. Being a Liberal candidate in Alberta, where the Conservative party can run a puppet and get it elected, was somewhat of a hopeless quest, but it gave me the opportunity to speak out against justice proposals I saw as reactionary and immoral. It also gave me a reason to resign from the position I had held for 33 years, and it was time for me to go. I had become disillusioned with a system that is slow to change and, in my view, in need of drastic change.

I will deal further with this in my next book.

APPENDIX A

ALLIES AND ADVERSARIES

The events recounted here were difficult for me. They were anxiety-filled years in which I lost friends or, perhaps more accurately, discovered that people I thought were friends weren't really friends at all. I spent many sleepless nights worrying about whether or not I would be able to keep my home in Canmore and what it was all going to cost me in the end.

But as the old Irishman said, "It is better to fight and lose than never to fight at all," and it was all worthwhile for the friends I made in the course of it. Naturally, there were those who disagreed with me. Now that I am reasonably sure of who my friends were and weren't, I add this appendix to say a bit about each of them.

ALLIES

Alan Hunter, QC (1937–2010)

Foremost among my allies was my lawyer, Alan Hunter. He became a good friend and mentor. I spent a number of very pleasant evenings visiting with him and his wife, Ginny, in their home in the Mayfair district of Calgary and at their summer place overlooking the Nicola Valley north of Kamloops, BC.

I'm not really sure why I chose Alan. I didn't really know him. We were on opposite sides in a lawsuit in the early '70s. He intimidated me but I was very impressed by his ability. I don't think I had spoken to him since, and then, some 35 years later, I needed a lawyer and he was the first person who came to mind.

I also didn't know until I attended Alan's office that Grace

Auger had articled with him and that he was a close friend of her husband, Dale Auger. I had met Dale's mother, Rose Auger, at an Aboriginal Justice Learning Network conference in Calgary in February of 1997. She was a renowned Medicine Woman and Indigenous rights activist, and she became my teacher and mentor at Morley.

Alan Hunter had in fact been following my activities at Morley with some interest, and so the connection was particularly fortuitous.

He had been admitted to the Alberta Bar in 1962 and appointed Queen's Counsel in 1981. He was an honorary professor of law at the University of Calgary. As a founding partner in Code Hunter LLP, he oversaw a diverse litigation practice with an emphasis on Charter cases, administrative law, Aboriginal law, and complex civil litigation including corporate commercial matters, fiduciary issues, contracts, torts and regulatory issues. He represented environmental groups and individuals on a pro bono basis. Alan was a member of the Canadian Bar Association and Calgary Bar Association, a Fellow of the American College of Trial Lawyers and the Federation of Defense and Corporate Counsel. He served as a bencher and president of the Law Society of Alberta, board chair of the Alberta Law Reform Institute and director of the Environmental Law Centre, and had received awards for distinguished service from the Law Society of Alberta.

Judge Hubert (Bert) Oliver (1922–2000)

Bert was the first person I went to after being ordered to move from my home in Canmore. He was the ACJ when I was appointed to the bench. We had had some serious disagreements along the way, but in the last years of his term we had come to an understanding and eventually became friends. He once told me I was the only judge, apart from other administrative judges, that he had ever invited to his home for dinner. He had been a colonel in the Judge Advocate General's office for many years, and he seemed to have a military attitude about not fraternizing with the enlisted men.

Judge Pierre Dubé (1941–2002)

I met Pierre when he was the resident judge in Peace River. Before I was appointed to my own circuit, I liked to do relief work in rural areas and often went there. We became friends and he was the only one of my fellow judges who actually supported me with money. He sent a series of cheques to my lawyer to be applied against my fees. In the end the money was refunded to him when the court ordered costs on a full indemnity basis.

When Chief Judge Wachowich was to be replaced, Pierre applied for the position. I remember our conversation being something to this effect:

"I've applied for the position of chief judge."

"You're kidding."

"No, I'm serious, and I've been interviewed by Havelock."

"I don't know how you could even talk to that guy. He's the worst justice minister we've ever had."

"Well, I did talk to him, and in the interview he asked me what things I would do if I were the given the job. I told him one of the first things would be to bring an end to the litigation between you and the chief judge's office."

"If you had any chance at all of getting that job you probably blew it when you said that. I think he's the real adversary in my lawsuit. I don't think Wachowich even understands what it's all about. But good luck to you, Pierre. I could use a friend in that office."

"Stranger things have happened."

Judge Manfred Delong

Manfred and I were probably about the two most opposite judges on the bench. He was a former chief Crown prosecutor and I had been a defence lawyer before my appointment as a judge.

Appointed to the Provincial Court in 1991, he was a very academic judge and researched everything he did. I don't like to read, and I especially don't like reading law, so I would often ask him for the answer to legal questions. I was always confident that his answers were correct.

When Premier Ralph Klein and Justice Minister Jon Havelock made public statements criticizing my order for the investigation at Morley, Delong produced a paper on the *sub judice* rule indicating that such public comments could in fact be contempt of court. The rule prohibits making public statements intended to influence the outcome of a judicial proceeding.

Manfred was the only other judge who assured me he would contribute to my costs if it became necessary.

Judge Raymond Bradley

Bradley (as he always signed himself) was an Edmonton judge who tried to make peace for me with Chief Judge Wachowich and then with Chief Judge Walter. He wasn't successful, but I appreciated his effort.

Judges John Maher and Frank Maloney

On Bradley's initiative, Judge Maher and Judge Maloney arranged a rather unusual mediation between me and Chief Judge Wachowich. Again I appreciated the effort, even though it was unsuccessful.

Judge John James

Appointed to the Provincial Court in 1992, John was better connected to the judicial grapevine than I was. He gave me valuable background information, otherwise known as gossip. He also leaked the story of my transfer to Bob Beaty at the *Calgary*

Herald. In 2000 he resigned from the bench to return to practice with the firm of Heenan Blaikie.

Judge Lynn Cook-Stanhope

Lynn was a judge of the Family and Youth division of the Provincial Court in Calgary. After I applied for judicial review of Chief Judge Wachowich's order to transfer me, I wanted to ask the Alberta Provincial Court Judges Association to give me some support for the legal fees I was incurring. I was in such a state of anxiety that I did not feel I could attend the meeting, so I asked Lynn to make the motion for me and gave her a lengthy brief I had prepared in support.

Judge Don Norheim

Don was the resident judge in Jasper while I was in Canmore, and as such we were the jurists at either end of the Icefields Parkway. Lynn Cook-Stanhope asked Don to present the motion to the association, which he did, and she spoke in support of it.

Chief Judge Gail Vickery (1942–2014)

In May of 2006, Judge Vickery was the first woman to be appointed to the position of chief judge of the Provincial Court of Alberta. She didn't play a big part in the events I recount in this book, but she made my last years as a sitting judge much more pleasant than the ten years prior to her appointment had been.

She had been a partner in the firm of Macleod Dixon and was developing their international office in Almaty, Kazakhstan, at about the time I ordered the investigation at Morley. She told me she was dealing with the vagaries of tribal tyranny in Kazakhstan when she heard about my efforts back home in Canada, and she was very supportive. If only she had been the chief judge in 1994, I believe I could have accomplished something.

In 2010 when I had finished writing *Bad Medicine*, I gave her a copy of the manuscript and asked for her comments. I was quite anxious about whether or not I could publish it while I was still sitting as a supernumerary judge, and I was pleasantly surprised when she told me she thought it was a great book and had no objection to my publishing it.

Jim Ogle

Jim Ogle was Ernest Hunter's lawyer, but in acting for Hunter on the government's appeal of my order for the investigation at Morley, he was successful in having that order upheld, at least in part, and in doing so was a huge help to me. He is now the assistant chief judge for the Provincial Court, Calgary Criminal Division.

Tina Fox

Indigenous court worker, director of the Eagle's Nest Women's Shelter, member of the Stoney Tribal Council for six terms, BA in Aboriginal and First Nations counselling, currently the Elder and counsellor at the Nakoda elementary school at Morley, Tina has publicly supported me throughout my difficulties and been a friend and mentor.

Yvonne DePeel

Yvonne came to Morley from Saskatchewan, where she had been the principal of the Beardy's and Okimasis school. The school had a serious problem with violence and through her efforts it was enrolled in the League of Peaceful Schools, an initiative sponsored by the Saskatchewan Department of Justice.

As the superintendent of schools for the Stoney Education Authority from 2001 to 2010, Yvonne made huge improvements in education for the Stoney people. I believe her firing by the Stoney Nation CEO at the time, Greg Varricchio, under Chiefs

David Bearspaw, Cliff Poucette and Larry Labelle, was a crime against the Stoney children.

Roland Rollinmud

The Stoney Elder and artist who created the cover illustration for *Bad Medicine*.

Bill McLean

A Stoney Elder and son of Chief Walking Buffalo, Bill invited me to Caux, Switzerland, to celebrate the 40th anniversary of his father's world tour promoting the concept of Moral Rearmament (now called Initiatives for Change).

Rose Auger

The Cree Elder and Medicine Woman who introduced me to the Sweat Lodge. She was a great friend, teacher and mentor.

Greg Twoyoungmen

My friend and ally in the fight for justice for the Stoney people. Lifelong critic of John Snow and advocate for democracy on the reserve. Greg wrote a paper titled "The Plight of My People" in which he compared the problems of the Stoney to those of the Irish – both arising from domination by England. His comparison made sense to me and was a big part of my bonding with the Stoney community.

Wilfred Fox

Stoney Elder and friend, brother-in-law to Tina Fox. He once told me he knew a lot more about his reserve after I started asking questions.

Bert Wildman

Stoney Elder and friend. I loved to hear him laugh.

Marjorie Powderface

Indigenous court worker. Bert's daughter, and grandmother of Riley Powderface. Marjorie was my first connection to the Stoney community. It was through her advice to go to the Eagle's Nest that I met Tina Fox.

Riley Powderface

Bert's great-grandson, Marjorie's grandson and a big part of my bonding with the community. Marjorie said he was named for me. One of my most pleasant memories of Morley is of my children Carlyn and Jamie chasing around the Chiniki restaurant with Riley and calling him Rileypowderface as if it were all one word.

Ed Whalen (1927–2001) and Nomi Whalen

Ed was a Canadian television personality and journalist known worldwide for hosting the popular TV series *Stampede Wrestling*, and was the voice of the Calgary Flames from 1980 to 1999. He also had 50 years of perfect attendance at Rotary.

Nomi is a former commissioner on the Human Rights Tribunal as well as a former Calgary city councillor and, until her retirement in 2016, a very active marriage commissioner.

Ed and Nomi's marriage was the second for both of them, but it lasted 34 years. When Nomi divorced her first husband, her lawyer was Milt Harradence. It was the only divorce file Milt ever did, and he did it because he was a friend of Nomi's. Later, Nomi was instrumental in getting Milt to participate in the mediation that settled my complaint to the Judicial Council.

Ed and Nomi had a weekend cottage across the Larch cul-de-sac in Canmore where we lived, and we became good friends. They were very sympathetic to the plight of the Aboriginal people and very supportive of me in the turbulent years of my "Indian wars."

When Ed died in 2001 Nomi invited me to speak at the

memorial held for him at the Saddledome. One of the other speakers was Ralph Klein. Ralph and I exchanged pleasantries on that occasion and he asked me if I was now finished with all of my litigation with the chief judge. I was tempted to ask him how much of a part he had played in the whole situation, but Ed's memorial did not seem like the place to start an argument. The event put me on the speaker's platform along with Bret "The Hitman" Hart and Calgary mayor Dave Bronconnier as well as Premier Klein. It was quite an experience for me, but the best part was being able to pay tribute to a beautiful man whom my children, along with thousands of other Alberta kids, called Grampa Eddie. Carlyn was 8 and Jamie was 6 at the time.

JUDICIAL INQUIRY BOARD

The board was of course required to be neutral, but this panel treated me well and conducted their hearing with the extraordinary proviso that if I didn't like their ruling I could challenge their jurisdiction after the fact. The members of the board were Justice Edward MacCallum, Judge Ken Hope and Judge Margaret Donnelly.

MEDIATION PANEL

Although I was disappointed in the outcome of the mediation of my complaint against Chief Judge Wachowich, Assistant Chief Judge Stevenson and Chief Judge Walter, I owe this panel a debt of gratitude for convincing me to drop a proceeding that was doomed from the beginning. The panel was composed of Herb Laycraft, Milt Harradence and Percy Marshall.

Chief Justice Herb Laycraft

James Herbert Laycraft was a prominent Calgary lawyer appointed to the bench in 1975 who served as the Chief Justice of Alberta from 1985 to 1991. I didn't have any dealings with him in my brief career as a lawyer, but he presided over the Judicial Council hearing that related to the most embarrassing event of my career, back in the early '80s.

I had been the sitting judge on the case of a young fellow I'll call "Paul Joseph Clark," who had set fire to a stray kitten he had taken in. One night while Clark was barbecuing and drinking, the kitten defecated on the rug. In his alcohol-fuelled anger at this, Clark thought he could teach the cat a lesson by putting a little lighter fluid on its tail and setting it on fire. He said he just expected a flash that would frighten the animal. But because of the alcohol he had consumed, he probably used more fluid than he realized, and there was a serious fire that caused severe injuries and the cat had to be put down. It was an extremely ugly incident, and the media had a feeding frenzy over it.

Charged with animal cruelty, Clark pleaded guilty. His lawyer asked for a presentence report, so the matter was adjourned. Several court appearances ensued, and every time, the accused's name would be on the radio and in the papers. The reports invariably stated he faced a six-month sentence.

Probably because of the coincidence of the accused's first two names, the media coverage reminded me of the attention drawn by the Paul Joseph Cini case a decade earlier (see the section just below on Milt Harradence). I felt tremendous compassion for this young man who was being so pilloried in the press. I was also aware of a number of people who would come to every appearance and sit in the front row of the courtroom. They were members of the SPCA and I had the impression they wanted to see the maximum penalty imposed. Balfour Der, who has since become quite a famous defence lawyer, was the prosecutor and he went on at some length describing the horror of the incident and at one point referred to the taking of a human life. He corrected himself, but the drama of his presentation went on.

Throughout the proceedings I was thinking that this young

man – my recollection is that he was only 19 – must have been going through tremendous stress from the publicity and the anxiety of wondering what would ultimately happen to him. I too reacted negatively – to the pressure I was feeling to impose a severe sentence. So, when submissions on sentence were over, I said I accepted the accused's version that he had not intended the horrifying consequences of an act of stupidity committed when he had had too much to drink, and that the proceedings together with all the media attention had already been a significant punishment. I sentenced him to one day in jail.

I have no second thoughts about that disposition. Media attention has caused me huge anxiety in my life, and I believe it must have been terrifying for that young man.

The embarrassment came later. A reporter for the *Calgary Sun*, Johnnie Bachusky, approached me and asked if I would agree to an interview with him. He said he was doing a series of profile articles on judges, and because I had been in the media in relation to a number of matters, he thought I would be a good subject. He said he had done one article on Justice Mary Hetherington, and when I phoned her and asked her about it, she confirmed she had done the interview and was looking forward to his article.

So I met with Bachusky for lunch and we talked about my career. Several times he alluded to the cat case and I declined to discuss it. At the end of lunch he asked me several times if I liked cats. After resisting to answer, I told him I didn't have any feelings one way or another but that I was extremely allergic to them and being near them made me sick.

This is the embarrassing part. The headline on the front page of the *Sun* the next morning read "'Cats make me sick': Judge Reilly."

The furor this created was devastating. Fortunately, I had arranged to take my children, Sean and Tara, skiing at Panorama the day after the interview. I really needed that time to let my nerves settle down, and we had a few great days on the mountain before I had to come home and face the aftermath of my greatest faux pas.

Years later, in the course of the Ernest Hunter complaint, I was extremely critical of the chief judge and the Judicial Council in their handling of that matter. But I had no such feelings about the Bachusky incident. In the first place, I freely admitted I had really screwed up in making that fateful admission to an opportunistic reporter. After that, though, I believe I handled it about as well as I could have under the circumstances.

When I was informed that the chief judge of the day, Con Kosowan, wanted to see me, I flew to Edmonton and met with him. He told me he was being deluged with calls demanding my resignation, and that the worst aspect of the matter was that the article was published the very day the appeal of the sentence I'd delivered in the cat case was being heard. Chief Judge Kosowan, unlike Chief Judge Walter later, actually understood the *sub judice* rule and its application in contempt of court matters. He told me he felt he had no other choice than to refer the issue to the Judicial Council, and that I should retain a lawyer. He also told me I would not be assigned to sit until the matter was concluded.

I asked Jack Major, QC, if he would act for me. He was one of the most prominent lawyers in Calgary at the time and was subsequently appointed to the Alberta Court of Appeal in 1991 and to the Supreme Court of Canada in 1992. He retired from the bench in 1995 and went back to the firm of Bennett Jones. (One of the great things about my somewhat checkered career was that it gave me opportunities to be represented by the very best lawyers.)

Major's focus was just to get the matter heard as quickly as possible, and his stature in the legal community made it possible for him to do that. The hearing took place in a boardroom at the Calgary courthouse. The wait had been a very anxiety-filled time for me, but the hearing itself was a positive experience. Major had me wait while he went in to discuss procedure with the council. When I was invited to come into the room, I was immediately put at ease by Queen's Bench Chief Justice Ken Moore. He asked me if I would like a cup of tea, and when I accepted he got it for me. Justice Laycraft chaired the meeting–hearing. Major admitted that the interview text and its headline were accurate, even if taken way out of context, and that it was published the day of the sentence appeal. I apologized for my grievous error and the embarrassment I had caused to the court.

Herb Laycraft concluded the matter in what I thought was an almost fatherly way. He told me I probably shouldn't have spoken to Bachusky at all, and that I certainly should have been a lot more guarded in what I said, but he could see I had been "sandbagged," and the proceedings were sufficient without further consequences to me.

Justice Milt Harradence (1922–2008)

Milt Harradence, QC, had been one of the most prominent criminal lawyers in Canada before being appointed to the Alberta Court of Appeal in 1979. He was also one of the most flamboyant. He had served in the RCAF in the Second World War and continued flying after the war, engaging in low-altitude aerobatics with former military aircraft.

When I represented Paul Joseph Cini on the charges arising out of the hijacking of Air Canada flight 812, we entered pleas of "not guilty by reason of insanity." I had been a lawyer for less than two years and I was very concerned about my ability to present the defence evidence and challenge the Crown's psychiatrist on the issue of insanity. The case was getting national media attention and it seemed everyone knew I was Cini's lawyer.

One day before the trial, as I was going into the courthouse library, Milt Harradence approached me and asked how I was doing. I told him I was worried about how I was going to handle the evidence in the Cini trial, and he spent hours in the library coaching me on the presentation of my evidence and the challenging of the Crown's. The seriousness of the charges would have warranted a lawyer of Harradence's stature, but he didn't take legal aid cases and I was doing the work on a legal aid certificate. So even though Cini was stuck with a very junior lawyer, I had the benefit of coaching from one of the best. Cini was convicted in spite of my efforts, but I was always grateful to Milt Harradence for the help he gave me in getting Cini the best representation possible to him in the circumstances.

Judge Percy Marshall

Percy Marshall was simply my favourite Provincial Court judge and colleague. Appointed to the bench in 1974, he was always cheerful, laughed easily and loved to be conspicuously insincere in his praises. My friend and colleague Judge Dave Tilley had introduced me to Marshall at a judges conference. Dave had arranged to play a game of pool with Percy and invited me to join them. Percy would exclaim over the easiest successful shot that it was an amazing feat, a shot Minnesota Fats would have been proud to make.

I immediately liked him, and when he spoke seriously he would repeat his motto, "Always speak to the good in a man." Dave teased Percy that he was so good at doing this that he could sentence a convicted criminal to ten years in prison and do it in such a pleasant manner that the convicted would thank him for it. Percy retired from the bench in 2004, and from 2005 to 2011 he further served as a member of the Occupational Health & Safety Board.

ADVERSARIES

Edward R.R. Wachowich (1929–2012)

Ed was a popular Edmonton lawyer and a successful businessman. He was a partner with Con Kosowan in the firm of Kosowan Wachowich. He loved to hunt, maintained a lodge east of Red Deer, and for many years co-hosted an annual dinner for Edmonton lawyers at which the main course was wild game. Wachowich was instrumental in the construction of Chancery Hall and Century Place, impressive Edmonton office buildings. One of his clients in the late '60s and early '70s was the Edmonton Eskimos football club.

His partner Con Kosowan was appointed to the Provincial Court in 1976 and was chief judge from 1985 to 1989. Wachowich was appointed to the Provincial Court in 1985 and succeeded his former law partner as chief judge in 1989.

The fact that Ed was appointed while Don Getty, a former Eskimos quarterback and frequent guest at his hunting lodge, was the premier of Alberta may be just a coincidence. I was inclined to think his appointments as judge and chief judge involved something more than his legal ability.

I could never feel any anger towards Ed for his role in my difficulties. I just saw him as an old man who wanted to maintain the status quo. Even though I made allegations against him of being politically motivated, I believed that to a large degree he was a pawn and the victim of manipulation by his assistant chief judge, Brian Stevenson.

Brian Clare Stevenson

I regard this individual as the villain of my story. This is ironic because, if you Google his name, you will find pages of accolades, mostly for his work with Lions Clubs. Stevenson was the international president of the Lions in 1987. Lions Clubs International says the following:

> In addition to his work as a Lion, past president Stevenson has served as president of the Calgary Social Planning Council, as a board member of the Calgary United Way and as a member of the City of Calgary Social Services Committee. He has also served as president of the Alberta Provincial Court Judges Association and as chairman of the International Year of Disabled Persons Committee for the province of Alberta. In 1996 the City of Calgary recognized his numerous voluntary contributions by awarding him the Grant MacEwan Lifetime Achievement Award of Merit. In 2002 Judge Stevenson was honoured by Her Majesty Queen Elizabeth II with her Golden Jubilee Medal, and in 2005 he received the Alberta Centennial Medal for his service to the community.

Brian Stevenson was appointed a judge in 1974, and became an assistant chief judge in 1992.

One thing he did that most impressed me was when he struck down a statute in the case of *R. v. Big M Drug Mart*. On May 30, 1982, a large drugstore was charged with carrying on the sale of goods on a Sunday contrary to the Lord's Day Act. Stevenson heard the trial and acquitted Big M on the basis that the Lord's Day Act was unconstitutional. It was a feather in his cap when his seemingly controversial decision was upheld by both the Alberta Court of Appeal and the Supreme Court of Canada.

I recall Stevenson saying in the judges lounge that he was going to do this. He said it in what for him was a typically flippant manner. I didn't think he was serious. It was always a little difficult to determine when he was being serious. I subsequently developed a similar problem with knowing when he was telling the truth.

One of the many ironies of my story is that I was thinking

about Stevenson and the *Big M* case when I decided the controversial *Hunter* case. I was pretty sure the matter would be appealed and that the Court of Appeal would overrule me. I was hopeful that it might be further appealed to the Supreme Court of Canada, and I expected that if it were, I might be part of a precedent-setting case in relation to Aboriginal offenders.

Ernest E.J. (Ernie) Walter

Walter was another Edmonton lawyer, appointed to the Provincial Court in 1993 and appointed chief judge in 1999. He was the first chief judge appointed to a seven-year term. Previous appointments to the position were for life, which meant until mandatory retirement at age 70.

Ralph Klein (1942–2013)

I considered myself one of Ralph's supporters as mayor of Calgary, as MLA and as premier of Alberta.

The first time I met him was at the Café dello Sport, the restaurant across the street from the St. Louis Hotel, which was his better-known watering hole. I was drinking with some of the court staff and had probably had more than I should have. I saw Ralph sitting with Rod Love at the next table, but I couldn't place him. I said to Lorna Cook that I knew that guy from somewhere but couldn't think where. She shook her head somewhat scornfully and said it was Ralph Klein, and Rod Love with him. I liked Ralph's public persona, and being somewhat uninhibited from the consumption, I went over and introduced myself. I'm afraid I might have been somewhat of a nuisance but he either didn't remember or didn't hold it against me.

When I celebrated my 40th birthday in 1986 I invited him to my party. I had recently divorced and was living in a very modest little house in Bankview with a big deck in the backyard. It was a very informal gathering of about a hundred of my closest friends. The main beverage was beer served from a system that would have made Rube Goldberg proud. Ron Starchuk, whose family owned the St. Louis, had given me an old icebox that his father had converted to hold a keg of beer. There was a tube that ran from the keg to a spigot on the door and a tube that came out of the side of the icebox, which pressurized the keg. It was hooked up to an old compressor that my nephew, Dave Furneaux, had given me. There was a big flywheel on an electric motor that turned the pulley on the compressor. There was a pressure gauge on the compressor and if it was set right the beer flowed perfectly. It flowed so well that we ran out in the middle of the afternoon. Fortunately Stu Laird was there. He managed the Boston Pizza at Westbrook and volunteered to go and get us another keg. This was 1986, remember, before Ralph privatized the sale of liquor, and it was a Sunday afternoon, so getting a keg of beer was a tremendous accomplishment, not to mention somewhat illegal. Ralph and his wife, Colleen, arrived just as we were installing the second keg and he seemed highly amused by the whole scene. It obviously wasn't exactly what they were expecting, as they were dressed for something a little more formal.

I list Ralph among my antagonists because he was quoted in the *Calgary Herald* as saying my order for the investigation at Morley was contrary to his policy of dealing with First Nations on a government to government basis. Whether he took any direct action against me or not, I don't know. I believe his comments about me may have motivated others to take the action they did. Did Henry II have to order his men to rid him of the meddlesome Becket?

Jonathan Havelock

As minister of justice and attorney general in 1997, Jon Havelock ordered the appeal of my order for the investigation at Morley.

In January 1998 he ordered the creation of the Alberta Justice

Summit, and it was held in January 1999. The purpose was to increase public confidence and participation in the justice system. In explaining the purpose of the summit he specifically mentioned me by name.

I believe the judiciary generally saw Havelock's efforts as political interference with the judicial system. I also believe he was the justice minister most disliked by the judiciary. The fact that I was engaged in conflict with him probably earned some approval for me from my fellow judges.

Ernest Hunter

The accused in a domestic assault matter who later swore a false statutory declaration against me.

Judicial Council 1

Chief Judge Walter, Justice of Appeal J.A. Côté, Justice J.B. Dea, Mr. T. Claxton, Mr. A.F. Kiernan and Mr. R. King.

This is the council that made the decision to refer the Hunter complaint to a judicial inquiry board. It should have been a neutral decision maker, but I name it as my antagonist. Chaired by Walter, with whom I was in continual conflict throughout his tenure, this council made the most onerous decision it could have made against me, and did so without giving me notice or a hearing.

Judicial Council 2

Justice of Appeal J.A. Côté, Justice J.B. Dea, Mr. A. MacLeod, Mr. A.F. Kiernan and Mr. R. King.

When my lawyer explained to Chief Judge Walter why he was unfit to sit in a matter that involved me, Walter disqualified himself. The council then reheard the matter, again without giving me a hearing, and confirmed their decision. Four of the five members of the second council had sat on the first as well and presumably remembered what Walter had said when he chaired the first meeting.

Jean Côté

1966: Gold Medallist at Oxford University; Law Clerk at Supreme Court of Canada
1968: Admitted to Alberta Bar
1974: Author of *Introduction to the Law of Contract*; co-author of *Court Procedure Guide*
1968–1987: Partner in the firm Reynolds Mirth Côté
1987: Appointed to Alberta Court of Appeal

John Berchmans (Berky) Dea

1955: U of A Law School
1956: Admitted to Alberta Bar
1978: Appointed to District Court of Alberta
1979: Appointed to Court of Queen's Bench

Cpl. Bill Young

The Banff Mountie who laid a complaint against me.

John Snow (1933–2006)

The Chief I criticized for ruling his reserve like the dictator of a banana republic and who instigated several complaints against me.

Terry Munro

Principal of Munro & Associates litigation consultants. Assisted John Snow in his efforts against me.

APPENDIX B

THE TALK I NEVER GAVE

A MOCCASIN IN TWO WORLDS

I want to thank the organizers of this event and especially Barb Bedard for inviting me to participate and giving me this opportunity to be on a panel with Tom Meekison and Mike Cardinal.

After accepting the invitation, however, I had misgivings. I was sure I would be the least knowledgeable of the group, but my wife said she thought I was a good choice because I am probably the most newly informed and the most recently ignorant of the panel.

Her comment "recently ignorant" was good. I believe that the biggest problem facing the Aboriginal stepping into the world of the dominant white society is our ignorance about them. And when we have known something for a long time, we tend to forget we were once ignorant about it, and we don't allow for what others don't know.

For example, I went to a three-day program on Aboriginal justice in Saskatoon in 1989. There were a number of Aboriginal women on the program who talked at length about abuses in residential schools, and I didn't know what they were talking about because I had never heard about residential schools.

I'm embarrassed to admit my ignorance, but I believe it is important to reflect on it. I was 43 years old and I had been a judge for 12 years, but I had never heard of residential schools. And I believe the reason I hadn't heard about them was because the same policies of the Canadian government that were designed to eliminate Aboriginal culture were also designed to keep white

Canadians ignorant of what was going on. This is not a political comment, but a historical one.

These people were trying to tell us about problems they have in white society and I didn't get the information they were attempting to share with me, because I didn't have the necessary background knowledge.

I now know that residential schools were a program of the Canadian government primarily designed to destroy Indian culture. It was the view of the 19th-century politicians that Indians were uncivilized savages and that the best way to deal with the problem they constituted for the government was to take all of the children away from their families and turn them into white Christians.

The horrors of this program cannot be overstated. It destroyed the fabric of Indian society by tearing families apart and it is probably the greatest single reason for the dysfunction that exists in so many Indian communities today. I now listen to stories about these schools in a much different way.

A few months ago a lady from Saskatchewan who is now in her 80s was at our house for dinner. She told us about being in a residential school when she was 13 years old. Now, that's an age when teenagers are very self-conscious, and Indian teenagers are the same as whites in this respect. There were some visitors at the school and she was curious about them, so she sneaked up the stairs to have a look. One of the nuns caught her, smacked her over the head with a tin cup, then took her into a washroom and shaved the hair off half of her head. The nun said, "If you want to meet visitors, come and meet them," and took her in front of the visitors with her head half shaved. But our dinner guest could not continue telling us her story, because she had started crying. The humiliation of that incident is still with her 70 years later, and I now believe that this kind of experience was virtually universal with generations of Indian children.

Before I go on, I want to mention that one of the greatest difficulties in speaking on this subject is the resistance that comes from both sides of the cultural divide. If you suggest there are problems in Aboriginal society, some of the people in that society will react badly, with denial, allegations of racism, threats of lawsuits. If you suggest that white society may have some responsibility for the problems in Aboriginal society, the resistance will be equally enthusiastic: "Well, I didn't do it." "I've never hurt an Indian." "I didn't even know Custer."

I believe I was fortunate in that I was trained to listen to both sides of the story from an early age because of the circumstances of my childhood. My father was born in Sherbrooke, Quebec, in 1890. He was 56 years old the year I was born, 1946, and he retired when I was 10, so he was more like a grandfather than a father. He was a schoolteacher and well read, and he loved history. He had met Sir Wilfrid Laurier, and one of his favourite quotes from Laurier was, "I love my God, and next to God I love my Canada."

So when I was a little boy, I would go to school and get the Walt Disney version of Canadian history. Almost all of our textbooks were written in Ontario, and they basically gave us the white Anglo-Saxon Protestant, Orange Lodge version. At home I would get the Irish Catholic Quebecker version.

For example, in school I learned about Sir John A. Macdonald, Canada's first prime minister. A father of Confederation. A man whose vision was responsible for this great country stretching from sea to sea. *A mare usque ad mare.* At home, Pop's reaction was, "Man of vision. Hah! That brandy-swilling drunkard never sobered up long enough to see across the room."

At school we learned that Macdonald worked hard to build a railway to tie this country together. At home I learned that the railroad was built to make money by exploiting undeveloped land, and that it didn't matter how many Indians and Métis they displaced to do that. I learned that the country was built to serve the railway, not the other way around.

At school we learned that the addition of more provinces was done peacefully, the only exception being the North-West Rebellion, in which a crazy half-breed who heard voices took up arms against his own country and was properly hanged for doing so. At home my father told me it was Louis Riel that was the man of vision, and that he was murdered by Protestant Orangemen because he was a francophone Catholic and because he was interfering with their railway.

My father was a second-generation Quebecker and his family were some of the people Macdonald was speaking of when he said he would hang Louis Riel though every dog in Quebec barked for his life. (It's been my experience that when you talk about people that way, they will react badly.)

Now, I'm not trying to convince you that my father's version was any more correct than the other. I do say there is always more than one side to a story, and if we want to understand each other, we have to be ready to listen to each other.

My father unfortunately didn't give me the unofficial version of the Indian situation and that may have been because he accepted the official version. As I say, he was born in the 19th century and grew up in an age when white Christian superiority was a socially acceptable attitude. This attitude is politically unacceptable today, but it did not become so until that terrible lesson Adolf Hitler taught the world when he carried it to such an extreme that it motivated the murder of six million people.

I feel the level of resistance in this room begin to rise. I'm not saying we are a bunch of racists, but I am saying that the policies of the past were racist and that their effect will continue if we don't know about it, acknowledge it and ensure that it does not continue. I don't believe Aboriginal people hate whites for what has happened, but I do think they want us to acknowledge how it has hurt them.

I was at a funeral at Morley last year. (I have been to too many funerals at Morley.) One of the Elders came up to me at the cemetery and said, "John, will you come and look at something with me?" He took me to his parents' grave. They had died on the same day in the 1950s. He told me that in those days, Fish and Wildlife had, in its great wisdom, decided that the deer and elk population was declining because there were too many wolves, so they embarked on a program of putting out poisoned meat to kill wolves. My friend's father went hunting one day and killed a moose. He field dressed it and carried home as much of the meat as he could. The next day he went and got more of it, and his mother prepared it for supper. The day after that his mother and father and two of his cousins who had been staying with them were all found dead. People deemed that what must have happened was that wildlife officers came upon the meat and, believing it was abandoned, poisoned it to kill wolves.

The Stoney Elder told me this story without any apparent anger or hatred or need for revenge. He just wanted me to listen, and to acknowledge his hurt.

What I have learned about Aboriginals over the last couple of years, more than anything else, is how much they have been hurt.

My dad taught school at Western Canada College in the 1920s and one of his fellow teachers, and a man with whom he had a lifelong friendship, was John Laurie. Laurie was a great friend of the Indian people of Alberta. He was the founder of the Alberta Indian Association and he was instrumental in obtaining the removal of a section of the Indian Act that had prevented treaty Indians from voting.

Laurie had been adopted by a Stoney family and I knew he was buried on the reserve, but I didn't know where. I was visiting with some people from Morley last spring and asked if they could tell me. They did, and one of the women got tears in her eyes and said in her gentle Indian way, "When you go there, look at the other grave markers. They will tell you a story." So I went and it was the most brutal story I have ever been told.

I have a son who was born in 1970, and to me he is still just a boy. In that little cemetery that serves the Wesley people, a community of about 1,000, there are dozens of graves of Stoney youth who had been born since 1970 and are already buried there. (Olive Dickason, in her book *Canada's First Nations*, says that among Canadian Aboriginals under 25, the suicide rate is the highest in the world.)

I believe that one of the big problems white people have in dealing with the plight of Aboriginal people is that they are afraid that "putting things right" would mean we would all have to leave and go back to where we came from, and since that isn't possible, the conclusion seems to be that we just can't do anything, so we just shouldn't even talk about it.

My message to those with a moccasin in two worlds is that I acknowledge your difficulties and your suffering, but you should not expect all white Canadians to understand you, and you should know what we think about ourselves and what we think we know about Aboriginals.

First, we like to think of ourselves as nice people. If you try to tell us we are not nice people, we will react badly and defensively. We are taught that this land was settled peacefully, and that we made treaties with the Indians in which we acted honourably and fairly, and we treated you well. When you killed off all of your buffalo, we brought you beef and grain and taught you how to farm. We put you on reserves and provided you with Indian agents to look after you because you weren't able to look after yourselves. (How you managed to get by for 50,000 years before we got here is something we never bothered to ask.) We built schools and staffed them in order to teach your children to read and write. We have basically done a tremendous service by bring-ing you the modern age and helping you advance through thou-sands of years of development in only a few centuries, and the real reason for the few problems you have is that the advancement we have brought you has been a little too fast.

This is what we have been taught and this is what you will be faced with in many of your dealings with members of our society. At the same time, I encourage you to have hope. I believe that the majority of Canadians are people of good will, and that they would not agree with the way you have been treated, and the way you are being treated, if they knew about it.

With the increasing education and awareness that is occur-ring in our present age, I am hopeful that changes are happening that will allow you to take your place in Canadian society, not as assimilated people who have been turned into white people, but as proud, independent Aboriginal peoples who will be acknow-ledged as the real founding races of this great country, and will be accorded the place in society that is rightly yours.

All of Canada will benefit from a renewed relationship. This will happen when we really get to know each other. The organizers of this event should receive the highest praise for this Aboriginal Awareness Week. As a matter of fact, it is mentioned as the kind of event that is needed to promote cross-cultural understand-ing, in the *Report of the Royal Commission on Aboriginal Peoples*, volume 5, "Renewal: A Twenty-year Commitment," chapter 4, "Public Education: Building Awareness and Understanding." The RCAP report was a tremendous undertaking and contains a wealth of material on every aspect of the Aboriginal situation in Canada. Unfortunately the information is buried in its own length.

I would like to have seen one more, short volume, and I may write it myself. It would be called Taking Responsibility. It would focus on the information that points to the fault of the Canadian state in creating the current hardships facing Aboriginals, with a view to encouraging white society to accept its responsibility for the current plight of the Aboriginal people. It would also focus on the information relating to fault of Aboriginal people and the solutions that are available to them today, to encourage them to accept their responsibility to improve their own future, and I believe many are doing this.

My greatest disappointment with the RCAP report is that in all of the recommendations that are made in relation to education and awareness, there isn't one to produce preschool and primary-school books and programs about Aboriginals for use in all non-Aboriginal schools across the country, so that our children will know each other. I believe that the hardships which Aboriginal people have suffered for so many years would not have been allowed to happen, and would not be allowed to continue, if we knew more about each other. We should have been learning this as children and we should be teaching it to our children.

I thank you for this opportunity to speak.

APPENDIX C

FROM DISSENTING REASONS FOR JUDGMENT BY BC COURT OF APPEAL JUSTICE ROWLES IN *R. V. GLADUE*

[October 24, 1997]

...[49] The enactment by Parliament of s. 718.2(*d*) and (*e*) of the Criminal Code provides statutory recognition of the principle of restraint in the use of incarceration in sentencing. Canada's high incarceration rate as contrasted with other Western industrialized countries and the disproportionately high number of Aboriginal people Canada incarcerates has been referred to repeatedly in reports and studies on sentencing. Recent reports on sentencing include the 1982 federal government white paper entitled *The Criminal Law in Canadian Society*, the 1987 Canadian Sentencing Commission report known as the Archambault Report (*Sentencing Reform: A Canadian Approach*, J.R. Omer Archambault, chairman), and the 1988 report of the Standing Committee on Justice and Solicitor General (*Taking Responsibility*, David Daubney, chairman). The many inquiries and reports on Aboriginal people and the justice system are referred to in *Bridging the Cultural Divide: A Report on Aboriginal People and Criminal Justice in Canada*, prepared by the 1996 Royal Commission on Aboriginal Peoples. Two themes are constant in these reports: the overly extensive use of incarceration and the high rate of Aboriginal offenders who are incarcerated.

[50] In *Volume 1: The Justice System and Aboriginal People: Report of the Aboriginal Justice Inquiry of Manitoba* (1991) at 402–403,

reference is made to the findings of the Canadian Sentencing Commission (the Archambault Report).

The Canadian Sentencing Commission has pointed out that:

> The Criminal Code displays an apparent bias toward the use of incarceration, since for most offences the penalty indicated is expressed in terms of a maximum term of imprisonment. A number of difficulties arise if imprisonment is perceived to be the preferred sanction for most offences. Perhaps most significant is that although we regularly impose this most onerous and expensive sanction, it accomplishes very little apart from separating offenders from society for a period of time. In the past few decades many groups and federally appointed committees and commissions given the responsibility for studying various aspects of the criminal justice system have argued that imprisonment should be used only as a last resort and/or that it should be reserved for those convicted of only the most serious offences. However, although much has been said, little has been done to move us in this direction.

The commission recommends that Parliament incorporate a statement of purpose and principles in the criminal law. Sentences, it contends, should reflect "the least onerous sanction appropriate to the circumstances."

[51] That recommendation came to fruition on 3 September 1996 when the new Part XXIII of the Criminal Code came into force. In 1994, when the new sentencing provisions were first introduced into Parliament as Bill C-41, the Minister of Justice acknowledged that many of the Bill's provisions flowed from recommendations of the Archambault Report and the Daubney

Committee Report. In the House of Commons Debates (20 September 1994 at page 5873), the Honourable Allan Rock (then the Minister of Justice and Attorney General of Canada) stated:

> A general principle that runs throughout Bill C-41 is that jails should be reserved for those who should be there. Alternatives should be put in place for those who commit offences but who do not need or merit incarceration. ...
>
> It is not simply by being more harsh that we will achieve more effective criminal justice. We must use our scarce resources wisely.

[52] When considering how the principles contained in s. 718.2(*d*) and (*e*) are to be construed and, particularly, how the clause "with particular attention to the circumstances of Aboriginal offenders" is to be given effect, it is useful to refer to s. 8 of the Interpretation Act, RSBC 1996, c. 238, which provides that:

> Every enactment must be construed as being remedial, and must be given such fair, large and liberal construction and interpretation as best ensures the attainment of its objects.

[53] Legislative debates may be considered for the general purpose of determining the mischief Parliament was attempting to remedy with the legislation: see *R. v. Heywood*, [1994] 3 SCR 761 at 787–789.

[54] From the many commission reports and the parliamentary debates on Bill C-41, I think it is clear that the mischief subsections 718.2(*d*) and 718.2(*e*) were designed to remedy was the excessive use of incarceration in the criminal justice system in Canada and the disproportionately high number of Aboriginal people who are incarcerated.

[55] The over-representation of Aboriginal people in the Canadian criminal justice system is well documented. For a review of these findings see *Bridging the Cultural Divide:*

A Report on Aboriginal People and Criminal Justice in Canada (Royal Commission on Aboriginal Peoples, 1996) at pp. 28–33. Over-representation of the magnitude found in the studies results, in part, from what is referred to as systemic discrimination. The operation of systemic discrimination is described by Tim Quigley in "Some Issues in Sentencing of Aboriginal Offenders" in R. Gosse, J.Y. Henderson and R. Carter, eds., *Continuing Poundmaker and Riel's Quest* (Saskatoon: Purich Publishing, 1994) at 275–76:

> Socioeconomic factors such as employment status, level of education, family situation, etc., appear on the surface as neutral criteria. They are considered as such by the legal system. Yet they can conceal an extremely strong bias in the sentencing process. Convicted persons with steady employment and stability in their lives, or at least prospects of the same, are much less likely to be sent to jail for offences that are borderline imprisonment offences. The unemployed, transients, the poorly educated are all better candidates for imprisonment. When the social, political and economic aspects of our society place Aboriginal people disproportionately within the ranks of the latter, our society literally sentences more of them to jail. This is systemic discrimination.

[56] The clause in s. 718.2(*e*) of the Criminal Code "with particular attention to the circumstances of Aboriginal offenders" invites recognition and amelioration of the impact systemic discrimination has on Aboriginal people.

[57] A prior criminal record with sentences of imprisonment is often viewed as indicative of an offender's inability to reform. There are some circumstances which may work in concert to exaggerate the instances of criminal records for Aboriginal persons. In "Some Issues in Sentencing of Aboriginal Offenders," supra, Quigley notes, at 275:

Prior criminal record as a factor can have an undue influence on the imprisonment rate for Aboriginal people due to the snowball effect of some of the factors listed above. If there are more young Aboriginal people, if they are disproportionately unemployed, idle and alienated, and if they are overly scrutinized by the police, it should not be surprising that frequently breaches of the law are detected and punished. Add to that the greater likelihood of being denied bail (which increases the chance of being jailed if convicted), the greater likelihood of fine default and the diminished likelihood of receiving probation, and there is a greater probability of imprisonment being imposed. Some of the same factors increase the chances of the same person reoffending and being detected once again. After that, every succeeding conviction is much more apt to be punished by imprisonment, thus creating a snowball effect: jail becomes virtually the only option, regardless of the seriousness of the offence.

[58] Historical disadvantage is not unique to the Aboriginal population but the courts have explicitly recognized the negative role which incarceration has played in the cycle of poverty, lack of education and unemployment, violence and abuse in the Aboriginal population. In *R. v. M.(R.B.)*, 1990 CanLII 5416 (BCCA), McEachern CJBC observed:

It appears self-evident to us that in any population there will be some disadvantaged members who, for many reasons, are likely to fall, or more likely to drift, into a life of idleness and crime. Society must be protected from them as best it can, but in some cases it is unrealistic to think that some of these unfortunate persons can be rehabilitated once the cycle starts, by successive and increased periods of imprisonment, especially when, upon release, they are returned to the same environment, lifestyle, frustrations and temptations which contributed to their misfortune in the first place.

This, of course, is especially the case with those of our citizens who have not had the advantages of a stable family structure in their formative years, or were harmed before or at birth, or afterwards by some form of alcohol syndrome, or from other physical or cognitive impairment or from the additional misfortune of abuse in childhood. It appears this accused may suffer from all of these disadvantages.

This all too typical collection of misfortunes is not limited to our native Indian populations, but may be more numerically prominent amongst them, partly because of historical disadvantages of which some, such as this accused, may be the unfortunate product.

Some of these persons are able to overcome their disadvantages, some may be able to benefit from the disciplines which society imposes by imprisonment or otherwise (although I suspect their number is small if not minuscule), but many, of which I suspect the accused is typical, are not capable of reforming themselves. For them, each sentence, including those of increasing severity, are only stages of the cycle that, if allowed to continue, will probably become permanent, so that a life, which is always precious, becomes wasted.

What is required, in this and many similar cases, is intensive guidance, encouragement, training and supervision on preferably a daily or frequent basis by a person or persons in whom the accused has confidence.

[59] While it has long been accepted that the measure and effectiveness of the punitive aspect of incarceration should be examined within the context of the offender's specific

circumstances, s. 718.2(*e*) emphasizes the need for specific recognition to be given to the potential effect of incarceration on Aboriginal offenders.

[60] According to the *Report of the Aboriginal Justice Inquiry of Manitoba* (1991) at p. 405, Aboriginal people have traditionally dealt with unacceptable conduct in a different manner from that embedded in the Canadian penal system:

> Instead of exacting vengeance and punishment, the intent in Aboriginal communities was to demonstrate the community's disapproval of the behaviour, to counsel the offender, and to return the peace and order to the community without using imprisonment.

The conception of justice as restorative of the community may be relevant to the degree to which "justice" may be seen to be done by Aboriginal people. Particularly in isolated Aboriginal communities, the need for rehabilitation, reintegration and reconciliation may be essential to the community's cohesion. The Manitoba Report concluded at 395:

> We are firmly of the view that it is more important to determine what has caused a person to act in an inappropriate way, and to deal with the cause of the behaviour, than it is to sentence a person for longer periods to satisfy a public demand for punishment or retribution.

[61] While an appreciation of an offender's Aboriginal community and culture is a simpler task where the offender lives on a reserve, the influence and application of Aboriginal concepts of justice becomes substantially more complicated where the offender lives in an urban setting. This issue was considered in the Manitoba Report at page 408:

> ... it is suggested that if the accused has no connection to

his or her Aboriginal culture, then it should no longer be a factor to take into consideration in sentencing. ...

Great care must be taken in these cases, because the influence of Aboriginal cultures is present, although difficult to detect. As we have noted earlier, it is important to distinguish between a person's lifestyle, which for some individuals may appear to be one of complete integration into the mainstream, and his or her culture, which is reflective of the values in which a person was raised and which continues to shape that person's behaviour. Thus, it is important for the courts to satisfy themselves as to the true influence of Aboriginal culture. The acceptance of outward appearances is not sufficient. In fact, where the influence of Aboriginal culture is difficult to detect, this itself may be a factor that the courts should take into consideration.

[62] In *Bridging the Cultural Divide: A Report on Aboriginal People and Criminal Justice in Canada* (1996), the Royal Commission on Aboriginal Peoples stated at 280:

The realities of life in many reserves and northern communities mean that people often have to leave to pursue education or find employment. Some, particularly women, have left to escape violent situations; others, such as people with disabilities, leave because of the lack of services on reserves. Leaving their reserves or communities does not mean that these people have abandoned their culture, their traditions or their understanding of who they are. (Emphasis added [by BCCA].)

[63] While assessing the impact of an Aboriginal offender's heritage may be more complex where the offender does not live on a reserve, it cannot be regarded as irrelevant in the sentencing process.

[64] The courts have, for some time, accepted the principle that alternative sentences for Aboriginal offenders are appropriate where the offender resides in an isolated Aboriginal community and where that community is able to take responsibility for, and provide and administer its own sanctions for, the offence. The advantages of sentencing circles are referred to in *R. v. Moses* (1992), 71 ccc (3d) 347 at 356 (Yukon Terr. Ct.). The impact of imprisonment on the Aboriginal offender when removed from his community was recognized many years ago in *R. v. Fireman* (1971), 4 ccc (2d) 82 (Ont. ca).

[65] In urban settings, however, there are frequently resources within the communities which are tailored to the needs of Aboriginal offenders.

[66] In *Bridging the Cultural Divide*, the Royal Commission on Aboriginal Peoples cautions against limiting a consideration of community-based programs to reserve communities (at pp. 280–82):

> There is often an unspoken assumption that Aboriginal justice systems will develop in rural or northern communities and that urban Aboriginal people, because they have chosen to live in the city, have no choice but to deal with the non-Aboriginal system if they come into conflict with the law. This ignores the facts about Aboriginal people today, however, and makes the promise of culturally appropriate justice systems an illusion for almost half of all Aboriginal people in Canada – the half that live in towns and cities. ...
>
> In many urban areas, Aboriginal people have a quite well developed network of social and cultural agencies. ...
>
> Reserves and rural or northern communities dealing with alcohol or drug abuse problems often have to send people hundreds or thousands of miles away for treatment. Anger management programs and the like are also rare in these

types of Aboriginal communities. Urban centres, by contrast, tend to have more Aboriginal-specific services available.

[67] For the reasons the Manitoba Report gives, a determination of whether imprisonment of an Aboriginal offender is necessary should involve a consideration of the various resources available, whether the resources are on the reserve or in the urban community.

[68] In the present case, it is my respectful view that the learned trial judge was in error when he concluded that, in sentencing the appellant, it was unnecessary to consider the appellant's Aboriginal background because the appellant and the deceased were "not living within the Aboriginal community as such" and they were "living off a reserve and the offence occurred in an urban setting."

[69] Nothing in the legislation suggests that the application of s. 718.2(*e*) is limited to Aboriginal people living on reserves.

[70] The fact that the appellant was not living on the reserve did not alter her Aboriginal heritage or her cultural ties and it did not alter the significance of those factors in her rehabilitation.

[71] The evidence shows that the appellant and her family and at least part of the deceased's family were living in Nanaimo at the time the offence occurred. There was also evidence of a centre in Nanaimo called the Tillicum Haus Native Friendship Centre at which social, educational and counselling programs were available to Aboriginal people. It was this facility which the appellant attended to upgrade her education and to take counselling for alcohol abuse. In other words, within an urban setting, the appellant had available to support and assist her in her rehabilitation various social, educational and counselling resources at Tillicum Haus.

[72] As earlier indicated, it is the appellant's submission that the trial judge placed too much emphasis on the principles of

general deterrence and denunciation while disregarding the substantial efforts the appellant had made at rehabilitation during the 17 months she had been on bail. In his submissions on behalf of the appellant, Mr. McKinnon made clear that he was not arguing that denunciation should play no part in determining the appropriate sentence. Instead, he argued that denunciation of an offender's conduct can only be assessed on the basis of the circumstances of the particular case and offender.

[73] To support his submission in that regard, Mr. McKinnon referred to the following passages in the reasons of the majority in *R. v. Pettigrew*, 1990 CanLII 5417 (BCCA), in which Taylor J.A. said:

> Yet even where, as here, the crime involved is regarded as one of particular gravity – the careless taking of a life – the extent to which it should be considered morally reprehensible, so as to call for "denunciatory" punishment, can still be assessed only on the basis of the circumstances of the particular case and offender. In the absence of any prescribed minimum penalty, imprisonment can be imposed on this ground only if the circumstances of the case and of the offender call for such a response. In weighing the matter, the court must consider, among other things, whether any adverse effects which a denunciatory punishment would have on the rehabilitation of the offender can be justified in the overall interests of the protection and advancement of society.
>
> I do not think it would often be thought appropriate today that the denunciatory aspect of punishment should be the predominant consideration in a manslaughter case in which there is a want of deliberation or motivation and where the accused is a disadvantaged person and a first offender.

And at p. 397:

The [post-sentence] report which we have now received says that Ms. Pettigrew is a Metis, that she was born in the Northwest Territories, that her parents both used alcohol heavily, and that she was abused during her childhood. She has consumed alcohol since an early age and her life has been marked by a series of misfortunes, several of them tragic. Her childhood circumstances and life experiences, as now disclosed, make a sentence based wholly on "denunciation," "rejection" or "abhorrence," in my view, difficult to justify.

[74] In the present case the crime committed by the appellant must be viewed as a serious one, for a life was taken. The circumstances surrounding the offence are tragic for all, including the children of the appellant and the deceased.

[75] The circumstances of the offence include provocation, superimposed on an undiagnosed medical problem affecting the appellant's emotional stability. The circumstances of the offender included her youth and emotional immaturity. The appellant had had alcohol abuse problems but no history of other criminal conduct or acts of violence.

[76] The issue in this case is whether the sentence of three years imprisonment puts undue emphasis on the principles of general deterrence and denunciation and whether the trial judge erred in declining to give consideration to the provisions of s. 718.2(e) of the Criminal Code, which provides:

718.2. A court that imposes a sentence shall also take into consideration the following principles: ...

(e) all available sanctions other than imprisonment that are reasonable in the circumstances should be considered for all offenders, with particular attention to the circumstances of Aboriginal offenders.

[77] As I have already stated, appellant's counsel made it clear

that he was not arguing that denunciation should play no part in determining the appropriate sentence. I agree that general deterrence and denunciation are important factors to be taken into account in this case but I also respectfully agree with the observations of Justice Taylor in *Pettigrew*, supra, that "[i]n weighing the matter, the court must consider, among other things, whether any adverse effects which a denunciatory punishment would have on the rehabilitation of the offender can be justified in the overall interests of the protection and advancement of society."

[78] While defence counsel at trial made reference to the appellant's having taken alcohol abuse counselling and having upgraded her education, there was little more said about rehabilitation, and the trial judge did not have the benefit of a presentence report.

[79] The material we have before us includes an affidavit from the appellant in which she has provided further information concerning her Aboriginal heritage and her efforts at maintaining that heritage for herself and her children. In her affidavit, the appellant states that she has applied to become a full status Cree and her application is pending before the Cree Nation at the Atikameg Reserve in Alberta. She has deposed that she still maintains contact with Reuben Beaver's mother, Mary Yellowknee, in Alberta. Mary Yellowknee is a status Cree and, according to the appellant, she is assisting her with her status Cree applications for herself and her children. The appellant's daughter, Tanita, has been granted full status as a member of the Cree Nation.

[80] The measures the appellant took to rehabilitate herself in the 17 months before she was sentenced are readily apparent from the material now before us. Included in that material are letters from Tillicum Haus Native Friendship Centre, a probation officer from the Ministry of the Attorney General regarding the extent of the appellant's compliance with her bail order, a medical doctor regarding the appellant's difficulties with hyperthyroidism,

which was not diagnosed until after the offence, and the Indian Homemakers' Association of BC.

[81] The material to which I have just referred, which was not before the trial judge, shows that the appellant made a considerable effort "to get her life straightened around," as Mr. McKinnon expressed it, while she was awaiting trial. The success she has had in that period of time shows that the appellant is likely to be a good candidate for further rehabilitation.

[82] The importance of rehabilitation in this case does not end with the appellant, but extends to her children, her family and those in the wider community with whom she lives.

[83] In my opinion, a sentence of three years imprisonment was excessive in this case. The principles of general deterrence and denunciation had to be reflected in the sentence, but the sentence could have and, in my view, should have been designed to advance the appellant's rehabilitation through a period of supervised probation.

[84] Taking into account all of the circumstances to which I have referred, including those matters contained in material which was not before the learned trial judge, I would grant leave to appeal, and allow the appeal to the extent of reducing the sentence to one of two years less a day, to be followed by a three-year period of probation during which the appellant would be required to report to a probation officer and to take such counselling, including substance abuse counselling, as the probation officer may direct.

APPENDIX D

FROM REASONS FOR JUDGMENT BY ALBERTA QUEEN'S BENCH JUSTICE MASON IN *REILLY V. WACHOWICH*

[September 2, 1998] ...

[45] This court has the jurisdiction to review the chief judge's decision in this matter. The chief judge's adjudicative independence is not at issue. What is impugned is a decision purportedly made pursuant to his powers under the [Provincial Court Judges Act (PCJA)] and as a chief judge. Any such decision is made from his position under that Act as a statutory delegate and as a chief judge. Judicial review by this court is therefore available. What really is at issue is the extent of the chief judge's delegate powers under the PCJA and his inherent jurisdiction. ...

[46] In a Rule 129 application, the onus is on the applicant to prove that the matter should be struck out. Counsel for the chief judge has failed to satisfy me that this court does not have jurisdiction to conduct a judicial review in these circumstances.

[47] The chief judge's decision raises the constitutional issues of the adjudicative independence of Provincial Court trial judges and the institutional independence of that court. These issues cannot be circumscribed by provincial legislation. The decision also invites an examination of the statutory powers (i.e., administrative, supervisory and disciplinary) of the chief judge under the PCJA in the context of the reassignment of the judge and the transfer of his residence.

[48] Counsel for the chief judge urges me to characterize the chief judge's directive as administrative, supervisory and

disciplinary. He then argues that the directive was within the chief judge's unfettered and unreviewable power. However, while certain actions by a chief judge will not be reviewable, I cannot agree that a chief judge has completely unfettered powers. At the core of adjudicative judicial independence is the freedom of individual judges to hear and decide cases without interference by the government, any organization or group, any individual or even another judge. See *Beauregard v. The Queen*, ... [1986] 2 SCR 56 at 69–73, which was quoted by Lamer CJC in *R. v. Lippé*, ... [1991] 2 SCR 114 at 136–38. At 138, Lamer CJC asserts that adjudicative judicial independence is free from all government interference, including the "Chief Justice." ...

[49] In the present situation, counsel for Judge Reilly has alleged that the chief judge's directive is unconstitutional, as interfering with the adjudicative independence of Judge Reilly and, by extension, that of the entire Provincial Court. That is a serious allegation that must be examined thoroughly on judicial review.

[50] Judicial review is not excluded by the operation of s. 16(1) of the PCJA. That section forbids an action against a judge. The underlying matter here is not an action <u>against</u> the chief judge but an application for judicial review. Moreover, I have difficulty with counsel for the chief judge's contention that the wording of s. 16(1) should be interpreted as more strict than the strictest privative clause that legislatures have ever enacted. Section 16(1) cannot be so interpreted, and *Shaw v. Trudel* does not stand for such a proposition. It speaks only to the immunity of judges from civil actions against them, when acting in their adjudicative roles.
...

[52] The existence of the Judicial Council does not exclude judicial review. Judge Reilly will be asking that the chief judge's decision be declared a nullity. That remedy is not available from

the Judicial Council. Nor is the Judicial Council able to assess the constitutionality of the chief judge's decision.

[53] I am also not persuaded by counsel for the chief judge's argument that no review is required because the principles of natural justice do not apply to this type of decision. Counsel for the chief judge submitted that the requirement for natural justice principles depends on the circumstances – different levels and components of natural justice are required in different circumstances. While I agree with that general proposition, the issue of which, if any, natural justice principles apply in this matter are for the judicial review application itself. The potential issue of the "chilling effect" on future decisions of Judge Reilly and other judges is also a matter for the judicial review itself. ...

Disposition

[55] There will be a judicial review of the chief judge's decision to reassign Judge Reilly and to transfer his residence from Canmore to Calgary. The chief judge will file a return, as required by Rule 753.13. ...

FURTHER READING

Books, articles, reports

Canadian Judicial Council. *Ethical Principles for Judges.* Ottawa: Canadian Judicial Council, 1998. Accessed 2014-06-28 (pdf) at is.gd/ CS1AiN.

Cawsey, Allan, et al. *Justice on Trial: Report of the Task Force on the Criminal Justice System and Its Impact on the Indian and Métis People of Alberta.* 3 vols. Edmonton: Alberta Justice, March 1991.

Dickason, Olive Patricia. *Canada's First Nations: A History of Founding Peoples from Earliest Times.* Toronto: McClelland & Stewart, 1992.

Fine, Sean. "Chief judges seen as too powerful: Senior jurist says 'ideological control' over courts must be curbed." *The Globe and Mail,* June 9, 1993, A4. Accessed 2016-09-22 as document ID 385255971 on ProQuest's Canadian Newsstand Complete via public library proxy server (requires library card).

Friedland, Martin L. *A Place Apart: Judicial Independence and Accountability in Canada.* Ottawa: Canadian Judicial Council, 1995.

Gossen, Diane Chelsom. *Restitution: Restructuring School Discipline.* 2nd rev. ed. Chapel Hill, NC: New View Publications, 1999.

Holmes, Joan. "The Original Intentions of the Indian Act." Conference paper for Pacific Business & Law Institute, Ottawa, April 17–18, 2002. Accessed 2014-05-01 (pdf) at is.gd/frukkS.

Lewis, Mark. "The Honorable Mr. Justice T. David Marshall." *Slaw,* Canada's online legal magazine, November 27, 2009. Accessed 2014-05-01 at is.gd/4ILECJ.

Lucas, Alastair. "Provincial Court Judges' Professional Allowances and Judicial Independence." *ABlawg.ca* (University of Calgary Faculty of Law blog), April 2, 2008. Accessed 2014-05-01 at is.gd/X5zzns.

Macdonald, David, and Daniel Wilson. *Shameful Neglect: Indigenous Child Poverty in Canada.* Ottawa: Canadian Centre for Policy Alternatives, 2016. Accessed 2016-06-05 (pdf) at is.gd/uHujHw.

Macdonald, Sir John A., Superintendent General of Indian Affairs, to Sir John Douglas Sutherland Campbell, Marquess of Lorne, Governor General of Canada. *Department of Indian Affairs Annual Report,* 1880: 8. Cited at n98 in Joan Holmes, "The Original Intentions of the Indian

Act." Conference paper for Pacific Business & Law Institute, Ottawa, April 17–18, 2002. Accessed 2014-05-01 (pdf) at is.gd/frukkS.

MacEwan, Grant. *Tatanga Mani: Walking Buffalo of the Stonies.* Edmonton: M.G. Hurtig, 1969.

Marshall, T. David. *Judicial Conduct and Accountability.* Scarborough, Ont.: Carswell, 1995.

McCormick, Peter J. *Judicial Independence and Judicial Governance in the Provincial Courts.* N.p.: Canadian Association of Provincial Court Judges, April 2004.

Morton, James C. "*Gladue* Factors." *Morton's Musings* (blog), September 19, 2014. Accessed 2014-09-28 at is.gd/Xxf5Fa.

Quigley, Tim. "Some Issues in Sentencing of Aboriginal Offenders." In Richard Gosse, J.Y. Henderson and R. Carter, eds., *Continuing Poundmaker and Riel's Quest.* Saskatoon: Purich Publishing, 1994.

Reilly, John. "Book Review: *Ghost Dancing with Colonialism*, by Grace Woo." *Alberta Law Review* 50, no. 1 (2012): 219–223. Accessed 2014-06-28 (pdf) at is.gd/hRoawa.

Royal Commission on Aboriginal Peoples. *Bridging the Cultural Divide: A Report on Aboriginal People and Criminal Justice in Canada.* Ottawa: Royal Commission on Aboriginal Peoples, 1996. Accessed 2018-11-30 (pdf) from is.gd/gDDwlo.

———. *Report of the Royal Commission on Aboriginal Peoples.* 5 vols. Ottawa: Canada Communication Group, 1996. Accessed 2018-11-30 (pdf) from is.gd/Y1SepA.

Schmeiser, Douglas A., and W. Howard McConnell. *The Independence of Provincial Court Judges: A Public Trust.* N.p.: Canadian Association of Provincial Court Judges, 1996.

Staples, David. "Successful native justice program set to expand." *Edmonton Journal*, May 21, 2006, A1. Accessed 2016-07-28 as document ID 253297884 on ProQuest's Canadian Newsstream via public library proxy server (requires library card).

Truth and Reconciliation Commission of Canada. *Honouring the Truth, Reconciling for the Future: Summary of the Final Report.* Ottawa: Truth and Reconciliation Commission of Canada, 2015. Accessed 2018-11-30 (pdf) at is.gd/9hMvB2.

Woo, Grace Li Xiu. *Ghost Dancing with Colonialism: Decolonization and Indigenous Rights at the Supreme Court of Canada.* Vancouver: UBC Press, 2011.

Cases

Beauregard v. Canada, [1986] 2 SCR 56, 1986 CanLII 24 (SCC). Accessed 2014-05-01 at canlii.ca/t/1fts8.

MacKeigan v. Hickman, [1989] 2 SCR 796, 1989 CanLII 40 (SCC). Accessed 2014-06-28 at canlii.ca/t/1ft26.

Ref. re Public Sector Pay Reduction Act (PEI). See Ref re Remuneration of Judges etc.

Ref re Remuneration of Judges of the Prov. Court of PEI; Ref re Independence and Impartiality of Judges of the Prov. Court of PEI, [1997] 3 SCR 3, 1997 CanLII 317 (SCC). Accessed 2014-09-12 at canlii.ca/t/1fqzp.

R. v. Big M Drug Mart Ltd., [1985] 1 SCR 295, 1985 CanLII 69 (SCC). Accessed 2014-06-24 at canlii.ca/t/1fv2b.

R. v. Brady (1998), 59 Alta LR (3d) 133, 1998 ABCA 7 (Alta. CA). Accessed2014-05-01 at canlii.ca/t/5str.

R. v. Campbell (1994), 25 Alta LR (3d) 158, 1994 CanLII 5258 (Alta. QB). Accessed 2014-05-17 at canlii.ca/t/1p6kv.

R. v. Gladue (1997), 119 CCC (3d) 481, 1997 CanLII 3015 (BCCA), accessed 2014-05-01 at canlii.ca/t/1dzcq; affirmed [1999] 1 SCR 688, 1999 CanLII 679 (SCC), accessed 2014-05-01 at canlii.ca/t/1fqp2.

R. v. Heywood, [1994] 3 SCR 761, 1994 CanLII 34 (SCC). Accessed 2014-05-01 at canlii.ca/t/1frnd.

R. v. Hunter (1998), 63 Alta LR (3d) 229, 1998 ABCA 141 (Alta. CA). Accessed 2014-05-01 at canlii.ca/t/5sql.

R. v. Ipeelee, [2012] 1 SCR 433, 2012 SCC 13 (CanLII). Accessed 2014-05-01 at canlii.ca/t/fqq00.

R. v. McDonnell, [1997] 1 SCR 948, 1997 CanLII 389 (SCC). Accessed 2014-06-28 at canlii.ca/t/1fr3d.

R. v. Twoyoungmen, [1998] 4 CNLR 262, 1998 ABPC 135 (CanLII). Accessed 2014-06-15 at canlii.ca/t/5r8k.

Reilly v. Wachowich (1998), 64 Alta LR (3d) 227, 1998 ABQB 741 (Alta. QB). Accessed 2014-05-01 at canlii.ca/t/5qo1. [Sept. 2 reasons for judgment as to jurisdiction; respondent ordered to file return to originating notice of motion.]

Reilly v. Wachowich (1998), 68 Alta LR (3d) 189, 1998 ABQB 754 (Alta. QB). Accessed 2014-05-01 at canlii.ca/t/5qoc. [Sept. 8 application by respondent to vary stay of relocation pending judicial review decision.]

Reilly v. Wachowich (1999a), 71 Alta LR (3d) 214, 1999 ABQB 309 (Alta. QB), accessed 2014-05-01 at canlii.ca/t/5p8x; affirmed Wachowich v. Reilly

(2000), 84 Alta LR (3d) 201, 2000 ABCA 241 (Alta. CA), accessed 2014-05-01 at canlii.ca/t/5rq3. [Apr. 26 reasons for judgment allowing application for judicial review; Sept. 5 dismissal of respondent's appeal.]

Reilly v. Wachowich (1999b), 77 Alta LR (3d) 208, 1999 ABQB 639 (Alta. QB). Accessed 2014-05-01 at canlii.ca/t/5p07. [Aug. 16 decision on costs.]

Reilly v. Walter (2006), 59 Alta LR (4th) 108, 2006 ABQB 383 (Alta. QB), accessed 2014-05-01 at canlii.ca/t/1ngoq; affirmed *Reilly v. Chief Judge of Provincial Court of Alberta* (2008), 85 Alta LR (4th) 1, 2008 ABCA 72 (Alta. CA), accessed 2014-05-01 at canlii.ca/t/1vx1p. [May 24 dismissal of application re professional education allowance for Caux conference; Mar. 3 dismissal of applicant's appeal.]

United States v. Leonard (2012), 112 OR (3d) 496, 2012 ONCA 622 (Ont. CA). Accessed 2014-05-01 at canlii.ca/t/fss8m.

Valente v. The Queen, [1985] 2 SCR 673, 1985 CanLII 25 (SCC). Accessed 2014-05-01 at canlii.ca/t/1ftzs.

Wachowich v. Reilly (2000). See *Reilly v. Wachowich* (1999a).

Statutes

Constitution Act, 1982, being Sched. B to the Canada Act 1982 (UK), 1982, c. 11, s. 11(d). Accessed 2014-06-28 at canlii.ca/t/ldsx.

Criminal Code, RSC 1985, c. C-46, s. 718.2(*e*). Accessed 2014-06-28 at canlii.ca/t/529tl.

Judicature Act, RSA 2000, c. J-2, Pt. 6: Functions of Judicial Council and Complaints Procedure. Accessed 2014-05-01 at canlii.ca/t/525bm.

Justice Statutes Amendment Act, 1998 (Bill 25) [in force 1998-08-31, inserting Pt. 6.1, re complaints against judges, into the Judicature Act, RSA 1980, c. J-1; see now Judicature Act, RSA 2000, above]. Accessed (pdf) 2014-05-01 at is.gd/FmVGE7.

Justice Statutes Amendment Act, 2000 (Bill 20) [in force 2001-04-01, amalgamating provisions of the Provincial Court Judges Act (see below) into the Provincial Court Act, RSA 1980, c. P-20, and enacting new provisions re appointment, jurisdiction, judicial functions etc.; see now Provincial Court Act, RSA 2000, below]. Accessed (pdf) 2014-05-01 at is.gd/ylBooK.

Provincial Court Act, RSA 2000, c. P-31, s. 9.51(1). Accessed 2014-06-28 at canlii.ca/t/522m8.

Provincial Court Judges Act, SA 1981, c. P-20.1, s. 16(1) [see now Provincial Court Act, RSA 2000, c. P-31, s. 9.51(1), above]. Accessed 2014-08-15 at is.gd/MUUl3f.

Provincial Court Judges and Masters in Chambers Compensation Regulation, Alta. Reg. 176/1998, s. 4.1. Accessed 2014-05-01 at canlii.ca/t/51x7c.

INDEX OF NAMES

JOHN REILLY is the bestselling author of *Bad Medicine: A Judge's Struggle for Justice in a First Nations Community*, *Bad Judgment: The Myths of First Nations Equality and Judicial Independence in Canada*, and *Bad Law: Rethinking Justice for a Postcolonial Canada*. After 33 years in public service as a circuit court judge, Reilly retired, having become disillusioned with the Canadian criminal justice system and in particular its treatment of Indigenous people. Still publicly active and openly critical about the law, politics, and the legal system, he now seeks to challenge people to rethink the true meaning of justice, the need for drastic changes in the criminal justice system in Canada, and the need to change our attitudes towards Indigenous people. John lives in Calgary, Alberta.